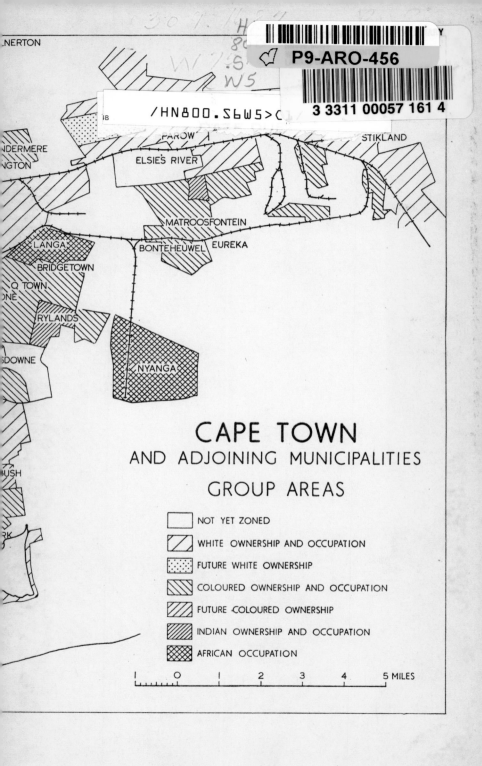

NERTON

NDERMERE
NGTON

PAROW

STIKLAND

ELSIE'S RIVER

MATROOSFONTEIN

LANGA

BRIDGETOWN

BONTEHEUWEL   EUREKA

Q TOWN
ONE

RYLANDS

SDOWNE

NYANGA

USH

RK

CAPE TOWN
AND ADJOINING MUNICIPALITIES
GROUP AREAS

NOT YET ZONED

WHITE OWNERSHIP AND OCCUPATION

FUTURE WHITE OWNERSHIP

COLOURED OWNERSHIP AND OCCUPATION

FUTURE COLOURED OWNERSHIP

INDIAN OWNERSHIP AND OCCUPATION

AFRICAN OCCUPATION

1   0   1   2   3   4   5 MILES

LANGA

LANGA

A STUDY OF
SOCIAL GROUPS
IN AN AFRICAN TOWNSHIP

MONICA WILSON
& ARCHIE MAFEJE

CAPE TOWN
OXFORD UNIVERSITY PRESS
LONDON   NEW YORK
1963

Oxford University Press, Amen House, London E.C.4
GLASGOW NEW YORK TORONTO MELBOURNE WELLINGTON
BOMBAY CALCUTTA MADRAS KARACHI LAHORE DACCA
CAPE TOWN SALISBURY NAIROBI IBADAN ACCRA
KUALA LUMPUR HONG KONG

SET AND PRINTED
IN MONOTYPE TIMES BY
THE RUSTICA PRESS (PTY.) LTD.
CAPE TOWN, SOUTH AFRICA

CONTENTS

    1. Types and Range of Membership   113
    2. Sports Clubs   114
    3. Music and Dance Clubs   126
    4. Raising Funds   131

7   CLASSES AND LEADERS
    1. Category and Class   137
    2. The Choice of Leaders   143

8   ARBITRATION IN DISPUTES
    1. Disputes among Migrants   153
    2. Disputes among Townsmen   161
    3. The Arbitrator   168

9   CONCLUSION   172

    Appendix: The Law Regulating Movement to Town   182
    Select Bibliography   185
    Index   189

ILLUSTRATIONS AND MAPS

ACKNOWLEDGEMENTS

The fieldwork on which this book is based was financed by the National Council for Social Research of the Department of Education, Arts, and Science, to whom acknowledgement is made. Opinions expressed and conclusions reached are, however, those of the authors and are not to be regarded as representing the view of the National Council for Social Research.

A grant in aid of publication was made by the University of Cape Town from its very limited resources and is gratefully acknowledged. We owe our thanks to the Department of Geography in the University of Cape Town for drawing the two maps.

We are indebted to the people of Langa for their friendly co-operation in the investigations, and to the Langa Administration for permission to work in the township. An account of the tensions inherent in the system under which poverty drives people to seek work in town, and the policy of the government is to exclude many of them, should in no sense be taken as a criticism of individuals administering the system.

Field work was carried out by Dr. A. R. W. Crosse-Upcott from July 1955 until March 1957, and by Mr. Archie Mafeje, who is himself Xhosa-speaking, intermittently between November 1961 and September 1962. The formulation of the problems, the direction of the field work, and the writing of the book was done by Professor Monica Wilson. The study was planned as a complement to another investigation carried out by Dr. Sheila van der Horst and Mr. G. V. Doxey into the character, mobility, and turnover of the African labour force in the Cape Peninsula, and to investigations of the Coloured community of the Western Cape, and of the housing and administration of Africans, undertaken by the University of Stellenbosch. The material on the labour force is ready for the press and has been used in the preparation of this draft; that on the Coloured community and on housing and administration has not yet been published.

Various members of the School of African Studies in the University of Cape Town have read and commented on this account. We are particularly grateful to Professor H. J. Simons, Dr. A. C. Jordan, Dr. D. P. Kunene, and Dr. Peter Carstens for their help; and Dr. Audrey Richards of the University of Cambridge. We should like to acknowledge also the great stimulus given to urban studies by the Institute of Social Research at Rhodes University, and the personal help of Professor Hobart Houghton and Professor Philip Mayer. Close parallels—and also differences—between the situation in East London and that in Langa are apparent.

School of African Studies
University of Cape Town
March 1963

Transkei
& Ciskei

O. F. S.

•BURGHERSDORP

GLEN

QUEENSTOWN⊙

•BEDFORD
ADELAIDE°   HEALDTOWN°   EAST   KK
FORT BEAUFORT° ALICE°°OLOVEDALE
                      FORT HARE
                              VICTORIA   MD

GRAHAMSTOWN⊙   PED

DRAWN BY THE DEPARTMENT
OF GEOGRAPHY
IN THE UNIVERSITY OF CAPE TO

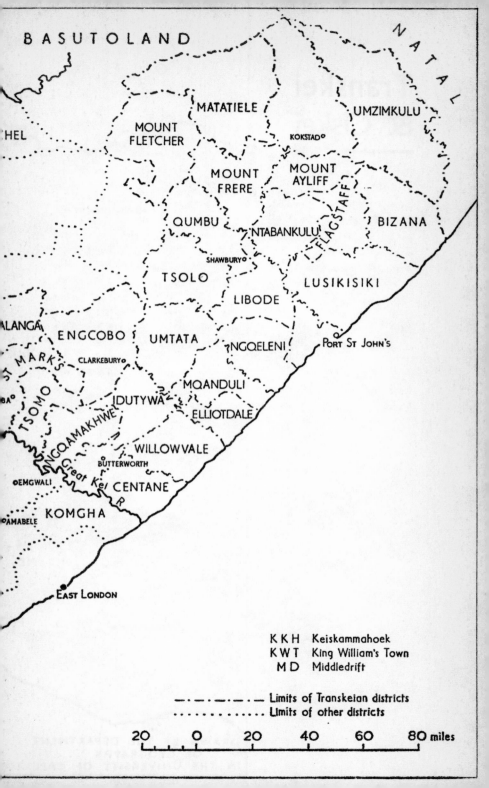

BASUTOLAND

NATAL

MATATIELE

UMZIMKULU

MOUNT FLETCHER

KOKSTAD○

MOUNT FRERE

MOUNT AYLIFF

FLAGSTAFF

QUMBU

NTABANKULU

BIZANA

SHAWBURY○

TSOLO

LUSIKISIKI

LIBODE

ENGCOBO

UMTATA

NGQELENI

PORT ST JOHN'S

ST MARKS

CLARKEBURY○

MQANDULI

TSOMO

IDUTYWA

ELLIOTDALE

NGQAMAKHWE

○EMGWALI

Great Kei R.

WILLOWVALE

BUTTERWORTH○

CENTANE

○AMABELE

KOMGHA

●EAST LONDON

K K H	Keiskammahoek
K W T	King William's Town
M D	Middledrift

—·—·—·—·— Limits of Transkeian districts

·············· Limits of other districts

20   0   20   40   60   80 miles

1 Introduction

1. THE FIELD OF STUDY

Cape Town is dominated by the colour cleavage which exists between black and white in southern Africa and confines colour groups to separate areas and occupations.[1] Langa is a township on the periphery of the city, very poor by comparison with most of the suburbs, and reserved for occupation by black Africans, most of them Xhosa-speaking. They are not the original occupants of the western Cape, but they have been there in appreciable numbers for a hundred years, mingling with the 'Coloured' people of mixed descent, and working along with them and white South Africans. The Africans come mostly from the eastern part of the Cape Province, where the Portuguese found them in the sixteenth century,[2] and the Coloured people count among their ancestors the aborigines of the Cape, the Khoikhoin people, or so-called Hottentots. The white settlers established themselves in 1652.

Xhosa-speaking people worked on the roads in the western Cape from the 1840's, and by 1879 many of the men had wives and children with them.[3] Except for a drop in 1911, the African population of greater Cape Town has increased steadily, and now forms 9 per cent of the total.

[1] For the contemporary South African background see Leo Marquard, *The Peoples and Policies of South Africa*, 3rd ed., 1962.

[2] G. M. Theal, *Historical Records of South East Africa*, vol. II. Cf. Monica Wilson, 'The Early History of the Transkei and Ciskei', *African Studies*, v, 18 (1959), pp. 167–79, for a discussion of the Portuguese and other evidence of the date at which Xhosa-speaking people were living south of the Umtata River.

[3] In 1879, 3,778 Xhosa working in the western Cape included 1,164 women and 1,472 children. In 1902 of 2,092 Tswana, 486 were women and 891 children: A 26–79 Cape of Good Hope, Department of Native Affairs, *Blue Book on Native Affairs*, 1902, pp. 85–95.

I am indebted to my colleague, Professor H. J. Simons, for much of the detailed evidence contained in this chapter, and in the appendix. He has made a study, extending over many years, of the movement of Africans to the western Cape.

1

Until 1926 there was no restriction on the entry of Africans into Cape Town. After that successive regulations[4] empowered the government to exclude them, and since 1955 large numbers of men and women[5] have been compelled to leave. A man is 'endorsed out' if he is without employment, and has not lived in Cape Town for at least fifteen years, or been with one employer for at least ten years; a woman if she is neither employed nor the wife of a man 'exempted' because of the length of his employment in town. The avowed policy of the government, reiterated since 1955, is that Africans must gradually and systematically be withdrawn from the western Cape. Employers are equally insistent that existing industries and farms cannot continue to operate without them.

POPULATION RETURNS*

TABLE 1: CAPE TOWN MUNICIPALITY

Year	White	Coloured and Asians	Africans	Total	African % of Total
1865	15,118	13,065	274(K)†	28,457	1·0
1875	18,973	14,093	173	33,239	0·5
1891	25,393	25,235	623	51,251	1·2
1904	44,203	31,318	2,147	77,668	2·8
1911	86,239	80,449	1,569	168,257	0·9
1921	111,784	89,259	8,684	209,727	4·1
1936	152,244	135,621	13,583	301,448	4·5
1946	180,805	171,767	31,258	383,830	8·1
1951	186,660	214,334	40,215	441,209	9·1
1959	196,560	307,350	72,711	576,621	12·6
1960	188,545	269,172	39,254	496,971	7·9

TABLE 2: GREATER CAPE TOWN

1865	20,966	17,118	707(K)‡	38,791	1·8
1875	25,256	19,250	202	44,688	0·5
1891	40,956	37,318	781	79,055	1·0
1904	104,421	62,534	7,492	174,447	4·3
1911	86,708³	80,801	1,581	169,090	0·9
1921	117,027	94,582	8,893	220,502	4·0
1936	173,412	156,651	14,160	344,223	4·1
1946	220,401	216,315	35,197	471,413	7·5
1951	247,442	280,413	49,793	577,648	8·6
1960	278,555	374,609	65,025	718,189	9·0

* *Census Reports. Social Survey of Cape Town No. SS.* 2 1941; University of Cape Town. City of Cape Town, *M.O.H. Annual Reports.*

† 'Kaffirs' only—i.e. Xhosa-speaking only, excluding Sotho.

‡ Includes troops.

[4] For details see appendix.

[5] Between January 1959 and March 1962, 26,211 Africans, 28 per cent of them women, were ordered to leave the western Cape Province: *House of Assembly, Debates,* 30 March 1962, c. 3542.

What drives men to town is poverty: they must earn or their families in the reserves go hungry:[6] and wives or widows often come also to help support families at home. But poverty in the town is bitter also, and the real wages of Africans are not increasing.[7] It was calculated that in 1961 the income of 50 per cent of the African families in the Cape Town municipal area was less than is necessary to keep a family[8] at a 'minimum level of health and decency'. The figure for the Peninsula Africans *as a whole* is estimated by an experienced social worker at over 80 per cent.[9] Langa is not as poor as the African settlements outside the municipal area, but there is acute malnutrition even in Langa.[10]

The African labourers who first came to Cape Town were housed by their employers, some in compounds specially designated for them, such as that for dock-workers which was already in existence by 1890, but others were scattered throughout greater Cape Town on their employers' premises, or wherever a room could be found near by. Repeated attempts have been made to separate them from the rest of the community, and confine them to 'locations'. In 1902, after an outbreak of plague had attracted notice to the condition of the slums, a 'government reserve' was established on the outskirts of the city, at Ndabeni. 'Natives who were living under insanitary conditions in the slums of Cape Town were offered accommodation at a low rental in Ndabeni.' Some moved out, but between 5,000 and 6,000 continued to live within the city. The influenza epidemic of 1918 again drew attention to the slums and the City Council first took over Ndabeni, and then

[6] D. Hobart Houghton and E. M. Walton, *The Economy of a Native Reserve*, *Keiskammahoek Rural Survey*, vol. II, 1952, *passim*.

[7] 'Since the war although the real wages (money wages at constant—1938—prices) of White employees in industry have risen by over a third, the real wages of the non-White workers have barely increased at all': O. P. F. Horwood, 'The Employment Provided by Manufacturing Industry', *Industry and Trade*, vol. 56, no. 3, March 1960, p. 97.

[8] Personal communication from Professor E. Batson, Director of the School of Social Science, University of Cape Town. Professor Batson has directed a social survey of Cape Town which has been carried out over twenty years. Cf. bibliography.

[9] Dr. O. D. Wollheim, Warden of C.A.F.D.A., statement at Archbishop's seminar on Poverty, 30 March 1962.

[10] For the budgets in a squatters' camp in the Cape in 1952 see M. Lipschitz and N. M. Greshoff, 'Living Conditions in a Squatters' Camp', *Race Relations Journal*, XXI, 4, 1954, pp. 1–38.

proceeded to establish a new township, Langa, which was to be a model in housing and planning. The chairman of the Native Affairs Committee of the City Council visited a number of towns in South Africa and made recommendations to his council on the type of 'location' which they should build. Great stress was laid on providing married quarters, and it was suggested that families should be allowed to buy their own houses, but the council finally decided against this. Besides the houses for families, 'barracks' were built for single men, with large dormitories, and a limited number of 'flats' providing double rooms for men who wanted something a little better than the barracks (cf. plates 2, 3 and 8). Langa expanded fast, and for the first twenty-five years the married men with their wives made up a third to a quarter of the total. Since 1954 the government has refused to allow the building of further houses for families in Langa, but additional single quarters, known as the 'zones', have been built and the proportion of men to women has risen as high as 10 : 1, and is now over 8 : 1.

TABLE 3: POPULATION OF LANGA* (MONTHLY AVERAGE P.A.)

AFRICANS

YEAR	EUROPEANS	Male	Female	Children (under 16)	Total	Masculinity ratio (m : 100f)	TOTAL POPULATION
1930	—	1,116	324	320	1,760	344	—
1935	—	1,963	621	1,146	3,730	316	—
1939–40	25	3,655	874	1,509	6,038	418	6,063
1944–5	26	4,453	1,254	2,142	7,849	355	7,875
1949–50	37	6,558	1,433	3,026	11,017	457	11,054
1952–3	43	7,156	1,470	2,347	10,973	486	11,016
1953–4	39	7,320	1,650	2,938	11,908	443	11,947
1954–5	37	8,102	1,695	3,150	12,947	477	12,984
1956	38	15,004	1,734	3,282	20,020	865	20,058
1957	37	17,941	1,771	3,373	23,085	1,013	23,122
1958	28	18,697	1,807	3,485	23,989	1,034	24,017
1959	21	19,445	1,842	3,624	24,911	1,055	24,932
1960 (Dec.)	—	19,050	2,190	4,317	25,557	870	—
1961 (Dec.)	—	18,847	2,175	4,314	25,336	866	—

* City of Cape Town, *Mayor's Minutes; M.O.H. Reports*, 1960 and 1961 figures by courtesy of Administrative Office, Langa.

Although Langa grew fast the African population of greater Cape Town grew still faster, and in 1952 only a third was housed in officially recognized 'locations'; the rest were living scattered through the city and in squatters' camps on the periphery—Cook's Bush, Hout Bay, Elsie's River, Kensington, and Windermere. In 1956 an 'emergency camp' was established at Nyanga, and thousands of Africans were compelled to move there. No houses were provided—they were required to put up their own shelters in a specified area where water and latrines were provided, while their claims to live in town were examined. Those accepted as having a legitimate right to be in greater Cape Town are gradually being provided with houses to rent; those not recognized as having such a right are compelled to leave the area. But the removal from former slums and squatters' camps is in no sense complete: individuals and families tend to drift back to their old quarters, and shacks that have been forcibly destroyed appear again. The dwellers in old squatters' camps who had established some sort of community with their neighbours have the greatest objection to moving to a bleak site, miles from the city. The distance from work, the cost of building again, and living with strangers instead of in a known community make the moves bitterly unpopular.

TABLE 4: AFRICANS IN GREATER CAPE TOWN*

	Male	Female	Masculinity ratio (m: 100f)
1911	1,250	331	377·6
1921	7,073	1,820	388·6
1936	9,944	4,216	235·8
1946	24,293	10,904	222·7
1951	32,842	16,951	193·7
1960		65,025	

* *Census Reports*. It is in the interest of many Africans to evade numeration since they are living illegally in the urban area, and the actual population probably exceeds the official figure.

In South Africa two distinct things are often confused: slum clearance, and the compulsory segregation of people of different colours. Ndabeni, Langa, and Nyanga were all begun because people were living in squalor and the medical authorities were pressing for slum clearance, but they were all also planned as *segregated* areas, to which Africans would be confined. It was stated that the areas set aside for African occupation would be *permanently* assigned to them, but in fact they have been required repeatedly to move. Ndabeni was originally well outside the city boundary, but Cape Town was growing fast, and by the 1920's new houses for whites were impinging upon it, and the Ndabeni site itself was judged most suitable for factories. A new 'location' was selected, much farther out. Building began at Langa in 1923, and the township was officially opened in 1927. Thirty years later the process was repeated. New townships for white and for Coloured people are impinging on Langa; a proposal by the City Council to extend Langa was rejected by the Bantu Affairs Department. The new township of Nyanga was established still farther out. Only single men, and no further families, are admitted to Langa and it is the expressed policy of the Bantu Affairs Department that families already in Langa, though still in occupation of their houses, will be required to move to Nyanga. This process of removal of each generation is inevitable if a city is expanding and complete territorial segregation between racial groups is insisted upon. It could be avoided only if a city were planned in two sections, each to extend in an opposite direction. Such a plan has not been followed consistently in any city in South Africa, and it would be impossible in Cape Town, which is almost surrounded by sea and mountain.

The policy of segregation means that the poor are pushed farther and farther from their places of employment. Normally, in a city, the poor live nearest to the factories and docks, and the well-to-do farther out. In Cape Town, as in other cities of the Republic, each new African township has been farther and farther away, and the journey to work grows longer. Ndabeni was 4 miles from the city centre, Langa is 8 miles, and Nyanga 12 miles. It is true that new factories have been built in the direction of Langa and Nyanga, but the dock labourers, and the Africans employed in the city, must now live 8 to 12 miles from their work. Return fares to the centre of Cape Town are R1.65[11] a month for a season ticket by train from Langa, or 20c a day by bus, and R2.20 a month for a season ticket from Nyanga by train, and 38c a day by bus, i.e. 6–8 per cent of an unskilled labourer's wages if he travels in the cheapest way. From Ndabeni the return fare by bus was 6d. (5c).

Langa was established as a 'respectable' township. It was the headquarters of the administration, and of most of the churches, and a high school was built there. Families were led to believe

[11] R1 = 10s. or $1.40.

that they might settle there permanently. In 1927 there were
already men who had been in Cape Town for thirty years, and
who formed a settled community with sports clubs, and African
traders and eating-house owners.[12] Langa is still the most
'middle class' of the African communities in the Cape: its
inhabitants think themselves a cut above their fellows in
Kensington or Retreat or Nyanga. But it includes very diverse
types and houses are so scarce that people must take whatever
they can get. 'Decent people' and town toughs—*tsotsis*—live
all mixed up; a clergyman may have a beer-brewer as his next-
door neighbour. Many middle-class African families find
themselves compelled[13] to bring up children in a street in
which their neighbours have totally different standards of
hygiene, manners, and morals. This is a source of great anxiety
and frustration.

There has been much greater security of life and property
in Langa than in the townships of Johannesburg, but with
growing restrictions on entry, and the increase in the disproportion between men and women, disorder has increased.
Women are less safe, going about alone, than formerly, and
the tension between police and people is growing. In 1956 an
African minister said that Langa was 'rapidly losing its peaceful
atmosphere. This is due to the influx of bachelors from Windermere and similar slums. These men are now quartered in the
flats and barracks and zones so that it is now unsafe to go
beyond the married quarters after dark. Several assaults have
been reported recently.' Nowadays (1961), the police go to the
zones or barracks only in a large group and there must be
white police, who are armed, among them.

Friction with the police is directly related to raiding for
passes, and as restriction on residence is enforced more and
more rigidly, so raiding to discover who is in the area illegally

[12] Evidence given by the City of Cape Town to the Native Economic Commission, 1931. In 1931 there were 19 traders and 4 eating-houses in Langa, and
22 traders and 15 eating-houses in Ndabeni. All the licence-holders were Africans.

[13] Africans in urban areas were prevented from buying or renting land (save
with the permission of the Governor-General) by the Native Laws Amendment
Act of 1937, but those who were registered voters continued until 1959 to enjoy
the rights of 'exempted persons' who could *live* outside the areas specifically
set aside for Africans. Some continued to occupy premises they owned, but
their rights are now threatened by the Group Areas Act and they may be
compelled to move.

increases. Restriction on residence cannot, in fact, be effective unless an area is totally sealed off, or else the right of persons to be in the area is continually questioned, so some form of raiding for passes is the inevitable corollary of control of movement into Cape Town. There is also tension between people and police over the brewing of beer, which has increased as the proportion of single men has increased. In 1961 a large majority of Langa residents voted against the granting of a licence for the sale of 'European' liquor in the township. Three categories of people opposed it: the church people, the brewers, and the politically conscious—the last because Africans had not been consulted in the legislation that was passed permitting the wider sale of liquor.

Langa is administered by the City of Cape Town, but municipal action in relation to Africans is increasingly circumscribed by the central government.[14] The people of Langa are represented neither in Parliament nor on the city council, and therefore they have no control over their administration. A superintendent—who is always a white man—is appointed by the city council, and he is assisted by a staff of whites and Africans. There is an Advisory Board, composed of elected and nominated members, whose function it is to express the views of the people of Langa to the 'Native Affairs Committee' of the council; it ceased to function for a period, but an attempt has been made to resuscitate it recently. In Langa, as in most towns of the Republic, the Africans have grown more and more impatient of the advisory boards, which can take no effective action.

There also exists a 'Vigilance Association' which claims a membership of about 300 and represents the older and more conservative rent-payers in the married quarters of Langa. Committee members and office bearers are elected at an annual general meeting. It has repeatedly appealed to the administration against increased rents, police raids, poor sanitation and street lighting, the admission of girls to the zones at night, and other matters of public concern. It was also represented by a senior Q.C. at the investigation into the riot. The younger and more radical people refer to it contemptuously as X's (the Superintendent's) Association and regard

[14] Cf. appendix.

it, like the Advisory Board, as a 'collaborationist organization'. It has no statutory functions as the Advisory Board has.

The city council provides all the housing in Langa—as already noted no African is allowed to own land there (or, now, elsewhere in the Peninsula), and build for himself. The council supplies water and electricity and is responsible for roads and sanitation. It maintains a health service with free medical attention at a number of clinics,[15] and a day nursery, in Langa, and employs a welfare officer. A sports stadium has recently been built and there is a communal hall, where films are shown. The Administrative Office is mainly concerned with the control of movement—issuing passes to seek work, registering contracts, or 'endorsing out' those who are not employed or permitted to live in town; allocating accommodation and collecting rents. The African assistants employed in the latter tasks are each responsible for a section of the township and they are known as *wardsmen*. The central government is responsible for police and justice—a magistrate's court sits daily—post office, railway, and labour bureau.

Since entry into Cape Town and sojourning there are controlled, and the desire to enter to find a job or, for a woman, to join her husband, is so strong, the temptation to offer and accept bribes is great and a black market in passes is known to exist; indeed precise figures as to the cost of a pass are quoted even in remote villages in Tanganyika, and various cases were noted during the course of fieldwork in which a pass was said to have been obtained through bribery. Two whites and fourteen Africans, most of them clerks in the Native Administration Office at Langa, appeared on 6 January 1961 before a magistrate on charges of falsitas, or a contravention of the Prevention of Corruption Act. The Crown alleged that the men received money for stamping the reference books of persons illegally in the area, giving them permission to live and work in Cape Town instead of being 'endorsed out'. An African interpreter was also charged, it being alleged that he had accepted more than £200 from twenty-five Africans so that they could find work in the Peninsula.[16] None of the men from Langa was convicted, but four men from Stellenbosch, Paarl, and Welling-

[15] Until 1960 there was also a hospital with thirty beds, and a library.
[16] *Cape Times*, 5 January 1961; 7 January 1961. *Cape Argus*, 22 May 1961.

ton were convicted on similar charges. Houses are also eagerly
sought after, and some wardsmen are alleged to allocate a house
to whoever brings the largest 'present'. Those who have handed
over a present but fail to get the house have no redress. During
the period of fieldwork there were also numerous reports of
misappropriation of municipal materials, one particular
European being repeatedly named as being responsible for
large-scale thefts. Of the truth or falsehood of these charges
we have not got the evidence to judge, but it is certain that
corruption is *believed* to be widespread in the granting of
passes and houses, and in the use of publicly owned materials.
The attitude of one African clerk who admitted in conversation
to selling passes was: 'It's not very nice but a man's got to
live', and also, 'One must help one's fellows'.

Segregation and restriction on movement are not accepted as
right and good by any of the people living in Langa. There is
an all-pervading dissatisfaction with existing conditions and a
conviction that they are growing worse and worse. The whittling
away of political rights from 1936 onwards, the increasing
restriction on movement and rights of occupation; reservation
of specified occupations to certain racial groups; the rigid
control of education by the Bantu Education Department, and
prohibition on Africans attending the University of Cape
Town—all these exclude Africans more and more from the
common life of the community. Anger at pass laws is nothing
new—a former Minister of Native Affairs, Deneys Reitz,
speaking in the Senate twenty years ago, said that 'nothing
was so conducive to irritation, to bad feeling, to hatred, to
disturbance of race relations between black and white as the
pass laws', but it mounts as the enforcement of the law grows
more rigid and, more especially, as the law is applied to
women.

The policy of apartheid is rejected not only because of the
misery it engenders through restriction of movement and
employment, but also because, in the words of one informant,
'The basis of apartheid is deeper than mere territorial segregation; its basis is inequality, between white and non-white'.

The mounting tension led to a riot in March 1960 when police
fired on a crowd that had not dispersed when ordered to
do so, killing at least one man and wounding a number of

others.[17] The crowd set fire to a car and killed the Coloured driver in it, as well as burning various buildings. Many African leaders were then arrested. Nine days later 30,000 men marched through Cape Town to the central police station to demand the release of their leaders, and returned home peacefully, after a discussion between their leader and the Chief of Police, on the understanding that their leader would be given an interview with the Minister of Justice. Instead of being interviewed he was arrested, and that night Langa was surrounded by the military. Subsequently it was raided by the police, who seized what they classified as 'weapons' and 'stolen property'. In the view of the people the police conducted a systematic looting of property and beat up many men who were not at work, or who were on night-shift and at home during the day-time. During the judicial inquiry which followed, the pass system and low wages were repeatedly cited as causes of unrest in Langa.[18] The Commission also found that: 'People living at Langa were anxious and frustrated because they felt that there was no constitutional channel through which they could make their grievances known to the State.'

2. THE PROBLEM AND METHOD OF WORK

This, then, is the township in which we sought to answer two questions: the first, what are the effective social groups in Langa? and the second, when and why do they cohere, and when and why do they split or dissolve? The second question leads directly to one of the fundamental problems in social anthropology: What is the basis for the coherence of groups?

The difficulties of fieldwork in such a situation are too obvious to require elaboration, but they led to one distortion in the material of which readers must be aware. We did not investigate political organizations or trade unions. Questions were not asked about them early in the investigation because that would have aroused suspicion, and during the course of the study the two main political organizations, the African National Congress and the Pan-African Congress, were banned. Furthermore, two cases occurred in which journalists were imprisoned

[17] For an account of the events see M. Horrell, *Days of Crisis in South Africa*, S.A. Institute of Race Relations, 1960.

[18] The inquiry was confined to the events which took place on the day of the riot, 21 March, but references were made by witnesses to the causes.

for refusing to reveal to the police their sources of information on political matters. A very large number of the people of Langa take a lively interest in politics, and readers must make allowance for this fact.

2 Categories of People

1. CRITERIA OF CLASSIFICATION

The basic questions we asked were these: 'How do you identify people? In a crowd how do you sort them out in your own mind?' Two general criteria are immediately apparent: colour and sex. As has already been indicated, black, 'Coloured', and white are separated by a body of law and convention, and it is clear that most Africans in Langa, like most other South Africans, classify people in these categories.

Coloured and African sometimes associate in sports, or music and dance clubs, as we shall see, and they may work in the same factory, but for the most part they hold aloof. Derogatory Xhosa terms for Coloured people are often used: *ilawu*, derived from *ilawu lentaba*—a rogue, someone without customs and traditions, capable of doing anything; and *iqeya*—someone who drinks excessively; and the Coloured people reciprocate, calling the Africans uncivilized. In those parts of greater Cape Town or Johannesburg where people of different race have long lived intermingled, Coloured, Indian, and African boys are sometimes members of the same gang, but Langa is a segregated African area and the racial cleavage, coinciding with a territorial one, is dominant. Only in the city at work, and in the lunch hour, is there constant mingling (cf. plate II).

The distinction of sex is also very clear, an absolute dichotomy between men and women in occupation, manners, and dress being expected. For example, an African girl in Langa breaks the conventions if she wears trousers, and most Langa men disapprove strongly if a sophisticated girl dares to do so, though white and Coloured girls regularly wear trousers for sports, and at other times also. And, as we shall see, the migrants and the respectable people object very much to seeing a young woman smoke or drink, though her brother may do so without comment.

13

A third cleavage is that between the townspeople, the migrants, and the half-and-half type who are in process of being assimilated as townsmen but are not yet accepted. The townsmen live in houses as members of families, the migrants as single men in the barracks and zones, and the half-and-half group in the flats, spilling over into the zones, since space in the flats is limited, or scattered around wherever they can find a lodging or put up a shack.

The townsmen and the in-between types subdivide on the basis of local domicile—where they live in town—Langa people being distinguished from those in Nyanga, and both from those in Windermere and Kensington. The migrants, on the other hand, subdivide on the basis of where they live in the country, and groups of home-boys are formed, based on the village of origin. Thus locality is a basis of differentiation for everyone in town, but it operates differently for townsmen and migrants.

Class differences are clearly evident in town. They are closely related to education, but are also connected with the urban-rural cleavage, the townsmen looking down on the migrants as uncivilized or 'raw', while the migrants are shocked at the undisciplined behaviour of many townsmen. Many professional men and women—teachers, nurses, doctors, lawyers, priests, and ministers—live and work in the country, and they, if they move to town, are not classified as migrants, and are readily absorbed into the urban middle class, but the majority of countrymen are classed by the townsmen as 'country bumpkins'. Within the category of townsmen an important distinction is made between the *tsotsi* set, who are violent and boisterous, and the respectable, 'decent people', of which the educated section forms the middle class.

Age is also of importance in differentiating categories of townsmen. Among the half-educated, two main divisions based on age are recognized, *ikhaba* and *ooMac*, and the older men and women become, the more restrained their behaviour is expected to be, so that the distinction in behaviour between uneducated and educated is less among mature men and women than among teenagers. Among the migrants, age divisions are overshadowed by the divisions based on village of origin.

The categories emerging from a combination of the migrant-townsmen cleavage, class, and age may be summarized thus:

1. The migrant labourers, some of whom have never been to school at all, and others who have had up to eight years at school.
2. The semi-urbanized, with some education, who aspire to become townsmen.
3. The urbanized whose homes are in town.
    (a) Townee or *tsotsi* type, further subdivided on the basis of age into *ikhaba* and *ooMac*.
    (b) 'Decent people', some of whom form an educated middle class—the *ooscuse-me*—and others the respectable lower class.

The criteria of distinction between these categories is no such readily measurable thing as the number of years a man has worked in town, or the proportion of his life spent in town, the frequency of visits home, or even his individual land-rights or lack of land in the country; rather it is a matter of attitude and values. These are reflected in spending patterns. The migrant does not accept town values, and even though he may have worked in town for many years he still regards the country as his home. Except, perhaps, for occasional visits to town, his wife and children remain in the country, and in order to save and send them money he lives in the barracks or zones and pinches on food and clothes.

The semi-urbanized man behaves very much as a townsman while he is in town, and seeks to move out of the barracks or zones into the flats or a room in a private house, but he does not cut his ties with the country. His wife may or may not join him, but he still thinks of country life as better for an older, settled man. Many women remain semi-urbanized in their attitudes and values even though they have lived in town for some years and their husbands have become real townsmen. They continue to distinguish 'home people' (*abantu basekhaya*) from townspeople (*abantu basedolophini*). What draws the women back to the country is first their children, for neither parent may wish their children to be brought up in town, and secondly, the security afforded in the country by a close-knit group of kin holding land. A woman in town often feels that were her husband to die she would be helpless.

The urbanized man accepts town values—the values of an

industrial society—and regards the town as his home. 'He looks to the whites.' Although he may have been in town only for three or four years he is already certain that he will 'never go back to the country to build a hut', and his visits to the country are only holidays. His wife and children live with him in town, and even though a child may be sent to a grandmother in the country for a time it will 'come home' to town. The townsman seeks to achieve a European standard in food, dress, and furnishing, and spends his money on these things.

We do not know with any precision what proportion of the Langa population in each category is, but the men living in the barracks and zones total about 66 per cent, those in the flats 5 per cent, and the townspeople—men, women, and children— in the houses 28 per cent. Many of those forced to live in the zones would prefer to be in the flats or in houses, and they are, in fact, semi-urbanized. The townees perhaps form a third of the townsmen, the middle-class a third, and the 'decent people' of lower class a third. In greater Cape Town the proportion of semi-urbanized is considerably higher than in Langa, and the migrants lower: probably a third urbanized, a third semi-urbanized, and a third migrant is a reasonable estimate. The need for statistical verification of this is obvious.

Each of the categories defined must now be discussed in greater detail.

2. THE MIGRANTS

The *amagoduka*—those who go home—are looked down on by townsmen as country bumpkins; they are said to be ignorant, 'uncivilized' and are laughed at for being gullible. The migrants, for their part, despise the townees for their immoral ways and lack of discipline. The Christians from the country are shocked by the drunkenness, lasciviousness, and the violence of the townees, while pagans comment on their lack of morals (*isimilo*), ignorance of traditional custom (*amasiko*), and 'disregard for disgraceful behaviour'.

As has already been indicated, migrants and townsmen live separately in Langa, and they do not mingle very much. A true migrant is readily identified by his dress, his gait and manners, and his speech. Typically, he wears shabby trousers and a dilapidated hat, carries a billy-can, and smokes a long pipe filled with *twak*—a rank tobacco popular in the country. He walks with the grace and dignity of those who have spent their childhood on the veld, barefoot, but stares around him in town and is nervous crossing a street. He speaks the traditional Xhosa with relatively little modification, and in addressing people there is a certain formality and courtesy in his speech and manner. As for food, the migrants live mainly on mealies and bread, with beans or curdled milk, and small quantities of meat, tea, and sugar when they can afford it. Many of them suffer from scurvy. The monthly budget in three messes which were investigated worked out at R3.28 to R3.80 per man for food, R1.50 for rent, and R2 for fares, out of a wage of R26.50 to R27. Remittances home were reported to be R100 to R160 a year.

Women—the wives of migrants—are visible also by their dress and walk, manners and speech, and taste in food. They wear long skirts with black shawls and headkerchiefs—doeks— and low-heeled shoes, and they walk erect and magnificent, carrying any luggage they have on their heads. They are quiet in their manner and respectful to older people, and may even use the curious circumlocutions whereby a woman avoids mentioning the name of her husband's father, or words that rhyme with his name. Pagans are not seen in Cape Town in red blankets, as they still are in the eastern Cape, unless they have donned them especially for some celebration or a play, but country people, whether pagan or Christian, are easily recognizable.

The migrants, the *amagoduka*, are often referred to by towns-people as *amaqaba*—those who smear themselves with red clay—i.e. pagans, but in fact a great many of them, probably the majority, are 'school people' (*amagqoboka*),[1] and in the country distinguish themselves from 'reds'. Migration to the Cape has been selective. At first the Africans who came were mostly adult men who had had some schooling in the reserves, and had already worked either in the Johannesburg mines or a smaller town. Boys and illiterates went to the mines. Then sons of school families, even though not yet circumcised, began coming to Cape Town to look for their first job, and older

[1] *Amagqoboka* literally means converts, but is often used more widely for 'school people'. Cf. Monica Hunter, *Reaction to Conquest*, p. 6.

men who, though illiterate, had some experience of town life, came also. As a body the workers are much less 'raw' than those on the mines or some of the smaller towns, such as East London, and the 'school' group is relatively strong. The country–town cleavage tends to override the pagan–Christian cleavage which has been so important in the country during four generations, but which has now virtually disappeared from some rural districts, while surviving in others. As one informant, a house-wife of 25 with ten years' education,[2] insisted, not all the men in the barracks or zones are *amaqaba*, and *amaqaba* are to be found in the flats and houses also, but she had difficulty in defining the difference precisely. An educated man summed it up thus: 'The school people [*amagqoboka*] do not smoke and do not drink. Their language is more refined, and their topics of conversation are different from those of the *amaqaba*.' Even townsmen say that, on the whole, the migrants are hard-working and charitable—literally 'with humanity' (*banobuntu*)—whereas townees are often lazy and mean, but they are criticized as being 'apathetic' about working conditions and 'lacking any form of (political) leadership of their own'. As a pastor of one of the small churches, himself a retired railway worker, put it: 'They just come back from work and sit in their blankets.' Since restriction on movement and employment has increased, however, the migrants are identifying themselves more and more with townsmen on political issues.

Conversation among the migrants turns on stock and crops. They are always anxious for news from home about the weather —drought or rain means much to them—the condition of the cattle, and the fields. They discuss for hours the implications of the rehabilitation scheme, stock limitation and, closely connected with this, the position of headmen. The disturbances in Pondoland during 1960 caused great concern: 'It may start with the Mpondo, but it will affect everyone eventually', they said. Deaths in the home village are also discussed at length. Wages, the pass laws, and police raids are what concern them most in town and comment on them is bitter. 'The whites introduced the idea of a pass and the law requires that we carry

[2] Since the terminology used for school classes is not uniform in different countries, the approximate number of years spent in school is given. Twelve years' schooling prepares a candidate for matriculation at a university, or for the 'senior certificate' examination.

it, but the same law refuses us one. We stand in the queue at
Langa office for weeks without securing a pass, and sometimes
we have to return to the country without getting one. The
pass laws are really burning us.'

Young men talk about stick fights, and dances, and love-
making at home, and here the cleavage between pagan and
'school' people becomes apparent, for they attend different
functions in the country and only members of the 'in-group'
enjoy such reminiscences together. Older men—school and
pagan together—talk about the decay in morals of the younger
generation, and more particularly among townsmen, and they
talk of particular lineages and their relationships, and changes
in the social system. Few of them read regularly, but an
occasional man buys the *Cape Argus* or *Imvo*.

Three conversations overheard in a bus give some flavour of
migrants' attitudes and interests. The first reflects the meeting
in town of migrants from the same village:

A middle-aged man, 'school', and a migrant addressed two
young married women:

'Young lady do you remember me? Oh look at her, she is as
alert as her mother! Who is the other young lady sitting next
to you? Is she your sister? She looks so like you.'

'Yes, she is my younger sister, but who are you? I don't
remember you.'

'Do you know the homestead immediately across the stream
from your home?'

'Yes, I do! Are you F's father?'

'I am. I saw you growing up! You were children only yesterday, and now you are married women. To whom is your sister
married?'

'To X of P clan.'

'I see, that makes four of you, married daughters of Y. He
is a greater man now that all his daughters are married. Now
tell me what are you doing here in town, who is at home to
reap and plough when the time comes?'

'If you knew how I long to be back in the country you would
not inquire! I am weary of staying here, the five weeks I have
been in town seem like five years. One does nothing but go
up and down in these buses!'

Then a migrant complained to a townee about the iniquity of the change to a decimal coinage:

'If there is anything stupid this Government has ever introduced, it is this new money! And the way we are cheated in the buses! On every 4*d*. one loses ½*d*.'

'No, it's the same really, and the new system is easier to work.'

'What are you talking about when we are suffering so much with this new system!'

'Perhaps it is because of your lack of education, that you find it difficult'.

'To me it seems as if the educated are no better off.'

'That is nonsense!'

'By my sister's name what I am saying is true and straightforward, straight as a teacher's tie! Have you ever noticed a teacher's tie?'

And two migrants—men—talked about the proper way to treat a wife:

'Yes, it is good that women should run the house as white women do, but at the same time it is necessary that the man should have the over-riding authority so that when he wants to carry out a new plan he can do so without interference from his wife.'

'But at times it's a disadvantage to do things without consulting your wife.'

'Agreed, but all the same you will agree that sometimes it is necessary that one should make major decisions oneself, and act in a manly way [*ngobudoda*]. On such occasions women are often a disturbance because all they do is to talk endlessly.'

'Yes, you are right. Indeed, that is the trouble with town women, and that is why they dominate their husbands so. Have you ever in your life seen a man ruled by a woman?'

They finally agreed that women should be allowed some freedom, but subject to their husbands' authority.

Migrants work as milkmen in dairies, a job in which wages are low and the hours long; in building and construction; in the brickfields and cement works; in nursery gardens; and as dock

2

labourers.[3] Some of them also find jobs in certain factories and as petrol attendants in garages.

3. THE SEMI-URBANIZED

There are two types of partly urbanized men living in the flats in Langa, and in lodgings. They are all would-be townsmen who are 'trying to push in and be absorbed', 'trying to imitate townsmen', but some seek absorption in the *ooMac* group, and others with the 'decent people' in town. All of them are stigmatized as uncouth countrymen, *iibari*, by the townsmen proper, but the stereotype of *ibari* is the flashy young man, aspiring to *ooMac*. *Ibari* is probably derived from the Afrikaans, *baar* —rough, but it is also associated by some informants with *barbarian*. A film, *The Barbarians*, shown some years ago in Johannesburg, depicted the barbarians invading Rome, and it made a great impression. Educated Africans often refer to the uncouth as 'uncivilized', 'barbarians' or 'philistines', and after the film of *The Barbarians* the *tsotsis* in Johannesburg are said to have taken over the word and applied it to the new generation of countrymen who are in the process of being absorbed in town. The term is resented, and no man would ever use it of himself or of a friend in his presence.

The *iibari* mostly have at least a little education—indeed some of those living in the flats are much better educated than many townsmen proper—but they come from the country and have not yet been assimilated. Typically their dress is flashy, but not so fashionable as that of young townsmen. They wear suits with collars and ties, and their trousers have turn-ups. An *ibari* often has breakfast at an eating-house and lunches in town, and he spends far more on food than the migrant. One whose budget was investigated spent R15 monthly on food, as well as R7.20 on drink, and R3.25 on rent. He earned R32 a month. In their walk and speech the *iibari* are more urban than rural: their Xhosa is interlarded with English and Afrikaans words and they like to speak English in the street, or on buses and other public places.

The respectable men in the flats have links on the one hand with 'school people' in the country, and on the other with the

[3] Cf. S. van der Horst, forthcoming study on the employment of Africans in greater Cape Town.

'decent people' in town. They are conservative in their dress, and are never seen in the flashy clothes affected by *ooMac* and the *iibari* proper, and live much more economically. R9.83 a month was what a petrol attendant who messed with a friend spent on his share of the groceries, plus R1 for fuel. He earned R30 a month. Their language is that of country 'school people.'

Men in the flats do not live in tight-knit groups of home-boys as the migrants do, but their friends are often from the same home areas. Not all of them are necessarily countrymen; there may be a group from another town which has not yet been absorbed into Langa. For example, a party of men from Johannesburg came to build a power station in Cape Town; they lived in the flats and formed a gang of their own, in opposition to the Langa townsmen proper, and they too were classed as *iibari*.

The *iibari* are mostly 'angry young men', bitterly resentful of white domination, and aggressive towards everyone. They talk about starvation wages, iniquitous rents, and the restrictions of the pass system; and of how a man can make money and buy a car and travel to see Johannesburg, and Durban, and Port Elizabeth. Country matters are not of much interest to them; rather it is liquor, clothes, women, and jazz shows in town that they discuss.

Women belonging to the respectable section of the semi-urbanized are most commonly domestic servants who have followed their husbands to town and found jobs for themselves. Often they come as experienced cooks and housemaids, having worked first in country towns. They differ in their dress from the real countrywomen; a flowered foulard and hat, and shoes with heels, replace the print and doek and flat-heeled shoes of the *amagodukakazi*—the women migrants.

4. THE TOWNSMEN

The *townees* or *tsotsis* are also called '*location boys*', *ooclever*, *bright boys*, and *spoilers*, after a gang which terrorized Alexandra Township in Johannesburg. This type of urbanized young man is distinguished by his dress: wide-bottomed trousers without any turn-up, called *ivups*, which might be translated 'flappers';[4]

---

[4] *Vuphu*—the noise made by a garment wide enough to be blown about by the wind.

'skipper' shirts, sports coat, no collar or tie, and pointed shoes. He uses a mixture of Afrikaans and Xhosa slang—indeed the language of the *tsotsis* in Johannesburg, *mensetaal*, is said to be identical with that of white 'ducktails', and in Cape Town *tsotsi* and 'ducktail' speech approximates. The girls are equally extravagant in their dress and conspicuous for the fact that they smoke and drink, even in public, they slouch or mince in high heels, round shouldered, carrying their parcels in their hands. The men also walk differently from countrymen, with a much shorter stride, and jerkily.

The age-set from 15 to about 25 of the *tsotsi* type are called *ikhaba*, from *ikhaba* a half-grown mealie stalk. They also call themselves *die jong span*—the young team—and include boys and girls who have finished their primary school education and are not continuing, with a few girls who are still at school.

The *tsotsis* are violent and boisterous, given to smoking dagga and fighting with knives. They are a byword among the migrants and 'decent people' in town for their 'wildness', and the migrants will have nothing to do with them.

Ikhaba boys look for factory jobs and a few are delivery boys; they never work in dairies or in the building industry, and rarely in the docks. One attraction for them, as for others of the *tsotsi* type, in factory work is the opportunities it offers for pilfering, but the work itself is preferred to heavy labour, and hours are not so long as for milkmen. They also take the unpopular job of street-cleaner in Langa 'because they are often in trouble over passes and if a man works for the municipality he gets a pass'. Garage jobs are avoided because the hours are so long—forty-six hours a week—and often there is no whole day off in the week. The *ikhaba* prize a free week-end very highly.

The girls of the corresponding group—*ootsotsikazi*—seek jobs in factories or shops, or as waitresses in cafés, and some are domestic servants. Town girls like going out with *bright boys*— the *ikhaba* and their immediate seniors—because they are gay and sophisticated and provide a 'good time', but when it comes to marriage a middle-class man—a teacher or clerk—is preferred. The *bright boys* are not reliable and their income is irregular.

A little older than the *ikhaba*, from about 25 to 35, is the set called *ooMac*, from the Scottish *Mac*, which is a popular nickname among young men in town. They are expected to be more reasonable and responsible than the *ikhaba* boys—they no longer 'run around whistling in the location, or jumping on and off running buses, nor do they smoke dagga in public', 'but they are still wild'. Their wives, *ooMackazi*, being young married women, are expected to settle down as housewives, not going out to work, and not brewing beer as older women may, for a beer-brewer may be arrested, and for young women that is shameful. Their cooking is a good deal more elaborate than that of countrywomen, and by choice they eat food similar to that served in white homes. They like fish, which no conservative Xhosa will eat, and they even sing a song about the young man who treats his girl to 'fish and chips'. The budget for a family of four, two adults and two children, showed that R25.64 was spent each month on food; R1.68 on cleaning materials and R1.80 on fuel. The breadwinner was a taxi-driver earning R50 to R56 a month. Another family in the same category, with six members, spent R26.88 monthly on food.

Girls who have not married, but have had children, belong to this group also, and go about with *ooMac* men.

The men continue to seek work in factories, as they did when *ikhaba* boys, but they avoid, if possible, working in the same factory as migrants, for migrants are 'blind' and will not co-operate in the systematic pilfering that goes on. Because of the preference of both migrants and townsmen for working in separate concerns, and the habit of recruiting home-boys when any vacancy occurs (see below, [p. 50), there is a marked tendency for migrants and townsmen to congregate in different factories. A townsman will not apply for a job in a factory staffed mainly by migrants if he can find any alternative, and if many migrants are taken on the townsmen may leave. A case was cited of an educated young man who was offered a job as a clerk in the Langa Administrative Office, a post carrying considerable prestige, but he refused it on the ground that what he wanted was money, and he could make more by working in a factory, though the factory wages were not particularly good.

The pilfering is felt to be a means by which the under-paid get their own back, as the following conversation illustrates.

Two *ooMac* drove past a gang of road-workers supervised by two white foremen, who, as is customary, were watching, not working, and the one *uMac* remarked to the other:

'Look at those boers, all they do is to stand over those workers with their hands in their pockets, and yet when it comes to wages the money those two get is probably more than that drawn by all the workers combined.'

'Yes, as always, we do the hard work but are never paid for it. Under the circumstances how can people refrain from stealing?'

'The white business men also suffer a lot; the amount of stealing that is going on is much more than they realize. The gang is sitting on them! Nowadays no one bothers to go to a shop to buy things that are available in the location' (i.e. stolen goods).

Clothing, blanket, and boot-and-shoe factories are preferred to canneries, and soap-and-candle manufacturers, and flour-mills, for the work is cleaner. Work in a fish-processing factory is particularly disliked because of the smell.

Women of a generation older than *ooMackazi*, and who have not become respectable, are those who brew for sale, and whose customers drink on the premises, often rowdily. The disreputable woman brewer is characterized as one who 'shouts in the streets', and is seen drunk. Though elderly, her behaviour is not conventional, 'she is a funny old woman [*itopikazi elifani*]', the English word 'funny' being used in the sense of peculiar (see below, p. 28). There are no 'shebeen queens' in Langa with the prestige of those found in some Johannesburg townships; brewing and the sale of liquor are not highly regarded occupations even though they may be profitable.

Ikhaba and *ooMac* talk of the same sort of things as the *iibari*, but the *ikhaba* are also much taken up with styles of dress and tales of violence—robbery, housebreaking and murder; and both they and the *ooMac* discuss sport. Many of the *ooMac* are growing more responsible, as befits their age, and may be heard discussing among themselves how to treat a wife, or bring up children, or behave towards parents; or the position of the urban African, and the future of South Africa. Their wives talk about fashions and husbands, working conditions in domestic service, films, music, the difficulties of a

housewife, and how to bring up children. The men read the
Cape Times and *Cape Argus* and perhaps the *Bantu World*,
Imvo, and *Drum*, and the musicians among them, *Melody
Maker*. Their wives also like *Zonk, Bona, Femina, Golden City
Post*, comics, and love stories.

One *uMackazi* to another:
'Did you see X in her mauve? . . . She went past before
lunch-time. She was really smart. She looked sweet in mauve—
it suits her well.'
'I'm sure she had her nose in the air. What sort of shoes was
she wearing?'
'A modish sharp-pointed toe—probably a "Panther". . . .'
'Yes, she buys good clothes and dresses well, but she thinks
a lot of herself.'

uMac to *uMac*: 'Joe Ngidi is really a fine boxer. . . . You
know he defeated Mabena? . . .
'That Mabena is a wonder boy. I saw him once here in Cape
Town . . . he knows his footwork.'
'That reminds me of my days in the ring . . . footwork! I
excelled in that. One thing I like about Johannesburg is the
sport. Here in Cape Town it's very backward—people are not
interested. . . .'
'Cape Town is backward in everything, even the best
musicians come from Johannesburg. All the chaps do here is to
swim in the liquor.'

The second section of townsmen are the respectable people—
the 'decent people' as they are called—who are very critical of
the behaviour of *tsotsi* boys and girls. Many of them are
educated and essentially middle class, and some, indeed, suggest
that all the 'decent people' are educated, but this is not strictly
true. The educated people are referred to by others, somewhat
derogatorily, as *ooscuse-me*, and accused of being aloof and
conceited. They pride themselves on being respectably dressed,
and gentle and polite in their manner. 'They refrain from
talking at the tops of their voices' and are more refined in their
speech than the uneducated. School people are generally less
crude and more refined in their language than conservative

pagans and the change is still greater in the middle class.[5] English
is used in many situations among themselves, as Latin was
used by educated men in medieval Europe, and French by the
upper class in nineteenth-century Russia. It is the language of
communication within a group whose home languages differ.

Ooscuse-me include those in professional jobs—teachers,
lawyers, doctors, ministers of religion, nurses, secretaries—as
well as university students and others. Most of them take a
lively interest in national and international politics, and they
talk a great deal of such matters as African education, and
health, the legal system, and social reform. They read the
Cape Argus, and *Cape Times*, the radical *Torch* and *New Age*,
as well as *Drum*, *Zonk*, *Bona* and the *Reader's Digest*. The
women also like *Femina*.

Where earnings make it possible, food and furnishing
approximate to a middle-class white home. One family investigated, which had six members, four of them working, had a
joint income of R96 a month, and they spent R60.65 on food
R2.70 on cleaning materials and R4 on fuel. This was
exceptionally high—they entertained a great deal.

The 'decent people' generally support the churches (though a
good many *ooscuse-me* are not themselves churchgoers) and
this is one of the grounds of cleavage between 'townee' and
'decent'. Most *ooMac* and *ikhaba* deride Christianity.

Age divisions are less marked among the 'decent people'
than the townees: the majority in Cape Town are of an age
group corresponding to the *ooMac*, but there are also older men
and women, and their teenage children are mostly sent away to
boarding-school. These boys and girls tend to form a group of
their own in the holidays; those who are at school in Langa
may go around with the *ikhaba*, 'but they don't go to extremes'.
The difficulties of the middle-class people bringing up children
in town when the general pattern of behaviour for teenagers is
'wild' are obvious. There is evidence of sons from respectable
middle-class homes behaving like *tsotsis*, and of daughters
joining a wild set also, and bearing illegitimate children. For
this reason, parents who cannot afford boarding-school fees
may send their sons or daughters to relatives in the country,

[5] Dr. Vilakazi illustrates a similar change in Zulu. A. Vilakazi, 'A Reserve
from Within', *African Studies*, v, 16 (1957), p. 95.

and even young children are sent to the country expressly so that they should not 'learn town ways'.

Less well educated than the *ooscuse-me*, but still respectable, is the middle-aged and elderly type known as *amatopi* from topi, the pith sun-helmet worn by an earlier generation of Europeans—particularly missionaries and administrators—and so fashionable among an older generation of Africans. The younger section called 'wee topis' (*oomatopana*)[6] are mostly ex *ooMac*, from about 35 years old, and the *amatopi* proper are over 45. The *amatopi* generally—both younger and older sections—avoid factory work partly because they do not wish to become involved in theft cases; it would be a social stigma for a man of this age and type to be arrested; and they are mostly small business men:[7] general dealers, wood and coal merchants, tobacconists, hawkers, agents for wholesalers, and for the large hire-purchase business, taxi-owners, tailors, shoe-makers, hairdressers, tin-smiths, undertakers, cleaners in shops and offices, or caretakers. *Amatopikazi*, the wives and contemporaries of the *amatopi*, are housewives, and some are domestic servants. Men and women of this category are leaders in the churches, the Vigilance Association, the Rate-payers' Association, the Mfengu and Ntsikana celebrations, and the Advisory Board. The traders have their own African Traders' Association.

The *amatopi* are expected to act in a sober and responsible fashion like the educated 'decent people', and if a man does so he will be called *bawo* (father) by his juniors, but if he does not, and 'acts young', he will be addressed as *boetie* (brother) and referred to as a 'funny old man'. He is the parallel of the woman brewer and belongs to the townee rather than the respectable section of the community. Some *amatopikazi* may brew, and conduct an off-sales business in home-brewed beer, or in brandy, but they do it inconspicuously. If the trade becomes at all rowdy or noticeable they lose their status as 'respectable people'. Though they themselves are expected to have 'settled down', the *amatopi* 'understand wild boys', and are likely to be

[6] The form *oomatopana* (rather than *amatopana*) is not only a diminutive but has a jocular flavour implied in the prefix used, and the boy who addresses older men as *matopana* expresses familiarity rather than respect.
[7] There are 92 licensed trading premises in Langa and, in addition, the rooms of one doctor and one attorney. All licence holders are Africans. Figures by courtesy of the Administrative Office, Langa.

more sympathetic to *tsotsis* than the *ooscuse-me* are; they may, themselves, have been wild when young.

This brings us to a point of considerable significance: older men are *expected* to be much more sober and restrained than young men, and the crux of the complaint in town is that boys do not cease to behave as boys after circumcision. A contrast in behaviour between 'boy' and 'young man' was expected traditionally, but in town, among the *tsotsis*, it scarcely exists. It is, of course, generally true that the incidence of crimes of violence is much higher among teenagers than among older men—in England in 1955 one in three of all offenders found guilty of an indictable offence was under the age of 17[8]—but the expectation of a growth in restraint with increase in age appears to be even more marked in Langa than in London.

The conversation of the *amatopi* is often of national politics or local administration, of the various associations with which they are concerned, and of church matters, as well as of cars and business. They are ardent readers of English language newspapers—the *Cape Argus* and *Cape Times:* some of them also read such vernacular papers as *Imvo* and *Bantu World*, and religious publications. Their talk sounds familiar to white South Africans. Here, for instance, is a taxi-driver discussing cars with a friend:

'I see your "Plymouth" is still going strong.'

'May it continue . . . it's one of Manning and Patterson's[9] cattle. . . .'

'Yes, a "Plymouth" is a very good car, but I still prefer a "Chev". It can stand all sorts of conditions.'

5. THE PROCESS OF ABSORPTION

On their first trip from the country most young men stay in the barracks. There they are supervised by older men from the same village who urge the youngsters not to visit much in the location. They fear that if they do so they will squander their money and then they will not wish to return home because, penniless, they will scarcely be welcome. The older men who remain in the barracks are those who have rejected absorption themselves. But many men, on their second or third trip to

[8] Barbara Wootton, *Social Science and Social Pathology*, pp. 29–30.
[9] Referring to an Umtata garage.

town, do not return to the barracks but go to the flats, or seek lodgings in Kensington or elsewhere. They move partly to escape the supervision of the older men, but partly because of the intrinsic attraction to them of town life. Movement to the flats is selective; those who go are more likely to be those who have had some years' schooling, and those from Christian homes.

Mobility turns largely on education: teachers and other educated men and women from the country are very readily absorbed into the *ooscuse-me* group, though they have lived only a short time in town; but the uneducated, or those with only primary schooling, take longer to 'learn town ways' and become accepted. Professional men never stay in the barracks, and a young man who has been to a high school, coming to town for the first time, tries to make private arrangements with a friend to find him a place to live in the flats or in a private house. Of the original members of the *Statelytes* band (see below, p. 128) only two went through the barracks; the others came straight to the flats. Another example cited was a young matriculant from Healdtown who had school friends working in Cape Town and came straight to join them in the flats.

Joining clubs or associations is one of the ways of becoming integrated in town but, as we shall see, a number of the sports clubs and music clubs have a home-boy basis, so that a rugby player or jazz musician does not necessarily move immediately outside his home-boy group, but it will at least be a wider group than that from his own village (see below, p. 114). The more educated a man is, and the longer he spends in town, the more his associations depend upon like interest and personal friendship rather than upon coming from the same village, and he tends to move out of the home-boy club and join one in which the activity itself is the primary bond.

Women cannot stay in the barracks or zones, and wives of migrants who come to visit them live with friends in Langa, or Kensington, or Windermere, or elsewhere. As soon as a woman becomes a householder in her own right she is no longer a migrant proper but semi-urbanized, and women do not remain 'incapsulated' in a group from the home village in the degree to which men in the barracks do.

Migrants in Cape Town are mostly from the reserves of the Ciskei and Transkei, or from country towns; few come from farms, though migrants from farms are numerous in Johannesburg and East London; farm men moving to the Cape mostly go to Worcester or Paarl, and they divide into groups according to the districts from which they have come. The barracks and zones are, in fact, occupied by groups of home-boys, fluctuating in membership as individuals come and go from the country, but more or less stable as units from certain villages in the Transkei and Ciskei.

The migrants' recreations are largely within the groups of home-boys, but at week-ends there is dancing at the barracks and zones, pagans dancing the traditional dances and Christians the 'jive' popular at weddings in the country. Women are not permitted in the barracks and permits for them to visit the zones have to be obtained. This has been a source of much friction with the police. The present policy is to compel single men who have been living scattered through Kensington, Cook's Bush, Retreat, and elsewhere to move into the barracks and zones. They greatly resent being moved, and separated from the women with whom they have lived, and the Langa residents, for their part, look with great anxiety at the increase in the proportion of bachelors in Langa. 'What does X, the Location Superintendent, mean by establishing these zones? They are finishing our children.' X, it will be noted, is held *personally* responsible for the system he must administer. The complaint from parents that it is the migrants, and not townspeople proper, who make towns unsafe, and make it impossible to bring up families decently in town is an old one,[10] and has some substance in it: no town is likely to be very safe for families if a large body of single men is established permanently on its edge; but the least disciplined groups appear to be the *iibari*—those in process of being absorbed—and the teenage townees. The attitude of the townsmen proper to the migrants is ambivalent. They welcome them as customers—and many townsmen are trading in some fashion—though husbands and parents fear their influence on wives and daughters.

[10] Monica Hunter, *Reaction in Conquest*, p. 482. A similar complaint is made in Johannesburg.

6. AGE AND STATUS

Townspeople are classified partly by age, and which category they are put into depends on behaviour as well as chronological age. As noted above, 'a funny old man' old enough to be *itopi* may act as *uMac* and so be addressed as *boetie* (brother) rather than *bawo* (father). One of the characteristic changes in town is that both men and women are beginning to object to terms of address which suggest that they are older than they really are, or choose to be taken as. In the traditional Xhosa society status turned largely on age and it was never insulting to exaggerate someone's age; indeed, a white-haired African was once heard thanking a benefactor, a woman of 45, and assuring her that she was his 'grandmother'. The changing use of kinship terms is discussed later; here it is necessary to note that age and status are not so closely identified by townsmen as by country people, and the cult of youth has appeared; nevertheless 'the decent people' still pay respect to age.

Circumcision is not as absolute a cleavage between boys and men as it is in the country, but it is more important than it is in Johannesburg, firstly because Langa is relatively small and people know who is circumcised and who is not, and secondly, because the majority in Langa are Xhosa or Mfengu who practise circumcision, whereas in Johannesburg there are many Zulu who do not. In Johannesburg age is the most important criterion, and circumcised and uncircumcised may be members of the same group. In Langa they tend to be separated, but not sharply, as in the country. The age of circumcision is falling and is younger in town than in country, 15 to 16 being usual in town as against 20 in the country.

7. TERRITORIAL SEPARATION

Townsmen subdivide according to the locality in which they live. The Langa people distinguish themselves from those living in Nyanga, or Kensington, or Windermere, or elsewhere in the Cape. They regard themselves as somewhat superior (see p. 6); the majority of middle-class Africans in the Cape live in Langa, and the township as a whole is called snobbish by outsiders.

Langa boys and young men do not go freely to Kensington or Windermere; they fear to be attacked if they do so. Only if one has a friend in one of these slums will he visit alone, or a group may go together, warily, perhaps to attend a club to which they belong. Older men and women, and girls, go more readily, but still conscious that they are outside their home area, and migrants from the barracks may go because they are not townsmen of Langa. People from Langa and Nyanga visit one another constantly, though they have to secure passes to do so, and again the territorial separation is consciously noted. The boys of Nyanga are referred to as *'igenge yaseNyanga'*.

Within Langa there is a division between barracks, zones, flats, and houses, but not by streets among the houses as in the larger townships of Johannesburg. There, boys and young men keep to certain blocks of streets, and use only a defined route when travelling to and from bus or shops; they dare not stray for there are clearly marked 'territories' dominated by groups of boys and young men living within them, but Langa has no such divisions. A dangerous cleavage began to appear, however, when a large group of workmen came down from Johannesburg to build a new power station in Cape Town, and they were billeted in the Langa flats. They formed a gang in opposition to the Langa boys, and if a Langa boy alone met a group of the Johannesburg men he was likely to be beaten up. This was something new.

Langa then is, in a sense, 'the village' within which people move among familiar landmarks and faces. But with the great increase during the last years of bachelor accommodation in zones and barracks the cleavage between townsmen and migrants living in the different types of accommodation has become sharper, and security less.

Division into small communities within a city is familiar enough, as the following quotation indicates:

In London, as at least all Londoners know, we live in small groups of streets, the size of a small country town or large village, islanded between the traffic thoroughfares. The stores, banks, official buildings, the bus routes, the common property of everyone, mark the main thoroughfares, where we reach our frontiers and make contact with strangers; between the thoroughfares are the dwellings, the shops and pubs that serve small communities, knowing the needs and faces of individuals. Thousands of Londoners set off in the mornings from such inward-looking villages and are welcomed home to them at evening. . . .[11]

[11] William Townsend, 'The Idea of a Place', *The Listener*, 13 Oct. 1960, p. 620.

South African towns differ from this in that security of person is much more dependent upon remaining within one's own neighbourhood than it is in London. The danger in moving outside one's 'village' is less in the Cape than on the Reef, but it is increasing.

For the townsman, locality implies only the section of the city within which he lives, but for the migrant sub-groups based on *locality of origin* are of major importance. The migrant identifies himself as living, for example, in Langa, in the barracks, but to find him among the thousands of other migrants living in the Langa barracks one must know what locality he comes from. The conception is of such significance that it requires a chapter to itself.

8. LANGUAGE AND TRIBE

Division on the basis of language is much less important than division by colour for, as we have noted, Xhosa speech in town is interlarded with English and Afrikaans terms, and the language of the *tsotsis* approximates to that of the white duck-tails. The overwhelming majority of Africans in Cape Town are Xhosa-speaking, and the small number of Sotho-speakers and of 'Nyasa' (in which are included all those from north of the Limpopo) are treated as groups of home-boys. In Johannesburg a cleavage exists between Nguni and Sotho-speakers, both of whom are numerous, and divisions between Xhosa and Zulu, Sotho and Tswana, are also recognized, as well as separate categories of Shangaan and Venda, but these distinctions are of little significance in Cape Town. No fights on tribal lines such as occur in Johannesburg have been known in Langa: the alignment is between those living in barracks, those in the flats, and townsmen. Tribal cleavages are fostered by the government policy of 'ethnic grouping', which is stressed in the townships of the Reef. Left to themselves, people from the same district tend to live together when they first come to town, but gradually they are absorbed into the wider community. Compulsory 'ethnic grouping' slows up the process of absorption.

In Langa tribal names are used; people will often say: '*Kuhlala amaNgqika apho, amaGcakeka apho*', implying that men of the Ngqika section of the Xhosa (who were settled west of the Kei) live here, and of the Gcaleka section (who were settled east of the Kei after the border wars) live there; Thembu, Mpondo, Bhaca, Xesibe and Zulu (amaTshaka) are similarly spoken of as units. But tribal names from within the same linguistic group are rapidly being reduced to the same level as clan names. In town they are overshadowed by the country-town cleavage. For instance, Gcaleka as 'Transkeians' are rather slow to form any joint organization with the Ngqika who are 'Ciskeians', but directly an opposition with Cape Town boys is explicit then Gcaleka and Ngqika consolidate.

Tribal stereotypes exist on the same sort of level as stereotypes about Scotsmen, Welshmen, and Irishmen. The Xhosa are spoken of as 'a very hard people', '*ooclever*', precocious (*qavile*); the Pondo are 'wild'; the Mfengu 'sell-outs' and 'there are more Mfengu in the police'; just as Sandy is mean, Taffy a thief, and Paddy a shiftless spendthrift.

An impression of tribal solidarity is created by the celebration of 'tribal days'. The Mfengu commemorate their 'emancipation' from 'slavery' under the Xhosa on 14 May, the Xhosa commemorate Ntsikana, an early convert to Christianity, on 14 March, and the Sotho celebrate Moshweshwe Day, commemorating their famous chief, on 12 March. At each of these celebrations participants have, in the past, been encouraged to wear their traditional dress, or such modification of it as is considered decent, speeches have been made lauding the tribe, and songs sung and dances performed which were more or less traditional and exclusive to the group. 'Tribal days' began with commemoration by Mfengu Christians of their establishment within the 'Colony'; Xhosa and Sotho celebrations followed. They were popular forty years ago in the boarding-schools of the eastern Cape because they afforded the opportunity for a party with boys and girls together, and they have become regular occasions for celebration in urban townships.[12] The leaders have always been 'school people', not conservative pagans, and in no sense have the celebrations been really traditional. On the other hand, they have not been linked with modern political movements, and they have been approved by the township authorities and publicized in the English press.

[12] Cf. Monica Hunter, *Reaction to Conquest*, p. 459; Ruth Levin, *Marriage in Langa Native Location*, p. 15.

With the growth of African nationalism, sectional celebrations have come to be looked on with some suspicion, particularly by young people, and Mfengu and Sotho celebrations are now criticized in Langa for their exclusiveness. The Xhosa do not participate in Mfengu Day for, as one put it, 'this is a painful and unforgettable day when the Mfengu betrayed the Xhosa and sold them to the whites', 'What we are opposed to in the Mfengu celebration is discrimination [*ucalucalulo*]. You see, my wife is Mfengu, and how would I feel if she left me in the house to go and insult the Xhosa over there? That sort of thing can easily lead to the breaking up of homes.' A leading Xhosa was once asked to speak at such a celebration and refused, and many young people will not take part because they regard it as 'nothing but a way of reviving tribalism and thus splitting the nation [*isizwe*]'. The Sotho have also been accused of 'tribalism' in their celebration, and there has been disagreement among themselves about whether to celebrate or not. The Xhosa claim that in their celebration of Ntsikana Day they are *not* now being exclusive. Ntsikana was not a chief but, in his time, a radical who urged his people to listen to the missionaries and go to school.[13] He is now referred to as a 'Xhosa saint' and people are told: 'We are what we are today because we did not listen to what Ntsikane had to say . . . other nations are treading on us.' The main function of the committee concerned with the commemorating of Ntsikana is to raise funds for a scholarship which is given each year. Various schools nominate candidates and the committee selects one; four of the last six chosen were not Xhosa, but successively Sotho, Mfengu, Coloured, and 'Nyasa', so the claim of the organization that it provides 'a ceremony for everybody', and its aim is to 'promote progress among Africans', has some justification. The organizers are townsmen, of the middle class, a butcher, a shop-keeper, an insurance agent, and a salesman for a Cape Town firm, holding office in 1961. Some of them are also leading churchmen. The migrants from the barracks and zones do not take much interest in the proceedings.

'Tribal days' are parallel to the Caledonian Society's 'Burns

[13] John Knox Bokwe, *Ntsikana*, Lovedale, no date; Burnet Ntsikana, *The Life of Ntsikana*, Lovedale, 1902.

3

Nicht', or St. Patrick's Day celebrations, and might even be compared with the commemoration of the Day of the Covenant among Afrikaans-speaking South Africans, but no one of the celebrations rouses anything like the enthusiasm of St. Patrick's Day in New York, or the Day of the Covenant in Pretoria.

Since the establishment of Bantu Authorities in the country there has been much discussion and some anxiety as to government intentions regarding chiefs in town. In 1955 the Ngqika chief, Sandile, visited Cape Town and formally installed a representative. The same year the Zulu paramount, Cyprian, visited Cape Town. A Chiefs' Reception Committee exists, and it made arrangements for formal receptions on both occasions. Polite speeches were made and R300 was collected for the chief's expenses at Cyprian's reception, but there is bitter criticism of the institution of chieftainship, and particularly of chiefs visiting town, or seeking to assert any authority there, among people of all classes. The migrants in the barracks are often as outspoken in the matter as the *ooscuse-me*. Many people commented on the fact that Sandile's representative, though a Tshawe (the royal clan), was 'just a milkman' (one of the least honourable types of employment in town), and no one knew what his functions were to be, nor are they clear five years later. 'If Sandile wants help or donations he sends to Anta [his representative], but Anta has no authority, he cannot *instruct* men to do anything. If they refuse Sandile's requests he merely sends back word to the chief.' In 1960 one informant after another, when asked about chiefs, replied that he 'was not interested, they were just sell-outs', or words to that effect.

The position of a chief in the Ciskei has, for many years, been somewhat like that of the hereditary chief of a Scottish clan, as, for example, the MacLeod of MacLeod. The hereditary right carried considerable social prestige but little authority unless the chief also owned land or held some other office. In Pondoland and Thembuland chiefs carried more weight largely because they influenced the distribution of unsurveyed land. Now chiefs who hold office under the present system of Bantu Authorities have become so bitterly unpopular that it is commonly said: 'Chieftainship is finished.' A detailed study was made, and will be published separately,[14] of the reactions of

---

[14] A. Mafeje, 'A Chief Visits Town' (forthcoming).

people to the visit of a Thembu chief from the country, during 1961. This illustrates the ambivalence in the attitude of many people in town towards chieftainship: to refuse to receive the chief was very difficult for Thembu proud of their traditions, but to welcome him seemed to imply an acceptance of the system of administration through Bantu Authorities which is detested.

Those interested in language notice the difference in speech between men who come from the Ciskei and the Transkei, and between Mpondo, Bhaca, and Hlubi, as an Englishman may notice whether a man is from Yorkshire or Somerset, but the townsman is not much concerned with local country differences in speech or anything else. To him, the important criteria are townsman or migrant, and, within the group of townsmen, class.

The 'tribal' associations which flourish in towns of Rhodesia and the Congo are a function of relatively small language and cultural groups. In Cape Town one Bantu language — Xhosa — is dominant and its rivals are not other Bantu languages but English and Afrikaans. The numerous groups of home-boys are not differentiated by speech or tribal affiliation but by home village. Dialect differences have a local basis and adjoining villages may recognize the same chief, but the effective bond is to the village in which a man holds land-rights, actual or potential. Only in the minority groups, as among the Sotho of Basutoland or those from various Tswana chiefdoms, are there co-operating units which might be regarded as 'tribal' associations.

9. ILLUSTRATIONS

The categories defined become more intelligible if the biographies of individuals are studied, so sixteen case histories typical of the several categories are quoted below. The categories are not rigid but merge into one another, and members of the same family are sometimes differently classified. For instance, D 3, classified here as one of the 'decent people', but not *uscuse-me*, lives with an aunt who was classified in a budget survey as 'middle class', and M 2 is *uMackazi* though her husband is clearly *uscuse-me*. She attends church and is discreet in her behaviour, but she consciously and explicitly refuses to identify herself with the *ooscuse-me*, and her best friends are *ooMackazi*.

(i) *Migrants*

G was born in 1933, of semi-literate Christian parents. He went to school as a child, passing standard V in the village school, and standard VI at a school elsewhere in the Transkei. In 1949 he left school and went to work in the mines in Johannesburg for fourteen months, after which he returned home for nine months. Then he came to Cape Town and worked in a dairy for nine months—April to December 1951. Early in 1952 he found a job in a brickfield working there for six months, then moving on to a metal-work factory. He remained there for nine months, then went home to be circumcised in April 1953. He stayed at home until November 1954 when he went to Johannesburg on a contract to work on the mines. That completed, he came directly to Cape Town, and took a job as a delivery boy with a news agency. He worked for six months, then returned home for two months. In March 1956 he was back in town again, and found a job in a garage, first as a handyman and later as a driver. He has worked there ever since and has been home only twice, once for six months in 1957 when he got married, and again for six months early in 1960.

He lives with a group of home-boys from his own district in the Transkei: there are fourteen of them from the same village, and eight from other villages of the district, all in the same room in the barracks. Although he is a Christian—an Anglican—he does not attend church in town, nor is he a member of any club.

In answer to a question, he agreed that living in the flats would be pleasanter than living in the barracks, but to do so would be more expensive: 'Living in the flats induces people to spend too much money. . . . I am not a bee, I cannot eat honey while still making it. I have got nothing to do here in town except to make money, and then go home and open my own business if possible.'

His wife lives with her children at his parents' homestead. He is the heir.

(ii) *Semi-urbanized*

B was born in 1935 of Christian parents who lived in Qumbu District. His father was a school-teacher—now retired—and he grew up in the country, attending the village school and going on, in 1951, to a boarding-school for secondary education. He failed form I at the end of his first year at Healdtown, and had to leave, but he went to Shawbury where he remained until 1957. He claims to have got his senior certificate. He was circumcised in 1953.

He came to town in 1958 and worked with a building contractor for eleven days, then he got another job with a blanket manufacturer, and remained there for two years. Next he worked as a messenger in a stationer's shop, but he left after five days, because he 'could not bear being pushed around by half-educated white girls who have hardly passed their junior certificate'. He went home for a month in December, but returned early in 1961 and got a job as a salesman with a watch company, which he still holds.

He lives in the flats. During his first two years in town he lived with relatives—decent, semi-urbanized people—but left them because 'they wanted to control his life'. He is a member of the Bush Buck rugby club, and also of a five-man drinking 'syndicate'. He does not attend church. He is not yet married, and is not interested in whether he will settle finally in the country or in town. 'The question is irrelevant at this stage.' He is a typical *ibari*.

B 2 was born in 1936, in Tsomo district. His parents were peasants, and Christians. He passed standard VI in the village school in 1951 and went on to Healdtown. In 1953 he was circumcised. In 1956 he failed his senior certificate examination and was expelled in 1957 while preparing to write the examination again. He went to East London on a visit, and after two months went on to Port Elizabeth to look for a job. Failing to find one, he came to Cape Town in May 1958, and got a job as an office boy. He still has the same job, and in 1961 he went home, for the first time, on a month's holiday. He is not yet married, but is in love with a girl in town.

He is the only son in the family, and much attached to his father. He 'would not do anything that might hurt him', and 'he is the only person he would die for'. Though he would be content to stay in town if he could find decent accommodation, he will be 'bound to go back to the country and take over' on his father's death. He lives in the flats and belongs to no club.

B 3 was born in 1927 in the Engcobo District, his mother, but not his father, being Christian. He passed standard VI at a village school in 1946, and in 1947 went to Johannesburg for three months to work in the mines. He returned home and then, early in 1948, came to Cape Town, and worked in a dairy. In 1949 he went home for circumcision, and in 1950 returned to Cape Town to work in the same dairy, spending a full year. In 1951 he went home for six months, then returned to Cape Town and spent fourteen months working in a nursing-home, and two years in a paint factory. He went home for a month, in 1954, but returned to the same job and worked there without a break until 1959 when he went home for a month to get engaged to a country girl. He came back to his job, went home again in 1960 for three months to get married, and is again working in the same job. His wife lives with his mother and his younger brother: he is the eldest son, with land rights.

He would not now consider working on the mines, in the docks, in a dairy, or the building industry. He has been living in the flats since 1952, but dislikes the behaviour of the *iibari*: 'They are wild and they think of nothing else but drinking and running after women.' He himself is an excellent musician and is a member of the Happy Brothers choir, and a casino club. He attends rugby and soccer matches and is a member of the Methodist Church in Langa. He still thinks of the country as home. He is quiet and polite and in his speech and manner he resembles the 'school people' in the country. He does not smoke or drink. He has a few friends in the married quarters of the township whom he visits occasionally, and is much occupied with the choir.

(iii) *Townsmen*

(a) *iKhaba*

K 1 was born in Langa in 1937. His parents are Christians—Anglicans—and they have been in town for over thirty years. K 1 has never been to the country or any place other than Cape Town. He has a burning desire to visit Johannesburg. He attended a primary school in Langa, but left in 1949 when in standard V. He worked in an office as a 'tea-boy' from 1950 to 1952, then went to another office for a few months as a messenger, but lost that job because of pilfering. For eighteen months he worked in an acetylene factory, then got a job as a messenger for fourteen months, then moved to a job with the City Council, making cement slabs. After that he moved to a spinning and weaving factory and is still employed there.

He belongs to no club because in his view 'all the social clubs in Langa are for *ooscuse-me*'. At one time he was a member of the Langa Boxing club, now defunct. He does not attend church. He lives with his parents in Langa, but is a heavy drinker, and has repeatedly been charged with assault. He likes to speak the *mensetaal*, the jargon of the young townees. He is not yet married.

K 2 was also born in Langa and grew up with K 1, who is his contemporary, but he did not leave school until he had completed the primary course. This was in 1951. He started work in 1955, beginning as a labourer for the City Council, but in 1957 he was promoted to be a junior clerk in the Administration Office, and he still works there. He belongs to no church or club, and he drinks and goes about with the same group as K 1, but is less violent than he is.

(b) OoMac

M 1 was born in the Ciskei in 1931, and began his schooling there. His parents came to Cape Town in 1938 and he joined them in Langa in 1942, attending school in Langa until he completed the primary course in 1944. His father was a labourer and could not afford to send him to a high school so he stayed at home doing nothing until 1947 when he got a job as a messenger boy with a wholesale grocery. He has been with the firm ever since.

In 1949 he joined a jazz band, the City Jazz Kings, and played with them until 1954 when the club disintegrated. Now he is one of the leading members of the Disciples Jazz Band—'the ten and two' (there are twelve of them)—and is much attached to it. He also plays rugby for the Mother City club, and is a member of the Langa African Social and Cultural Association, but has no church connexion. He is a bachelor and lives in the 'special quarters'. He drinks fairly heavily but 'is rarely seen dead drunk'. 'He prefers to sleep in his room when drunk, he does not like the idea of being picked up in the street.'

M 2 was born in Langa in 1931. Her parents came to Langa in 1927, and her father was appointed a wardsman the year she was born. Her parents are Christians. She attended a primary school in Langa, and the high school, but left in 1949 after failing to pass the junior certificate examination. Her first job, in 1950, was as a domestic servant. After a year she left this place to become a shop-girl in Langa. That lasted for eighteen months, and then she worked as a doctor's receptionist for nine months. In 1955 she married a taxi-driver (see p. 66). A year later they got their own house. She has three children and has not gone out to work since marriage. She is a regular church-goer and a member of the choir, but there are certain difficulties with her husband because he is *uscuse-me* and she *Mackazi*. He, for example, is a member of the Ballroom Dancing club, and he wanted her to join also, but she refused on the ground that 'she is not interested in *scuse-me* activities because she is not one'. She prefers to go to the jazz shows in the Langa hall, which her husband detests. He 'does not know what she wants in skollie gatherings'. Her husband went no further in school than she did, but he is at home with *scuse-me* people while she is not.

M 3 was born in the Ciskei in 1934, and attended a village school until she had passed standard IV. In 1947 she went to Port Elizabeth to stay with relatives and completed her primary schooling (standard VI) there in 1949. Then she worked for two years as a waitress in a café, and in 1952 came to Langa to join her parents. She worked for three years as a housemaid, then became pregnant and spent 1957 looking after her baby. She spent three more years in domestic service, first as a housemaid and then as a cook until, in 1961, she became pregnant again. The father of her first child is not the father of the second. She is living with her father—her mother deserted him two years ago—and is caring for her younger brothers and sisters as well as her own child, and is working as a laundry agent.

Her father is a staunch churchman, and he, like all the older people in Langa, deplores the frequency of illegitimacy but can do nothing about it.[15] 'Look at M, my own child. This is the second child she is expecting. What shall I do with her? Shall I kill her or drive her out of the house? Of what use would that be? The best thing is to let my daughter enjoy life so long as she cares for her children properly. When God wills these bad conditions in society will all be over.' She herself is still attached to a church and is a member of a savings club.

(c) 'Decent people'—(young)

D 1 was born in Queenstown in 1932. She went to a primary school first in Lovedale, where she lived with relatives and then in King William's Town, and in 1948 she started at the Mantanzima Secondary School in Cala, but she had to leave after a year owing to ill health. For six years she was at home, doing nothing in particular until in 1955 she married a manual worker. Two years later they were divorced and she went to Johannesburg for a year as a domestic servant. In 1958 she returned to Queenstown and in March 1960 she came to Cape Town and got a job again in domestic service. She is of the type which 'won't spend all its money on the ever-increasing things town life offers because they have homes to return to one day'. She would not consider marrying an *uMac:* 'What should I do with a *tsotsi?* I have no time for them.' She belongs to no club, but is an adherent of the Anglican Church—not a communicant.

D 2 was born in 1927 in the Transkei, of Christian parents. He attended a primary school in Umtata, completing the primary course only in 1944. Then he went to Port Elizabeth, and attended a high school there for two years, but left before he had passed the second form. From 1948 to 1950 he worked in a drapery shop, then he came to Cape Town and got a job first in a small drapery shop, for a few months, and then in a large store where he remained

[15] The illegitimacy rate in Langa has fluctuated during the past twenty years, between 26·42 and 46·61 per cent of the total births. City of Cape Town, *M.O.H. Annual Reports.*

for three and a half years. Then, in 1955, he became an insurance agent, and is still so employed.

He is married to a girl from the Ciskei whom he met in Cape Town; he gave *lobola* for her, and has repeatedly visited her home. He is a member of the Western Province Ballroom Dancing Association, but refuses to take his wife to the meetings; he 'does not wish to introduce her to the corrupting town activities'. He considers it very important to visit his home in the country regularly for, he says: 'One's relatives always stand by one in times of trouble; town people cannot be relied upon. They only like you while things go well—as soon as everything goes wrong they desert you.' He is not a church member but is not opposed to church-going.

D 3 was born in Pondoland in 1938, and completed her primary schooling at a village school in 1954. She spent two years at a secondary school in Pondoland, but fell ill before completing the course and went home. In March 1957 she came to Cape Town, and took a job as a domestic servant; a year later she became a 'nurse-aid' at Groote Schuur Hospital. She has been home once on a month's holiday. She lives in Langa with an aunt, who also works at Groote Schuur Hospital as a skilled cook. She is well mannered and, though fashionable in her dress, she is not extreme. She is shocked by the behaviour of town girls. She is not a member of any club, nor does she attend church. If she is off duty on a Sunday it is her only free day in the week.

The aunt was born in the country, trained as a teacher at St. Matthew's, taught for some years and married, but she did not get on with her husband and was divorced. She came to Cape Town in 1934 and worked for some time as a domestic servant. Eventually she got a job as hospital cook, at which she earns R50 a month. She lives in Langa with her daughters and niece, a household of six. Three daughters are in domestic service. In another context the aunt was classified as 'middle class'.

(d) Amatopi

T 1 was born in 1874 in the Transkei, his mother being a Christian, but not his father. He passed standard VI at the village school in 1894 and in 1895 he came to Cape Town. He worked as a messenger boy in Sea Point until 1897 when he went home to be circumcised. In 1898 he began work in the docks as a foreman, then in 1899 he got a job with a tailor in Cape Town, as a messenger. He remained with him until 1945 when his employer died, and a firm, whose director was a cousin of his former employer, took him over. He is still with them as a messenger. The only break in his employment was from 1900–2 when he was attached to the army. He has been back to the country periodically on a month's holiday.

When he first came to Cape Town he was lodged by his employers, but in 1903 he moved to Ndabeni, and remained there until 1928 when he moved to Langa where a street is named after him. In 1908 he married a country girl and she joined him in Cape Town ten years later. They brought up their children in town. He has been chairman of the Langa Advisory Board, the Langa Vigilance Association, and the Mfengu Celebration Association, and a member of the Chiefs' Reception Committee. He is a member of the Methodist Church. He takes a lively interest in politics.

T 2 was born in 1909 in the Ciskei. She attended a village school and passed standard IV. In 1931 she married, and ten years later she went to East London to join her husband. In 1942 they came to Langa. Her husband died in 1947, but T 2 still lives in Langa with her children. Two daughters are working; she herself has never gone out to work. She is a member of the Full Gospel Church.

(e) Ooscuse-me

E 1 is a teacher. He was born in Langa in 1935, his parents having come to Cape Town from the Ciskei forty years ago. They lived first in Ndabeni, then in Maitland, and settled in Langa in the early thirties. They are leading church members and belong to the respectable middle class.

E 1 attended a primary school and the high school in Langa until 1954 when he went to Healdtown for three years to matriculate and train as a teacher. In 1958 he got a temporary post teaching in Langa and in 1959 a permanent post in a school in Retreat. He is still a bachelor and lives with his parents in Langa. He is a foundation member of the Langa African Social and Cultural Association, and on the executive committee; he is also a member of the Red Lion rugby club and a delegate from it to the Langa Rugby Union. The Red Lion club consists mainly of boys from Middledrift in the Ciskei—his father's home area. He did not join the Mother City club (as most town-born boys do) 'because the Mother City boys are rough and have skollie tendencies'. He is a member of the Methodist Church.

E 2 was born in East London in 1935, but grew up at his grandmother's in a village in the Ciskei, and attended the village school. In 1951 he went to Healdtown for five years and trained there as a teacher and physical training instructor. He came to Cape Town in 1957 and got a job in the Langa Administrative Office where he is still working, but he would like a permanent teaching post, and would gladly accept one whether in the town or in the country.

He is an instructor in the Cape Peninsula Athletics Association, and belongs to the Busy Bee rugby club, whose members mostly come from the part of the Ciskei in which he grew up. He is a member of the Methodist Church.

E 3 is a woman teacher. She was born in the Transkei in 1938 and attended a village school, then went to Emgwali for a three-year teacher's training course. In 1960 she got a post in Graaff-Reinet, and in 1961 she came to teach in Langa. She is a church member but belongs to no club.

3 Home-boys

1. WHO ARE HOME-BOYS?

For a migrant in town by far the most important group is that of his *abakhaya* or home-boys.[1] This is the group within which he lives and eats, and probably works.[2]

Home-boys are those who come from one neighbourhood (*isiphaluka*). The size of the area, which is important, varies with the number of men coming from it to Cape Town: often it is those from one rural village or 'location' under one headman, but if the village is large, and many of its members are in Cape Town, the effective group for most purposes will be those from a section of the village,[3] and if only one or two men come from a village they will join forces with others from the same magisterial district. All those from one magisterial district are recognized as home-boys in some sense, irrespective of numbers. As one informant put it: 'No matter where he comes from, if he pays tax in my district he is my home-boy.' But if there are fifty men in Cape Town from one district they do not all eat and sleep together, and they subdivide by villages and village sections. All the men from one village may be called together to discuss village business, or those from a district a matter concerning the wider group, and men who come from the area and fail to attend are criticized.

The largest territorial group combining is normally that from one magisterial district, but there are exceptions: for example, during the recent troubles in Pondoland, all Mpondo from Qawukeni (in eastern Pondoland) were combining to

---

[1] The English phrase is often used by Xhosa-speaking people. It is comparable in its implications to the 'old boys' of a school, and is not derogatory as is 'boy' when used by an employer.
[2] Cf. Philip Mayer's excellent account of *amakhaya* in *Townsmen or Tribesmen*.
[3] On villages and village sections cf. Monica Wilson *et al.*, *Social Structure*, pp. 4–22; *Keiskammahoek Rural Survey*, vol. III; W. D. Hammond Tooke, *Bhaca Society*, pp. 53 ff.

collect funds to help those at home. However, the chiefdom, even where chiefs survive as in Pondoland and Thembuland, is unimportant as a basis of grouping in town: village or village section and magisterial district are what matter.

An uneducated dock-worker of 25, who comes from Matatiele district and lives in the barracks, explained how home-boys hung together: 'We don't break away from each other when we come to town. It is proper and essential that we meet often to discuss developments at home, and hear who is ill, or who had died.' Asked whether the home-boys who met regularly together were those from one village or those from the whole district, he replied that he remembered no occasion on which all Matatiele men met, but he could imagine such a situation occurring, for example if there were trouble, as in Pondoland, with people at home arrested, and those at work would have to help by collecting money to send home. 'There are many Matatiele men in Cape Town and it would be difficult for them to meet regularly. It is more convenient for those from each village [ilali] to meet separately because, after all, they know each other at home, and what concerns them most is what is happening in their own village.'

An uneducated man of 40 from Tsolo, also living in the barracks, confirmed this, and added the point that so many Tsolo men were in Cape Town that 'if they all met wouldn't X [the Superintendent] think that we were preparing for a war?' Instead, people meet by neighbourhoods (iziphaluka, and later he identified neighbourhood with ilali) to discuss appeals for financial help from home in such matters as the building of a new church, the employment of an additional teacher in school (for which the parents must pay); and also matters like cattle culling and the rehabilitation scheme.

Men from Basutoland, Bechuanaland, or Zululand, who are few in number, may act as a group of home-boys for certain purposes. For example, a number of Kgatla men living in Langa, some of them in flats and some in the married quarters, acted together for mutual aid, providing money for the train fare home of one in difficulty, or for the burial of a comrade. This group even subscribed to send the corpse of one man home for burial. Such groups of men, who may not even have known each other before coming to town, are somewhat different from the close-knit unit of those who grew up in one village, herding, fighting, and going to parties together. Moreover, a Sotho who has grown up in town regards his contemporaries with whom he has grown up as his home-boys, rather than those who come from Basutoland (cf. p. 122). Those from north of the Limpopo are lumped together as 'Nyasa', but they have even fewer bonds uniting them than odd Sotho or Zulu, and they live scattered through the Peninsula and tend to be assimilated rather to the families of the Coloured girls, whom they usually marry, than to any organized African group. Only one 'Nyasa' man was located in Langa.

Home-boy loyalties override traditional tribal cleavages. For example, a Xhosa and a Mfengu[4] from the same village are home-boys irrespective of the traditional tribal enmity, and a man from Mount Frere district who was not a Bhaca would never be excluded from the group of home-boys on account of the tribal difference, even though his fellows knew very well that he was not a Bhaca by origin.

2. MUTUAL OBLIGATIONS

Men from one village or village section occupy the same room in the barracks, and cook and eat together, using a common supply of the staple foods such as mealie meal, samp, beans, and curdled milk. Delicacies such as meat and fruit are bought by individuals and shared with special friends, but for the staple supplies each man contributes a stipulated sum every month.

Two such groups may occupy one room. For example, in Room X in Langa barracks there are twenty-five men of varying ages. All come from Y magisterial district in the Transkei, fifteen come from one village and ten from another some miles distant. The fifteen men occupy one side of the 'stable' (isitali) as the barrack-rooms are called. They have their own food supplies and utensils and eat quite separately from the other ten, who have their own mess. Food is bought in quantities large enough to last for a month. Contributions are equal irrespective of age and status, and one young man, who has had nine years' schooling, is responsible for shopping.

[4] Cf. Monica Hunter, *Reaction to Conquest*, passim. Wilson *et al.*, *Social Structure*, passim.

He reports on his expenditure. Cooking and washing up is done by the young men, *amakrwala* (newly circumcised), or boys, *amakhwenkwe*, and the young men are served with a dish separate from that of the senior men. As a senior man put it: 'The wheel of fortune rotates, we have also been juniors.' The normal division is on the basis of age, but an educated visitor may be invited to eat with the seniors, even though he is a contemporary of the juniors.

Rooms in the barracks are known by the district from which the occupants come. Each room has its official number, used by the Administration, but, in addition, the occupants often paint over the door the registration letters for motor vehicles in their home district, so that a room occupied by men from King William's Town is CD, one from Umtata CCY and so on, and all sorts of bilingual puns are made on the letters. CFD, for example, is interpreted as 'Come from Dikeni', eDikeni being the Xhosa name for Alice, the dorp in the district for which CFD are the registration letters. Whether or not registration letters are painted on the door, it is commonly known that men from King William's Town occupy such and such a room or rooms, men from Umtata such and such, so that a visitor, having forgotten his friend's room number (as used by the Administration), can easily locate him if he knows where he comes from. Outsiders will know where the men—or some of them—from a given magisterial district live, and they, in turn, will know where men from a particular village or village section are to be found. In the zones the rooms are smaller, but home-boys from one district tend to occupy a whole block. Then in each mess there will be ten or fifteen men, all from one neighbourhood, and thirty-five to forty in the block.

The occupation of rooms is, of course, very closely linked with the shortage of accommodation in town, and the restrictions on entry. New-comers may not find a place beside their home-boys and have to go elsewhere until someone in the home-boys' room moves out. But one of the major obligations of a man in employment in town to his fellows in the country is to help each of them in securing a pass, a job, and a room, when they wish to come to work, and an elaborate system has been evolved whereby when one man goes home a friend comes to take his job and his place in the room, so that the solidarity of the group of home-boys, both in barracks and in employment, has been maintained.

An analysis of the home districts of employees shows a marked clustering from certain districts in particular factories or types of work. In the study of African employment made by Dr. van der Horst there was found to be 'a tendency in five of the seven firms for the men employed to come from a few districts' and the dairy investigated 'drew half its labour from Keiskammahoek district'.[5] The advantages to the worker of the private exchange through home-boys was that he was sure of a job and a place to live; he knew, before he came to town, what the conditions of work would be, and he worked alongside friends. The employer, for his part, held his older employees responsible, in some measure, for the behaviour of the recruits they brought to him.

This system, satisfactory to employers and employees alike, has now been seriously limited by the government insistence on compulsory allocation of labour, whereby a new-comer may take employment only through the government exchange, and employers are obliged to apply to the exchange. The limitation on free search for employment on the part of the employee, and the right to employ whom he chooses by the employer, is a source both of inefficiency and of tragedy. An employer may be unable to re-engage a former employee, and an African, desperate for work, refused permission to register in a job offered to him. To many Africans directed labour, combined with influx control, appears as forced labour, and the system arouses intense bitterness.

The compulsory direction of labour tends to break up the groups of home-boys, but some restriction on entry to town, and a shortage of accommodation, probably help to maintain them. The individual from the country has been *dependent* upon the help of his country friends to secure entry, employment, and a place to live, and this has tended to delay his absorption into the group of townsmen, Such absorption does occur with many, as we have seen, but it is delayed by the strength of ties with others from the home village.

In Cape Town, then, a group of men from a small country

[5] S. van der Horst, in a forthcoming study on the employment of Africans in greater Cape Town.

village tend to live, and eat, and work together. They address one another as *mkhaya* or home-boy if they are men of some education: only the most conservative use clan names. Until recently, if one member of the group went home for a spell he was likely to be replaced by another from the country. Those coming and going carried the news to friends and kinsmen, and often those returning to the country were commissioned to take parcels, containing clothes and other things for a worker's family at home. Home-boys are responsible if one of their number falls ill or dies. The effective unit is the group from one village (*ilali*) under one headman. All the home-boys, wherever they may be living in the Peninsula, are summoned by the senior man of the group, to whom the man in trouble, or his immediate friends, report the matter. The senior man explains the purpose of the meeting, and if the members are satisfied that the case is a good one, they decide among themselves how much each should contribute. The amount varies both with the size of the group and the character of the man in trouble. The usual contribution per head in a group of twenty to twenty-five from Ngqamakhwe was R4, whereas in a group of over fifty from Tsolo it was only R1.50, but a lukewarm home-boy is likely to receive less than a keen and loyal one. Repeated failure to attend meetings and contribute means that a man drops out of the group altogether, and cannot hope for help if he is in trouble.

A man from Willowvale gave this explanation: 'If one of us dies, we come together and collect money; everyone comes, even the chaps who are living at a distance—letters are written to them. The amount collected from each depends on how many men there are. When the dead man has been buried the balance of the money is sent to his family.' Asked whether *everyone* in town who came from the village would indeed attend the funeral, he qualified his first statement. X and Y, one a member of the Statelyte band and the other a ballroom dancer (see below, pp. 128, 130) were mentioned as men from his village; he replied: 'No, remember that there are people who, on coming to town, abandon Xhosa custom.' Home-boys also help a man who is unemployed, or in trouble with the police, so long as he has remained loyal to the group, but it is noticeable also that, with the increase in unemployment during 1961 to

PLATE 1 A migrant worker

PLATE 2   Barracks occupied by migrants

PLATE 3   Zones with a group of home-boys

1962, they are less ready to treat unemployment as an emergency requiring contributions from friends.

The older men of the group are held responsible, by country relatives, for the welfare of the young men. They admonish them and constantly laud the values of the rural community against the immorality and dissipations of the town. They may even fine those who disobey them. A senior man in town who fails to look after a younger man from his village will be much criticized on his return home. Personal friendships outside the group of home-boys are permitted: a man may form a friendship with another migrant he meets at work, or with a respectable townsman, perhaps a fellow clansman or someone who came originally from his home village, but a young man should not be drawn away too often from his clique, otherwise, as the senior men well understand, he will soon leave them and join the *iibari* in the flats. In the barracks and zones an individual is expected to be satisfied with whatever his own group of home-boys can offer, and not to hanker after some activity in which the others are not interested. He is told: 'Don't do things on the side' (*Musa ukwenza izinto ezisecaleni*); 'Don't pull your own way' (*Musa ukutsalela kwelakho icala wedwa*); 'Don't be a goat amongst sheep' (*Musa ukuba yibokhwe ezigusheni*). 'It is this that makes life in the barracks intolerable for certain types of men, and they escape to the flats as soon as opportunity offers.' The assessment is that of an educated African, and here is the crux of the process of urbanization. A city allows of greater diversity than a village and some men seize the opportunity to exercise freedom of choice; others cling to the warm security of the group of home-boys.

In his very interesting analysis of the migrants in East London, Professor Mayer[6] has suggested that it is only pagans who remain 'incapsulated' in groups of contemporaries from the home village. This is not so in Cape Town. A very considerable proportion of the migrants are 'school people', and the bond of common home locality sometimes overrides the pagan–'school' difference. Both pagan and 'school' may be members of the same mess, living and working together; only in their recreations, and particular friendships, and speech,

[6] Philip Mayer, *Townsmen or Tribesmen*. We are indebted to Professor Mayer for the useful phrase 'incapsulated'.

is a separation between them apparent. This holds even though
they come from a village in which there is still a cleavage
between pagan and 'school'. And the senior member of the
clique will be held responsible for both pagans and Christians,
irrespective of his own convictions.

Many of the migrants attend local churches, and the younger
ones may join sports clubs. These clubs, and in a lesser degree
certain congregations, tend to have a rural and regional basis,
so that those home-boys who are Christian may all attend
the same church, and those who play football join the same
club, uniting not only with others from their own magisterial
district, but from a wider neighbourhood, such as the Ciskei,
or northern Transkei, or the Cape Midlands. The pagan–
'school' cleavage, so sharp in conservative areas thirty years
ago, appears to be stronger in towns adjoining reserves, such
as East London and Durban, than it is in the more distant
centres. As has already been noted, Cape Town, with its higher
wages, tends to draw the more sophisticated, whereas the
completely uneducated go either to the mines, or to a town
close by.

3. HAVE TOWNSMEN HOME-BOYS?

Groups of home-boys flourish in the barracks and zones.
There membership is automatic, a fellow villager being accepted
as of right. The group is clearly defined: people know who
their home-boys are at all levels, i.e. members of the same
village section, or of the same village, or district. The members
of the smallest unit live and eat together, owning food in
common; discipline is exercised by a recognized leader, and
many groups continue through time, for as one member leaves
another from the same village replaces him. In fact home-boys
in the barracks form corporate groups.[7]

In the flats and houses it is different. Common origin may
provide a basis for friendship and co-operation, and a townsman who originally came from Middledrift will call a friend
from that district his home-boy, and those who have grown up
in Langa are home-boys vis-à-vis country migrants, or workmen

[7] The *degree* of incorporation varies from one society to another and one type
of group to another. Cf. Monica Wilson, *Rituals of Kinship among the Nyakyusa*,
p. 3.

from Johannesburg, but no group holds together without some common interest other than the home tie. In the barracks every man questioned could define his home-boy group, but some of those living in the flats and many in the married quarters cannot do so. The corporate group is replaced by a network of friends. For example, inquiry into the closest friends of a young *uMac* (a regular and co-operative informant) showed that he had *different* sets of friends with whom he did different things; there were two with whom he drank regularly, and others with whom he visited girls, and the two sets did not mix. One of his friends, B, with whom he visited, explained that he (B) had another circle of acquaintances with whom he drank, others with whom he did business (in stolen goods), and others again with whom he played games. Two members of the Statelyte gang (see below, p. 128) still went about together in 1961; they worked for the same firm, and visited and drank together, but the people with whom they interacted did not form a coherent group. They drank with one set, attended 'shows' with another, did business with others, and so on.

Similarly, the young musician who is referred to on pp. 40–1 could give no list of his home-boys. He shares a room in the flats with a close friend from another district, and sings in the choir which his room-mate leads (see p. 129), but there is no group with whom he interacts constantly for a variety of purposes. Of the men from his home village he said: 'They don't interest me, I really don't know how they think, their minds don't coincide with mine. . . . Most of them are interested in liquor and they never stop talking nonsense.' When he comes across them in town he greets them warmly, but he refuses to involve himself with them. In the country *all* the boys in a village are in some measure bound together: all are involved, for example, in a fight with another village; no one can opt out. But in town a man can choose his friends. Some men in town continue to belong to defined groups of home-boys as is illustrated below in groups IV, V and VI. What factors determine the formation and coherence of multi-purpose groups as opposed to clubs pursuing a single common interest among the semi-urbanized and townsmen, is not yet at all clear; however, it appears that: (1) Groups of girls growing up in town, and young women, are more close-knit than those of boys. *Ikhaba* girls refer to themselves and others as members of specific groups, and young women—*ooMackazi*—form small gossip groups which are sharply defined. The range of activities of women is considerably narrower than that of men in Langa, and therefore they do not tend to associate with different sets of friends for different activities, as the men do. (2) The *ooscuse-me*, both men and women, tend to engage in more activities together, and be closer knit than the *ooMac*, because there are relatively few of them, and they remain somewhat aloof from people of other categories.

4. SIX HOME-BOY GROUPS

A study of home-boy groups in time throws some light on the manner in which some individuals are absorbed as towns-men and others remain attached to country ideals. Six groups were studied of men of different categories. Not all the individuals mentioned live in Langa, but each group has, or has had, members living there, and an account of all the members is necessary to illustrate the process of absorption.

Group I. Date of arrival in town 1925–30. School people, migrants and townsmen

A came to Cape Town in 1928 and, except for short periods in the country, has been there ever since. He is nearer 60 than 50. He completed the primary course in a village school. When he first came to town he lived at his place of employment in Woodstock, then in the late thirties he bought a house in Athlone and lived there with his wife until, in the early forties, she 'could not bear town conditions any longer and was very anxious to go home'. They sold their house and went home to the Transkei. He returned to town after some time and got a job as handyman at Groote Schuur Hospital; he is still working there, now as a foreman. He rents a room in Cape Town. Two of his sons are working in town, and they live in the Langa flats. His wife visits him occasionally. She does not in the least regret having sold the house in Athlone: 'Where would I be now with this mass removal under the Group Areas Act had I remained? I would be a homeless vagabond; I saved my soul by going home in time, and building myself a house which I can occupy until I die.'

A gave an account of the members of his original home-boy group with whom he spent his time when he first came to town—he spoke of them with great fluency and intimacy.

A 1 also came to town in 1928. He had just qualified as a teacher at Clarkebury. He lived in Claremont and worked in a garage there, soon becoming qualified as a driver. He was a devoted Christian and a member of the Claremont branch of the Grand Temple—a temperance society. In 1936 he married, and though he was willing to become a townsman his wife would not hear of it. He applied for a teaching post in the country and as soon as he got an appointment he left Cape Town, and has been teaching at the same country school ever since. He has land rights in the country.

A 2 was a friend of A 1, and lived with him in Claremont. He, too, had completed the primary school course and worked at a garage. He came to town in 1927, and did not return home for ten years. Then he married a country girl and remained at home for two years. On his return to town he went back to the same job and the same quarters, and remained there for fifteen years. Ill-health finally sent him home. 'He was ruined, the town way of life had got the better of him; he had taken to drink and was going to the dogs.' He died shortly after his return home.

A 3 lived next door to A at home, and was also a close friend of A 1 and A 2. When he arrived in town he worked in a factory in Salt River, and lived near by. After some time he became a night-watchman in the factory. He had been to school in the village but did not go far. At first, he went home from time to time to visit his family, but for the last fifteen to twenty years he has not been home at all. 'His family wrote him countless letters until, finally, they gave him up. His brothers have also tried to speak to him and persuade him to go home, but with no success.' He lives with a concubine and her children.

A 4 was the most senior man of the group. He came to town in 1925 and worked as a packer in a wholesale store. He lived in Signal Road, Cape Town, and was greatly respected by the group because he was so helpful to them. 'It was he who received us when we came to town for the first time.' He remained in the same job until he left Cape Town in 1947 and returned home. He had visited his family in the country from time to time but they never came to town. 'He was a good man and never did anything bad.' He was a Christian and had spent six years in the village school. He died at home in the country some time ago.

A 5 came to town in 1929. He lived in the barracks in Langa, and worked in a factory in Paardeneiland, eventually becoming a store-man there. He had completed the primary course at the village school. He married in the late thirties and left town in 1946 to take up a headmanship in succession to his father, who had died. A 5 had a brother working in the Cape but he was rarely seen by other members of the group because he lived and worked at the Strand, 30 miles from the city, and so was not an active member of the home-boy group.

A 6 came to town in 1927. He worked as an unskilled labourer in a number of jobs, and lived at St. Columba's Home in Cape Town. He was a devout churchman and went home at regular intervals until his retirement. 'He never really liked town.' He died at home two years ago. He has sons working in Cape Town.

A 7 was A's elder brother, but he came to town only in 1930. He worked in various jobs, a garage, a news agency, and in several shops, then in 1935 he got a teaching post at one of the primary schools in Langa. He taught there until 1941 when he was appointed to the school in his home village. His wife was not willing to settle in town though she visited him there occasionally, and while teaching in Langa he spent most of his holidays at home. He is now retired.

A 8 came to town in 1929. He lived in Langa and had a job in a shoe factory. He came of a 'school' family, but did not have much education. While working in town he visited his home regularly and in 1958 he settled at home and is now looking after his land and cattle like any other peasant.

A 9 came to town in 1928 and worked in a shop. He had a room in Van der Leur Street, Cape Town. 'He was rather quiet and never really took much interest in town activities.' He visited home regularly and finally left town in 1953. He had completed a primary school course and spent one year in a secondary school.

A 10, who was a brother of A 9, came to town in 1930. He worked with a building contractor for some time, and then got a job as a night-watchman. He lived with his brother. He had left school after six years' primary education and, though 'nominally a Christian, he never came near the church door'. He left town in 1956.

A 11 was a qualified teacher. He came to town in 1926, worked in a shop, and lived in Woodstock. He married in 1934, but his wife remained at home. In 1936 he went to Johannesburg to take up a teaching post and his wife and children joined him there.

A 12 came to town in 1930 and worked as a petrol attendant, remaining with the same garage all the time he was in town. He lived in Wynberg.

A 13 worked for some time in town but left in 1939 to take up a teaching post in the country. He had married a country girl. 'He was a bright boy and knew how to live in this world.'

A 14 came to town in 1928 and worked as a dock labourer, living at Sea Point. After some time he got a job with a wholesale firm and while he was there he began peddling soft goods during the week-end. By this time he was living at Langa. In 1927 he went home and married, and remained at home for two or three years. On his return to town he did not look for employment but became a hawker, and after a few years he opened a shop. He got a house in Langa and his wife and family joined him there. His business is still going well. He had little education, spending only four years in the village school.

A 15, who came to town in 1929, first worked in a dairy in Lansdowne, living in quarters provided there. In 1935, after a visit home, he took a job in a garage, and learnt to drive. He and a friend bought a car and used it as a taxi, but after some time it cost them more in repairs than they made by taxi-ing, so they sold it, but he wanted very much to remain independent. He scraped together a little money and opened a shop in Langa, which he is still running. His family lives with him there. Like A 14 he had little education.

A 16 came to town in 1927 and first worked in a brickfield in Mowbray, then he got a job as a messenger in the Langa Administration Office, and after some time was promoted to be a clerk. He went home from time to time on leave, until his family joined him in town; they have a house in Langa. He had completed the primary school course.

A 17 came to town in the late twenties and got a job in a shop. He is still with the same firm, and his family lives with him in town.

A 18 came at the same time and began work in a chemical factory with which he has remained ever since. His family joined him and he is settled in town.

This group did not live together—apartheid was less rigid in Cape Town thirty years ago than it is now—and there were sub-groups—gangs as A called them—based on locality: one in Claremont, one in Langa, and one in the city, but the members visited each other on Sundays, and they attended parties together.

The members did not all come from the same village, but from four or five villages of the same district. Nowadays when there are many men in town from one district there is a much more rigid subdivision by villages. The members were all 'school people', but the better educated—the teachers—associated freely with the less educated, suggesting that class differentiation was less marked than it is now.

Six of the original nineteen have settled in Cape Town; one, a teacher, is living with his family in Johannesburg; the informant is still working in town but visits home, and his wife is settled there. The other eleven have either settled in the country

or died there. Of those settled in Cape Town two are self-
employed, one is a clerk, and three are with the firms with
which they began work on their arrival. All have been joined
by their wives and children except one who is regarded by his
family as an 'absconder', for he has deserted his wife in the
country and lives with a concubine. Of the three qualified as
teachers, two have chosen to take country jobs, and there is
evidence that in at least three cases, that of two teachers and
that of the foreman at the hospital, the pressure to settle in the
country came from the wives.

Group II. Date of arrival in town 1937–40. *Migrant school people*

B came to town in 1937 and lived in Athlone with a home-boy.
He worked first as a garden boy, then with an engineering firm,
and then, in 1944, he got a job with a large retail firm where he is
still working. He now lives in Windermere. He comes from a 'school'
family, but he spent only three years in school. He is attached to the
Methodist Church, but does not attend regularly. In the late forties
he married a country girl and he has land and a house in the country.
His wife has never been to town: 'He is resolved that she should
never put foot in town for he could never allow her to live in such
corrupting conditions.' In fact he himself lives with a concubine,
but he goes home regularly and supports his family at home. He
looks forward to the time when he will return home for good.

He gave the following brief biographies of seven men who were his
home-boys when he first came to town:

B 1 came to town in 1938, after having spent one year at a secondary school in the Transkei. He lived in Langa, in the zones, and
worked as a delivery boy for a butchery. In 1943 he got a job in a
shoe factory and remained in it until 1947 when he went home
for good. When on leave in 1945 he married. Asked why B 1 left
town so young, B replied: 'You should remember that some young
men are well born, and when their fathers die they leave them with
a good inheritance.' B 1 comes of a well-known 'school' family—a
number of them are teachers. He is a member of the Anglican Church.

B 2 came to town in 1939, after two years at a secondary school in
the Transkei, and also lived in Langa in the zones. He worked for
some time in a shop, and then went home for a year. In 1943 he
got a job with a large retail firm but spent only two years there
before going home to be married. Since 1946 he has been working in
East London, which he prefers to Cape Town. He has his own land
and house in the country, and is a regular migrant. He is a member
of the Presbyterian Church.

B 3 came to Cape Town in 1940 and began work as a dock labourer. He lived in the zones in Langa. Towards the end of 1942 he went home but he returned in 1943 and got a job at the fisheries at Cape Point. He spent four years there, but went home in 1947 to be married. He has never returned to Cape Town, but like B 1 inherited his father's homestead. He completed the primary school course and is a member of the Anglican Church.

B 4 came to Cape Town in 1936 and began work at an hotel in Sea Point, and continued there until 1941. Then he got a job in a leather works. In 1943 he went home to marry, but he returned the following year to the leather works. By this time he was living with his other home-boys in the zones in Langa. He is still there, and in the same job, but visits his home from time to time where he has his own land and house. He is a member of the Anglican Church.

B 5 came to Cape Town in 1940 and began work in a dairy. He lived in quarters there, but moved later to the zones. He worked for a short time with a building contractor, and after a visit home, as a dock labourer. In 1948 he married at home but returned in 1949 to the docks, continuing there until 1960 when he left Cape Town for East London, to join other home-boys there who had promised him a good job. He spent five years at the village school, and is a member of the Presbyterian Church. He has land and a house in the country and visits home regularly. He still writes to his home-boys in Cape Town.

B 6 came to Cape Town in 1939, and joined his home-boys in the zones. He got a job with a mattress manufacturer, with whom he has remained ever since. He married in the country in 1947, and his wife and children are at his late father's homestead. He has land and visits home regularly. He spent four years at the village school and is a Presbyterian.

The seven men in Group II all come from the same village in the Transkei. All of them are 'school people' but none of them has been absorbed in town, though one lives with a concubine. Two have moved to East London—perhaps because it is nearer their homes—and two have remained in the country. While they were working in Cape Town six of the seven lived in the zones and two of them are still there.

Group III. Date of arrival in town 1946–7. *Pagan migrants*

C, a pagan, was born in 1926. He first came to town in 1946 and worked in a dairy for eight months. He returned home early in 1947, and remained there until August, when he signed a contract with a recruiting corporation for mine-work in Johannesburg.

After completing it he returned home again and in April 1948 was circumcised. In January 1949 he returned to Cape Town and worked in a brickfield until April 1950, when he returned home again, for eleven months. He came back to Cape Town in March 1951 and worked at the same brickfield until October. In November he took a job with another contractor and worked until July 1952, when he returned home again. He remained at home for nearly two years, until June 1954, then returned to Cape Town and started work with a paint factory. In April 1955 he went home for eleven months, but returned to the same job in March 1956. He continued working until September 1959, when he went home for fifteen months. During this time he married. His father is dead and C is the only son of his parents. He left his wife in the homestead with his mother and returned to work in Cape Town in February 1961, getting a job at the abattoir. He has land at home.

Since shortly after he came to Cape Town he has lived, when in town, in the same room in the barracks, with a group of boys from his home village. In the same room there is a second group of home-boys from another village of the same district. He had no schooling as a child, but has been attending a night school in Cape Town and has passed standard V (normally seven years' schooling for a child), and is now doing standard VI work. He is the only man in his room who buys a newspaper—the *Cape Argus*—and he owns a couple of primary school readers, and a grammar and Xhosa–English dictionary. He takes a lively interest in politics, but is not a member of any sort of club.

C described the members of his home-boy group as follows:

C 1 also came to town in 1946 and worked in the same brickfield as C. They both lived in Mowbray then, close to their work, with some senior men from their home village. C 1 continued working at the brickfield until 1958, with a break in 1948 when he went home to be circumcised, and one in 1953 when he went home to be married. He is a pagan and never attended school. He has land at home. During 1958 and 1959 he lived in the barracks, in the same room as C, but in 1959 he went home on a visit and when he came back someone else had taken his place, so he joined another group of home-boys in the zones. He now works in a steel factory.

C 2 came to town in 1946 and lived with his elder brother at Rondebosch. He got a job at the University, and has remained in it ever since. In 1948 he went home to be circumcised, and in 1955 he went home again to marry. In 1957 he had to move from Rondebosch to the zones, where he is now living. Like the other men in his group he is a pagan, and he has never attended school. He has land at home.

C 3 came to town in 1947 and began work with a building contractor. At first he lived with his elder brother at their place of work, but in 1954 he joined his home-boys in the barracks. He went home to be circumcised in 1948, and later on he went home to marry, but he is still in his original job. He is also a pagan and illiterate.

C 4 came to town in 1947 and lived with kinsmen in Claremont. He worked in a bakery. Like the others he went home in 1948 to be circumcised, and on his return was employed by a building contractor. Some time later he got a job in a biscuit factory, which he still holds. He lives with his other home-boys in the barracks. He is married and has land rights at home, and like the others he is a pagan and illiterate.

C 5 came to town in 1946 and lived with a kinsman in Rosebank. He worked in a garage. He went home with the others to be circumcised in 1948, and on his return worked in the same biscuit factory as C 6, but after some time he returned to the garage in Rosebank, where he is still. He lives with the others in the barracks, and like them he is married, and has land rights, and he is pagan and illiterate.

These seven men come not only from the same village but from the same section of it, and they were circumcised the same year, though not in the same lodge (*boma*) for they belong to different clans, the Gcina and Mvulane, and each had its own lodge. C could name others who are his contemporaries from the same village, but he did not list them as his home-boys because he did not go about with them when he first came to town. As he put it, 'Our minds don't meet' *iingqondo zethu azifani*, i.e. we don't think alike). The members of this group were scattered when they first came to town, but five of them now live in the same room in the barracks and a sixth member was with them and only moved elsewhere because he lost his place one time when he went home on leave. None of them have been absorbed in town.

Group IV. Date of arrival in town 1946–8. School people, semi-urbanized

D came to town in 1948 and lived in the barracks. He worked in a bookshop and after a time became a travelling salesman, selling books in various centres in the Peninsula. In 1949 he went home for circumcision but he returned to the same job and room. In 1952 he took a job with a steel-works, but continued to live in the barracks. He went home once in 1954, on a visit. In 1957 he moved to the zones, for a year, but in 1958 he got a room in town which he still occupies. From 1957–9 he worked with the *Cape Argus*, as a delivery boy, and since then he has been with a leather-works. He married a town girl in 1960—in a registry office. In 1953 he played for the Langa Blues soccer club, and in 1960 he joined a trade union. At one time he belonged to a savings club. He had completed the primary school course before coming to town, and while he was working he followed a correspondence course, hoping to complete the junior certificate, but he never wrote the examination. He is an Anglican. He gave the following account of his home-boys:

D 1 also came to town in 1948. He worked at an hotel and lived in Primrose Street with senior home-boys. In 1949 he went home to be circumcised and, on his return, he began work in a tobacco company with which he is still. He married a teacher in the country in 1953. She came to town for a year but did not like town life and has gone back to the country; she is not working. It is thought that when he invited his wife to town he hoped to settle in town: as it is, he visits home regularly. He has been a member of the Transkeian Lions rugby club, and he belonged to the same savings club as D. He completed the primary course at a village school, and is a member of the Anglican Church.

D 2 came to town in 1948, and got a job at an hotel and lived there. In 1949 he went home to be circumcised. In 1950 he returned and got a job with the tobacco company with which D 1 works and he is still working there. From 1950 to 1955 he lived with his home-boys in Primrose Street, then he took up with a woman in domestic service and he spends most of his spare time with her. They have no children and she is a lover (*umasihlalisane*), not a wife; he leaves his property with his home-boys in Primrose Street, not with her. He has a legal wife and two children in the country, but he has been home only three times between 1948 and 1961. His wife was a teacher. He completed the first form in a secondary school in the country, and he is a regular church-goer, something about which his friends tease him. 'He goes to church so regularly because he has got so many sins to pray for.' His friends regard him as somewhat irresponsible, but he is inoffensive and jolly. He also played for the Transkeian Lions rugby club.

D 3 came to town in 1949, and attended Langa High School for two years. His mother was a domestic servant and he lived with her in District Six. In 1952 he returned to the country for circumcision, and in 1953 he worked for the matriculation examination, but did not complete the course. When he left school, he worked in a barber's shop, and began selling soft goods in his free time. Now he works for a china-dealer during the week and in the barber's shop over the week-end. He is two or three years younger than the other members of the group and is not yet married. Nominally he is an Anglican, but he does not show much interest in the church. His mother is a staunch church member. He does not belong to any clubs. In dress and speech he is a regular townsman, whereas the other members of the group are semi-urbanized.

D 4 came to town in 1947, and lived in the barracks in the same room as D. He worked for the City Council. In 1949 he also went home for circumcision. He returned in 1951 and worked as a hawker, staying in the zones. After two years he got a room in the flats, then in 1957 moved to a room in the house of relatives who lived in the married quarters in Langa. At the end of 1958 he joined his other home-boys in Primrose Street. He is not married but has lived with various women, and he has not been home since 1951. He now works for the same tobacco company as D 1 and D 2. He is not a member of any club.

D 5 came to town in 1949 and began work in a dairy. He continued working there, even after he found his home-boys, because he did not have a pass. In 1953 he moved to a job in the docks. His home-boys helped him to obtain a pass and after getting it he went to live with them in town, and they secured a job for him at the tobacco factory at which D 1, D 2 and D 4 work. He is not yet legally married, but lives with a woman—a domestic servant—in concubinage. He was circumcised before he left home in 1949 and he has never been back. He completed the primary course in the village school and is a member of the Anglican Church. At one time he belonged to a savings club.

D 6 came to town in 1946 and worked as a house-boy in Sea Point. In 1948 he went home for circumcision. On his return, he got a job in an hotel where he remained for five years. By the end of that time he was living with his home-boys in Primrose Street. In 1954 he went home to be married to a country girl, and in 1955 got a job in a biscuit factory (at which C 4 worked) for a year. In 1958 he became a driver for the tobacco company with which D 1, D 2, D 4 and D 5 work, and he is still with them. From 1955 to 1959 he lived in Windermere. After marrying in 1954 he visited home every two years until, at the beginning of 1960, he brought his wife and family to town with him. He got a house for them in Nyanga, and when asked whether he would still visit the country he replied sharply: 'What for? What should I do at home? We are all here. My wife and children are here and that is proof that Cape Town is my beginning and end and I shall not go elsewhere.' He spent six years in a primary school in the country, and is an Anglican. He was a member of a savings club for five years, and is a responsible husband and father.

Only one of the seven men in this group visits home regularly and he brought his wife to town but she did not wish to stay. All the others are already almost absorbed as townsmen.

Group V. Date of arrival in town 1946–7. *Middle class, mostly urbanized*

E is a taxi-driver. He came to Cape Town in 1947 after being expelled from a secondary school in the Transkei on account of a strike by the boys. He was then in the second form. His first job was with a building contractor, but he remained only for six months. Early in 1948 he became a porter in an hotel, and got a room in the flats. He spent four years at the hotel and then took a job as a petrol attendant at a garage for a few months. There he learnt to drive, and before the end of 1952 he got a job with a taxi firm. Two years later he bought his own car and set up as a taxi-driver on his own. As he changed jobs he changed accommodation and friends. In 1951 he left the flats and got a room in Wynberg in the same house as a man from his home district. They had known each other as boys. From 1953 to 1954 he lived as a sub-tenant in the married quarters in Langa, and there he fell in love with a Langa girl. He married her in 1955 and they lived for two years as sub-tenants then, in 1956, got a house to rent in Langa. They still live there with their three children.

E is *scuse-me* in his outlook. He is a member of the Anglican Church, and of the Cape Peninsula Ballroom Dancing Association. His wife has rather different tastes (cf. p. 42). He regards the following as his home-boys:

E 1 came to town in 1947 and found accommodation in the flats. It was he who got E a place there when he arrived in 1948. They shared a room until E 1 left Cape Town for East London in 1950. E 2 took his place. E 1 worked in East London as a petrol attendant until 1952, when he got a job as a truck-driver, delivering coal, in Umtata. In 1953 he bought a car and returned to East London to use it as a taxi. In 1956 he married an East London girl, a nurse. He has a house in Tsolo, in the Transkei, where he lives with his family, but he still runs a taxi business which is flourishing. He has had two years' secondary schooling and comes from an educated family. He is an Anglican.

E 2 came to Cape Town in 1946, and began work as a house-boy in Muizenberg. In 1948 he moved to a job with a timber firm. At first, he lived at his place of work, but in 1951 he got a room in a private house in Wynberg, and it was here that he joined E. At the end of 1952 he went home to be married (E then moved to Langa), and on his return he went to live in Kliptown. He was still employed by the same timber firm but in 1954 E taught him to drive, and in 1955 they went home in E's car, bringing E 2's wife back with them. He then got a job as a taxi-driver, but in 1957 gave that up to work at a dry-cleaner's. The same year he built a temporary shelter for himself and his wife in Nyanga East (where only temporary houses are permitted) and at the end of 1957, with the help of E, he bought a small van which he uses for collecting clothes for dry-cleaning. He now has two vans and has employed a young man to help him. He lives with his wife in Nyanga, but remains on close terms with E, whose house serves as one of his depots for dry-cleaning. Their wives are also good friends and visit one another regularly. E 2 only completed the primary school course, but he is a good business man. He and his wife are happily married. Although they have a church connexion they do not attend at all regularly. Economically, they are in the same category as E and his wife, but they are less ostentatious in their spending—perhaps because E's wife is town bred, and E 2's wife came from the country.

E 3 came to town in 1947. He lived in the flats and attended Langa High School for some months, but did not complete a year, and began work in Langa as a shop assistant. In 1949 he got a clerical job in the Administrative Office in Langa, and married a nurse, whose home was in the township. They lived with her parents for six months, but in 1950 they were able to rent a four-roomed house in Langa—it was here that E lived as a sub-tenant. In 1958 he divorced his wife, remarried her nine months later, and divorced her again after six months. Three months later he married another woman, also a nurse. To escape the critical attitude of the Langa community towards her, he sent her to the country, and she is still working in a country hospital. He is still working in the Langa Administrative Office. He has a good car, is a member of the Thembu rugby club, a representative of it on the Western Province Rugby Board, and a member of the Peninsula African Socialite Association. He is, therefore, classed by others as *uscuse-me*.

E 4 came to town in 1947 after completing two years' secondary schooling. He lived in the flats, and worked for a time in a garage, but lost that job and for part of 1948 he had no fixed work and made his money by dubious means. In 1949 his mother died in the country and his home-boys—E, E 1, E 2 and E 3—collected money for his fare home. By this time he was almost destitute. He took the money but did not go home: he disappeared to Freegrond in the Simonstown area. His home-boys found him there six months later. Again, he had no money and he was very shabby. He was no longer known by his own name but passed as —— ——, a Coloured man. He was very light in complexion and spoke Afrikaans well, so could

easily pass for Coloured. As his home-boys soon found out, he had
become a racketeer. 'We could not do anything about him, we
knew he was finished, so we left him to his own devices', said E.
Later they heard that he was in gaol, and when he came out he
disappeared to Johannesburg. This was in 1954. Recently his
home-boys heard that he had been seen in Johannesburg where he
was married to a Coloured woman and living under yet a different
name.

E 5 came to town in 1946, after leaving high school in the second
form. He got a job at Freegrond as a houseboy and remained there
for nine months. Then, from 1947 to 1952, he worked at an oxygen
factory in Salt River. From 1947 to 1951 he was a sub-tenant in the
married quarters in Langa, but his wife from the country joined
him in 1951 and they lived in Kliptown. It was he that E 2 joined in
1952. He lived there until the end of 1956 when he decided that it
was too expensive to keep a family in town so he took his wife and
children back to the country and moved to the Langa flats. From
1952 to 1954 he worked as a petrol attendant in a garage, and then
he got a job with a bank where he is still employed. He is a member
of the Thembu rugby club, and on the committee of the Langa
Tennis Club. Though he lives in the flats he is *uscuse-me* in outlook
and behaviour, and spends most of his time with townsmen.

E 6 came to town in 1946 after seven years at a primary school
in the country. He lived at first with a brother at Elsie's River, and
worked for a building contractor. In 1948 he went to live in Freegrond, and worked in an hotel in Muizenberg for six months. He
got a job as a driver, on a forged driving-licence, and two days later
had an accident. He was fined for driving without a licence and lost
his job. In 1949 both his parents died within a week of each other,
and he went home for two months. On his return he worked at
an hotel for two years, again in Muizenberg, and he lived with
Coloured people. He had already changed his name to ———
———, and he spoke Afrikaans fluently. At the end of 1950 a
message came saying that his sisters needed him urgently, but he
refused to go home. Early in 1951 his sisters wrote to the Superintendent in Langa asking him to send their brother home: the
Superintendent referred the matter to his home-boys. Because they
liked him, and it was clear that they were in danger of losing him,
they accepted the responsibility. For two days they did not go to
work, but spent the time hunting for their friend. After a tiresome
search they found him and told him that he was wanted at home and
should return. E 6 would not see reason so they grabbed him and
took him to Langa and locked him up in E's room. In the morning
they gave him food and went to work. To their 'surprise and

annoyance' he had gone when they returned: they found the door forced open and E 6 had vanished—also some things from the house. They went to look for him early next morning, and found him. They talked to him seriously, and asked what was happening. He apologized and explained that he was going through a difficult time; his parents' sudden death had been a heavy blow, and on top of that the effects of bad government were hitting him hard, and that was why he was passing as Coloured.[8] He promised that he would not give them any more trouble. His home-boys saw the change that had taken place in him and did not trust him completely. After buying him a train ticket they tied his legs and hands and left him to the care of an elderly man. The latter, said E angrily, was 'madly fond of wine', and after his home-boys had gone to work E 6 produced some money and said to the old man: 'If only you could untie me I could buy some wine for us to drink.' The old man would not trust him but offered to fetch the wine himself. They began drinking: only one of E 6's hands was free and he complained that he could not enjoy his drink properly so the old man 'who was made more fatherly by the wine', extracted a promise that he would not make trouble and untied him. E 6 immediately seized him, tied him to the kitchen stove, put a bottle of wine next to him, and disappeared. Six months later he was sent home with an uncle, but he disappeared at Amabele junction, just before getting into the Transkei. Later he was arrested in Port Elizabeth for burglary and house-breaking and he gave his name as —— —— of Freegrond. His Coloured concubine [sent money to pay his fine and he returned to Cape Town. His home-boys went to see him but he was very rude to them, and refused to have anything to do with them. 'We then had to abandon our beloved home-boy.'

Only two of the men still have close connexions with the country: E 1 who runs a taxi business which plies between East London and the Transkei; and E 5 who brought his wife and children to town but found it too expensive. These two are largely urban in outlook and the other five are certainly townsmen.

A point of particular interest about this group is that they are a combination of boys from the same village, and boys from the same school, the two links not wholly coinciding. E 1, E 2, E 4, E 5 and E 6 all went to the same boarding-school; E 1, E 3,

---

[8] Passing for Coloured has practical advantages, for Coloured people do not carry reference books, nor are they subject to influx control, and their choice of employment and housing is much wider than for Africans.

E 6 and E 7 come from one village, E 2 from Tsolo, and E 4 and E 5 from Umtata. The two who were not at the same school came from the leader's village.

Group VI. Date of arrival in town 1950 *to* 1951. *School people, migrant and urbanized*

F came to town in 1950 and lived with a kinsman in Athlone. He was already 19 but went to school and completed his primary schooling in Athlone and spent three years at Langa High School. While at high school he began to work as a newspaper delivery boy. In 1953 he left school and got a job with a mattress manufacturer. He found a room in Rylands, and lived with a Coloured woman. His relatives and more conservative home-boys were much concerned about him, and tried to send him home. In 1955 they succeeded, and he returned the following year, a changed man. He told a field-worker that when he went home his mother cried bitter tears because she had completely trusted him, and when he absconded, her heart was broken. 'From then on,' he said, 'I decided never to break my mother's heart again, lest ill luck befall me.' On his return to Cape Town he went to live with his conservative home-boys in the barracks, and still does so, and in 1958 he married a country girl of whom he is very fond. He goes home regularly, and in the eyes of his fellows is a 'good boy'. His parents are pagan but he, and his younger sister, and his wife are members of the Anglican Church. He gave the following account of his home-boys:

F 1 came to town in the same year as F. They attended school together and lived near one another in Athlone, and worked together for the same news agency. F 1 was living with a classificatory father. He left school in 1952 and went to live in Rylands, where F was already with the Coloured woman. He continued to work for the news agency, but he was sent home by his classificatory father and home-boys from the barracks along with F, in 1955. Three of them were sent home together; a fourth home-boy refused to go. F 1 came back to Cape Town with F early in 1956 but F 1's pass was not in order and he was 'endorsed out'. He went to Johannesburg, and is still working there, but he married a country girl in 1957 and goes home to visit. He is the eldest son in his family—the heir. Like F he has pagan parents but has become a Christian.

F 2 came to town in 1950 and attended school at Kensington, where he lived with his mother. He completed the primary course, then left school and during the whole of 1953 he did nothing. In 1954 he got a job with a shoe-polish manufacturer, but he was losing contact with his home-boys whom he had known in 1950, and in 1955, when F and F 1 were sent home he refused to go. His home-boys admonished him, telling him of what was happening at home, but they could not persuade him to go. He left Cape Town for Johannesburg and has not been heard of since.

F 3 came to town in 1950. He had attended the same village school as F, F 1, and F 2, but he was a class ahead of them and had already completed the primary course before coming to Cape Town. He lived for three years in the barracks, and worked as a dock labourer. In 1953 he got a job with pipe manufacturers in Stikland and lived with a concubine. This happened almost at the same time as F and F 1 went to live in Rylands. His home-boys went to fetch him, as they did F 1 and F 2, but it was not until 1957 that he agreed to go home. He remained at home for two years, before leaving for Johannesburg. He was a nominal Christian with pagan parents, but when at home in 1958 he shocked all the Christians in his area by carrying off *two* girls as brides, at the same time. It shocked even the pagans, both because Christians do not ordinarily practise *twala* marriage,[9] and no man had ever been known to *twala* two women at the same time. F 3 argued that his 'kinsmen and clansmen wanted it. If they didn't why did they insist on sending me away from Cape Town where I could marry four wives for 10s.?' The two girls he carried off were returned ceremoniously by his kinsmen to their homes, the very day he carried them off. His action was in fact a rejection of all conventions. He has never returned from Johannesburg and there is little expectation that he will ever do so.

F 4 was completing his primary schooling in the country in 1950, the year his friends left for Cape Town. He joined them in 1951, working in a dairy in Lansdowne and living at his place of work. In 1953 he went home and married. His father, who thought that his friends (F, F 1, F 2, and F 3) were the sort of boys to abscond, sought to settle him by providing a wife, though he was still too young to marry, by Nguni standards.

In 1954 he returned to Cape Town and got a job at the same news agency as F and F 1; the same year he joined them in Rylands, and lived as they did, with a Coloured concubine. He was sent home in 1955, with F and F 1, by his senior home-boys whom he referred to as *imoogie*—country bumpkins. While at home he went off to work in a neighbouring wattle plantation, and did not return until his father fetched him. Then, in 1957, he came back to Cape Town and worked again at the news agency. He lived at first with friends at Claremont, but he moved to Rylands because his older home-boys

[9] For the implications of this see Wilson *et al.*, *Social Structure*, pp. 84–5.

were 'continually tracing his movements'. He has not been home since 1957, and though his father continues to send messages to his senior home-boys asking them to send him home, 'Nobody is prepared to bother himself about someone who does not know what he wants in life. We have decided to leave F 4 alone, to do as he pleases, until he is satisfied.' This was F's opinion.

One or two points emerging from these cases are worth stressing. The extent to which home-boys take responsibility for their mates and try to prevent them absconding (*ukutshipha*) —disappearing in the city—and neglecting family responsibilities is striking in groups V and VI. Control by the group is exerted, and very often accepted. But it is also clear that incapsulation is often voluntary; home-boys who have lived scattered come together from choice and cling to one another, in the warm familiar atmosphere of childhood friends.

There is greater differentiation of groups as the number of Transkeians in Cape Town increases, and diversity of tastes becomes more marked; having grown up in the same village or district no longer provides a community of interest strong enough in itself to hold a group together. The members of groups III, IV, V, and VI respectively, are homogeneous in education, employment, and tastes, much more so than the members of group I, who were diverse in these things but united by their common origin. This differentiation is further reflected in the feeling expressed by K 1 and M 2 of being excluded from middle-class associations (see above, pp. 41, 42). And some men belong to no home-boy group, even though they retain close links with their families in the country, because they differ in their interests from their home-boys in town: the musician from Engcobo is a case in point (see pp. 40–1).

Education facilitates absorption in town but not nearly all the 'school people' who work in Cape Town are absorbed. In group II none of the seven men—all of them from 'school' homes—was absorbed and in groups I and V there are examples of teachers and nurses, and other educated people, choosing to live in the country. It is also apparent that illiterate pagans may be absorbed, and boys from pagan homes may abscond as F 2 and F 3 did.

A woman who has grown up in town never wishes to live in the country—a woman's life there is too hard, drawing wood and water, and working in the fields—so if a man marries a town girl he is likely to be absorbed, but a countrywoman often presses her husband to return home, even though she may live with him for a period in town, as A's wife did. The duty of a wife in traditional Nguni society was to 'build up the homestead [umzi]' and 'no homestead can ever be built in town', so a married woman who encourages her husband to settle in town may be regarded by her husband's family—and her own—as a 'destroyer' 'not worth the position of a wife'. Her behaviour reflects on her family and upbringing, and all her husband's subsequent faults will be blamed on her. 'The wife is responsible for whatever bad actions her husband does.' Furthermore, 'a woman who has disgraced her home by absconding with her husband, and has failed her in-laws by encouraging their son to abscond, has nothing to fall back on. She would not be welcome either at her own home or her married home if she returned. She would be a friendless wanderer with nowhere to go.'

Some in a set of home-boys are often absorbed, while others are not, as in groups I, IV, V and VI. A man's relationship with his wife, her attitude towards town life, and his position in the family—whether or not he is the heir—are important in determining his choice, but the relative weight of these and other possible factors still eludes us.

Lastly, the case histories suggest that new-comers change their jobs frequently until they are suited, but after that many remain for years with the same employer.

4 Kinsmen

Residents in Langa are involved in a network of kinship relationships which extend not only to other townships or suburbs in the Peninsula, but to the Transkei and Ciskei, and the towns of Port Elizabeth, East London, Grahamstown, Queenstown, and other country towns of the Border and Midlands, and even Johannesburg, Pretoria, and Durban. A handful also have kin in Basutoland or Bechuanaland. The wide dispersion of families, the extent to which ordinary working men have travelled, and the size of the sums spent on travelling in proportion to wages earned,[1] are a never failing source of astonishment to the outsider. As for the middle-class, their kinship connexions now extend to Britain and America, Ghana, Nigeria, Tanganyika, and the Rhodesias, where a son or niece is studying, teaching, or nursing, or lives in exile as a political refugee. The number 'abroad' is small, but their impact on a large group of kinsfolk at home is enormous.

The range of kinship relationships which are actively maintained has not been adequately assessed. The town bred, in conversation, suggest that it is only primary and secondary relationships which are of much importance; parents and children, grandparents and grandchildren, siblings and their children visit and co-operate, but second cousins are not of importance to one another unless some bond, other than that of kinship, unites them.

Some detailed investigations suggested that a kinship circle of twenty persons was common among the town bred, but men and women who had come from the country could provide enormous genealogies: one clergyman compiled a genealogy of

[1] Third-class return fares from Cape Town to other centres are as follows: Umtata R20.46; King William's Town R17.73; Port Elizabeth R15.50; Johannesburg R19.44.

his mother's kin alone which included 159 persons, of whom less than 10 per cent were in Cape Town, the others being in Natal and on the Rand. Another large genealogy gives 25 per cent in Cape Town, 50 per cent in Mount Frere district, and 25 per cent elsewhere in the Transkei.

Kinsmen are bound by personal ties, but they do not now form defined corporate groups other than the elementary family, and more than three-quarters of the people do not even live in families, for they are men who have left their wives and children behind in the country, or young bachelors. Of the 87 per cent of men who are living as single men in Langa probably over half are married.[2]

In Cape Town houses are small—mostly two-roomed, and a few three- and four-roomed—and accommodation is so short there is seldom opportunity for kinsmen to secure adjoining houses, so extended families cannot live together even if they wish to. Inquiry from young married couples suggests that they prefer to live on their own: an *uscuse-me* housewife of 30 insisted that she would not care to have anyone at all, other than her husband and children, living in the house. Even her own mother would be 'like anyone else, she would be a constant cause of misunderstanding'! An *ikhaba* girl of 24, as yet unmarried, took the same view: 'Living with people (other than husband and children) is such a nuisance and it leads to quarrels.' A young man of 30, working as a clerk, would be glad if he could have *his* mother living with them: 'She would be so useful.' However, he would not consider having in-laws in the house: 'They would always be finding fault with one's treatment of one's wife.'

Contrast with this the traditional attitude expressed by a young married woman, recently from the country, and just visiting in town. When asked whether she would not prefer to live alone with her husband and children she replied with surprise: 'What sort of homestead [*umzi*] would that be? Have you ever seen a homestead of children? A homestead is a homestead because of the old people.' And when asked whether

[2] In Dr. van der Horst's sample 58 per cent of the labour force was married. Half of these did not have their wives in town. Of the men away from Keiskamma-hoek district 53 per cent were married, 21 per cent had their wives with them. D. Hobart Houghton and E. M. Walton, *The Economy of a Native Reserve*, *Keiskammahoek Rural Survey*, vol. II, p. 134.

she did not find it difficult living with her mother-in-law she
replied: 'Even if it is, when I decided to get married I expected
such things. My in-laws are my in-laws and it behoves me to
bear with them patiently, because on getting married I came
willingly to them.' That is the traditional ideal, nevertheless
many country homesteads do split because of friction between
mother-in-law and daughter-in-law.

2. THE LINEAGE AND MARRIAGE

Lineage segments were held together traditionally among the
Nguni, partly because the male members lived in one homestead,
and partly because they shared a common inheritance in cattle:
the fact that members participated in common rituals and
observed an absolute taboo on marriage with fellow clansmen
also bound them together. In Langa, not only do kinsmen not
share a dwelling, but no immovable property can be inherited,
for occupiers cannot buy their houses, nor can they build their
own, and there is no family herd to pass on. So the control and
inheritance of substantial property, on which a lineage organization depends, are absent. Only country ties, with rights over
freehold or quitrent land, or a less secure right to inherit a field
in a village with 'communal tenure', magnify patrilineal descent
and the unity of a group of male kin. Thus common residence,
and shared rights in inherited property, have disappeared
among townsmen, and the rule of exogamy, which forbade
marriage within the clan, is questioned. Traditionally clan
identity was constantly asserted by the use of the *isiduko*, the
clan name, as a polite greeting, and children grew up knowing
very well which of their friends and contemporaries fell within
the prohibited degrees of marriage and which did not.[3] In
the country *iziduko* are still commonly heard in greeting, and
conservatives in town, the pagan migrants, and elderly people
will use it, but among the townees, and younger people
generally, *iziduko* are out of fashion. The use of clan names has
been largely displaced by the use of surnames which are required
in all official contexts, and in dealings with whites. In an earlier
generation school families all took a name—usually that of a
male ancestor but sometimes that of an admired European—
as a surname.

[3] Cf. Monica Hunter, *Reaction to Conquest*, pp. 51–9.

A study of marriage made in Langa sixteen years ago showed only two breaches of clan exogamy,[4] but as identification of clansmen lapses, the rules are weakened, and a number of young men and women expressed the view that they no longer mattered. A country woman of 30 who has been in town for less than ten years, 'would never dream of marrying a fellow clansman', but a young man of 19 living in the same house said he would marry a girl of his own clan, 'Why should we use clans when whites use none? What is the use of not following their practice since we are following them in our way of life?' He had been born in town and gone to a Coloured elementary school. A man of 25, who had grown up in Middledrift district, in the Ciskei, but is now absorbed as a townsman, said that he 'would not marry a woman of the same clan as himself only because of parental pressure'. In everyday meetings he never worries about inquiring into clan names. A man of 28, born in the Transkei, with ten years' education and making a living as a hawker in Langa, with a clientele mainly among migrants whom he likes and respects, 'is not interested in clan names and would marry any woman he loves', but a small trader, with the same educational background and radical in many of his views, would not marry a clanswoman.

On the whole, the women questioned were more conservative than the men. A housewife of 31, with ten years' education, who has lived mainly in town, would not consider marrying, or even having a love affair with, a fellow clansman, and a contemporary of similar background said the same. Neither of them inquired about clan names in ordinary contacts, but both said they would withdraw from a love affair immediately if they found a man to be of their own clan. Another young woman of 35, married, and the second generation in town, with nine years' schooling, insisted that clan exogamy should be observed.

The only woman who was prepared to disregard clan exogamy was a domestic servant of 24, born in town, and with rather less education than the others quoted. She is a typical *ikhaba* girl, and said she would 'marry any person she liked', irrespective of clan. A young wife of 25, newly arrived from the

---

[4] Ruth Levin, *Marriage in Langa Native Location*, p. 14. One of these—a notorious case—is still mentioned.

Transkei, burst out at this: 'But to sleep with a fellow clansman is like sleeping with your brother; it's incest!'

These samples are sufficient to indicate that the attitude toward clan exogamy is changing; only a statistical study of the clans of recently married husbands and wives, their mothers and grandmothers, would show how far there is a change in practice.

Although many people in town do not pay any regard to clan connexions there are others to whom traditional rituals are still important. Pagan clansmen gather, irrespective of their village or district, for the celebration of funerals, and 'dinner-parties',[5] for new-born babies, and clansmen are also summoned in cases of serious illness, and when it is necessary to consult a diviner. Then too, if a man has been very lucky, as in winning at the races, he calls his clansmen together to thank 'the old ones' (*abadala*, i.e. the *shades*). Fellow clansmen are also invited to a wedding, but so are many other people. It is in the matter of settling *lobola*, or damages in case of seduction, that senior clansmen are especially responsible; they handle the matter if one of their clan is sued, whereas home-boys are only informed of what is happening.

One case was cited in which hospitality was offered and accepted on the ground of common clanship. A woman commercial traveller was visiting Saldanha Bay. The weather was foul and the 'Nyasa' headman had difficulty in finding her a place to sleep until one of the local residents learned that she was a member of his clan; though a total stranger he insisted on providing shelter and generous hospitality, and he scolded the headman for failing to inform him that one of his fellow clansmen was in need. Other similar cases are said to have occurred.

The importance of mother's kin is commonly increased by a high illegitimacy rate, and it has been shown how, in the Ciskei, illegitimate children are brought up as children of their mother's family, often in a homestead of which the head is herself a mother of illegitimate children, or perhaps a widow.[6] Mother-

---

[5] 'Dinner-party' is a common euphemism among Christians for the celebration that replaces the pagan 'bringing home' the shade of the dead, a year after the funeral. Its use for the ritual at the birth of a child is less familiar but since slaughtering a goat—the traditional rite—is illegal in town some circumlocution is not unexpected.

[6] Wilson *et al.*, *Social Structure*, pp. 93–106.

managed homes are one of the products of a high illegitimacy rate and of a higher death-rate for men than for women, such as exists in the Ciskei and probably also in Cape Town. Our informants agreed that homes in which the head was a woman were common, but again we lack statistics to show their frequency.

As already noted (p. 43), the illegitimacy rate is high, but marriage is felt to be important, and many couples in town marry either by Christian or civil rites with or without *lobola*, or enter into customary unions. Concubinage (*ukuhlalisana*) is common but not approved, and it is felt to be particularly shameful for young girls and young men to live in that way, and elderly men and women. 'Old people are expected to be symbols of a chaste life.' For a professional woman it is felt wholly wrong: 'If a staff nurse lived with a lover, openly, the whole of Langa would know about it immediately.'

Here there is a contrast between Langa and the community in Johannesburg described by Miss Longmore in *The Dispossessed*. The difference is due partly, no doubt, to a difference of category and class. Illegitimacy or bearing and begetting illegitimate children is a stigma among middle-class people as it is not among the *tsotsis*. In Langa the 'decent people', including the middle-class section of them, are numerous, whereas Eastern Native Township is a particularly poor township, but it should be noted that in Langa even the *ooMac* marry, and their wives are *expected* to settle down and become respectable.

In town polygyny does not exist, and it has disappeared from many country districts also,[7] but it has been partly replaced by concubinage. Many of the *iibari* have town 'wives' with whom they live, though they are already married in the country, and even those whose wives are in town may take lovers. Some men do not, in fact, wish their wives to come to town for they prefer to enjoy themselves with young women, leaving the legitimate wife to bring up the children in the country without any regular source of income.

The pattern of migration makes it even easier for a man to evade his responsibilities to his family than it is for a man to do so in a large city anywhere. Maintenance orders are

[7] Wilson *et al.*, *Social Structure*, pp. 92–3.

very difficult to enforce.[8] Many of the *ooclever* (i.e. *ooMac*), and some *ooscuse-me* men who are married, regularly take out other women to parties and picnics, women who are recognized as their 'girl friends'. It is fashionable to go off picnicking by car and wives are not taken. Men who do this are criticized in Langa, but the criticism tends to come from women rather than men. Most wives do not accept the existence of lovers with equanimity, particularly if much money is spent on them, and bitter quarrels ensue. There is no general acceptance among the women of a *right* to concubinage as there was to polygynous marriage in the traditional Nguni society, and they comment sadly on how women 'begin to look old very quickly' after marriage.

The higher an individual's social status the more social pressure is exerted on him, and it is interesting to note how this operates in Langa. Girls in Langa are not expected to smoke or drink—*ikhaba* girls and *ooMackazi* commonly do so—but 'what cannot be tolerated is a *scuse-me* girl who drinks and smokes'. The effective pressure to conform is loss of prestige, with a possible change in class standing. And marriage tends to be regulated more and more by class, so the *scuse-me* girl who wishes to find a husband of her own class must conform. 'It is considered stupid for a *scuse-me* bachelor to take out an ordinary location girl, or a domestic servant', and if an educated girl behaves like a *tsotsi* she will not find a *scuse-me* husband.

Both men and women marry in order to have children to whom they have a legal claim and in order to be respected as mature people. As one woman put it: 'What would be the point of getting married if one were not to have children? One might as well remain a spinster. Who would wish to live by herself, like an owl, without any children?' And another said: 'One can never settle down and be a respectable mother without getting married. At one stage or the other one has to grow up. One cannot remain an old maid for ever—it's disgraceful.' And again: 'It's nice to be Mrs. somebody [using the English title though speaking Xhosa] for once and do things in your own right as mistress of the house. It's unlike what happens in these concubinage relationships when a woman lives in constant fear

---

[8] D. G. Bettison, 'Child Maintenance in a Small South African Town', *African Studies*, v, 15 (1956), pp. 132–8.

of being deserted by the "husband". . . .' Again, 'We do enter into concubinage with men, and have illegitimate children, but it's not the right thing to do because such a relationship can come to an end at any time, and it's a bad thing for children to grow up without a father. . . . No permanent and established home [*umzi*] can come out of such a relationship.'

Men also attach very great importance to having children: 'It is proper for a man to leave someone bearing his name, before he dies. It is essential that a man's name should live after his death.' 'Marriage completes a man's life in every conceivable way. Once a man has married he settles down and becomes dignified and respectable. . . . There is always something lacking about a bachelor's house. He does not enjoy a full life.' 'Without a wife and children one has nothing to work for.' 'A home is a home by virtue of a wife' (*umzi ngumzi ngomfazi*).

Children are felt to provide security for both parents in their old age, and even young children give a woman more security than if she is childless and her husband dies. 'She can have a home if she has children, whereas if she lived alone everyone would laugh.' But in town very large families are not desired: middle-class people and others also mostly do not want more than three or four children. The tradition of family planning—deliberately spacing births—which is so deep-rooted in Africa, makes a transition to limitation relatively easy.

A change in the status of women, vis-à-vis men, is very marked. This was apparent thirty years ago in Pondoland,[9] and it is even clearer now, particularly in town. In South Africa and the Protectorates, in contrast to the territories north of the Limpopo, the education of women has grown along with that of men. At the most famous of the frontier schools, Lovedale, girls began along with boys, and that tradition was maintained in other schools and when university education for Africans started. Educated women were early employed as teachers, and later trained as nurses, and they readily found employment. The less educated, who had nevertheless profited from some years in school and begun to learn English, entered domestic service; now they are also employed in considerable numbers

[9] Monica Hunter, 'The Effects of Contact with Europeans on the Status of Pondo Women', *Africa*, vol. VI (1933), pp. 259–76. H. J. Simons, The Legal Status of African Women (unpublished).

in factories, and in shops, and cafés. In all this the development in the Republic has differed from that farther north where the education of women lagged far behind that of men, and women have been very slow to enter employment. The differences may perhaps be attributed to a difference in the traditional marriage age, which made it possible in the south for girls to work for a year or two before they married, whereas farther north they were commonly betrothed before puberty. However that may be, the fact that girls went to school, and women took up employment, both skilled and unskilled, has had a profound influence on family relationships. Women earn and save; very commonly they control the family budget; and many of them set themselves to educate their children. In one case noted the husband, a part-time travelling salesman, was very anxious to buy a car, and his wife vetoed it. Unmarried girls and older women take employment; middle-class wives with a professional training continue to work after marriage; but young married women in other classes are expected to stay at home. Whether working or not, however, the wife is often a personality. One of the fieldworkers reported that: 'Almost every township leader has a wife of equal, if not greater, efficiency and drive.'

The more equal relationship between husband and wife, as well as their withdrawal from a wider kinship group, is expressed in the change in eating habits. Often, now, a husband and wife eat together at table, whereas traditionally a man ate with other men of the homestead, and his wife with the other women.

3. KINSMEN, FRIENDS, AND CLASS DIFFERENCES

People were asked about the relative importance of kinsmen and friends to them. The specific question was: 'If you could find someone a job, and a friend and a kinsman were both in desperate need of work, to which would you give it?' Replies varied. A young factory worker, born in town, would help a cousin find a job rather than a friend. 'My cousin is my blood relative, is it not so?' A shop-worker of 25, with ten years' education, who originally came from the country but is assimilated as a townsman, would give accommodation or a job to a friend in preference to a cousin, but brothers and sisters would be helped before any friend. A middle-aged factory worker, with six years' schooling, who lives in a house in Langa but still visits the country from time to time, was much more insistent on kinship obligations: 'My relatives [*izizalwane zam*] are my relatives and it is my duty to fulfil my obligations to them. I am not yet a person lacking customs and traditions [*ilawu*] and I cannot possibly forsake Xhosa custom.' At the opposite extreme was a small trader of 30, with ten years' schooling, who said: 'Why should I be worried about other adults? Every man for himself. The time for being concerned with relatives is past and gone; the only people I care about are my mother and father, and my younger brothers and sisters who cannot yet make their own living.' Nevertheless this same man said he would not marry a clanswoman. A young woman of 24, in domestic service, with eight years' schooling, has a number of kinsfolk in town—brothers and sisters, father's brothers, and mother's sisters. Most of them she visits infrequently, but she is fond of one aunt, and would miss her very much if she left Cape Town. In her view she would look to a friend for help in sickness, in finding a job, or securing accommodation, as readily as to kinsmen, but in case of death then the obligations of kinsmen are dominant. She is a typical *ikhaba* girl. The traditional attitude was expressed by a young married woman of 25 recently from the country: 'I have got relatives. They can never let me go without money, shelter, and food. In times of sickness and death, in times of pleasure and happiness, my relatives are always with me.'

As has been shown, migrants live in neighbourhood units, and in these kinship plays the same part as it does in the home village. Some of the home-boys are probably kinsmen of the same lineage, or mother's kin, affines, or fellow clansmen, and claims on a kinsman or clansman are greater than on an unrelated neighbour, but it is, above all, on the *group* of fellow villagers that a man relies for help in securing a pass, a job, and accommodation. A general impression, difficult to document precisely but gained from the fieldwork as a whole, is that in town men look most often to home-boys whereas women look to their kin for help.

Traditionally, in Nguni society, there were certain tensions between brothers, particularly between the heir—a man's senior son who inherited the bulk of his property—and his junior brothers. Economic competition between brothers, and

disputes over inheritance, become more acute with the change
to a money economy: a young man who has worked hard and
earned as much as, or more than, his older brother, and handed
over most of his earnings to his father, is unwilling to see his
older brother control the inheritance. Furthermore, as polygyny
disappears competition between 'houses' (each group of full
brothers) ceases, but the competition between groups of half-
brothers was a strong sanction for the solidarity of each group
of full brothers. The growth of a money economy and the
disappearance of polygyny therefore tend to increase rivalry
between full brothers. On the other hand, the system of migratory
labour compels some co-operation between them, for one
brother is left in charge of the wives and children at home when
the others go out to work. The effect of these conflicts appears to
be that a man feels more free with his home-boys than with his
brothers or parallel cousins; there are fewer strings attached to
co-operation with them. Between sisters, and brothers and
sisters, there are no similar rivalries, and relationships between
them are easy in the changing, as in the tribal, society.

There are hints, also, of a change in the relative importance
of sons and daughters in a family. Traditionally sons, as man-
power, were essential to the well-being of the family and did
indeed support it; daughters contributed through their *lobola* to
family wealth, but they married out and left the group. In town,
some people say, sons are more irresponsible than daughters,
and once grown up they do not contribute to the home, whereas
'daughters listen', and continue to care for their parents,
particularly their mothers, so that close-knit groups of mothers
and daughters, familiar in the slums of Liverpool and London,
are beginning to appear in Langa also.[10]

Women maintain their connexions in town by constant
visiting, informal and usually not prearranged, unless one or
other party is working and visits must be timed to fit with a
day 'off'. Visiting is, however, governed by personal compatibility. Some kinsfolk see each other daily or at least weekly;
others only go when a funeral or some other family event
makes it unavoidable.

Kinship bonds override class: probably most extended

[10] M. Kerr, *The People of Ship Street*. M. Young and P. Wilmott, *Family and Kinship in East London*.

6

PLATE 4   Married quarters showing women washing after a funeral

PLATE 5   Married quarters and shop (right)

PLATE 6   iTopi, leader of an independent church

families include educated and uneducated, migrant and townsman, but people tend to marry within their own class—this is
particularly marked among the *ooscuse-me*—and some informants were quite frank about 'dropping' relatives whose way of
life differed very much from their own. An *uscuse-me* housewife
of 30, with ten years' education, explained that she has brothers
and sisters, mother's sisters, and cousins in town, and she
visits frequently those she likes. The basis of like or dislike is
personality and behaviour. She has aunts in Kensington, but the
way they live is such that she does not dream of going to see
them: 'They have become the real location type' (*bangenwe
yilokishi kakhulu*). She attends the weddings and parties of
those relatives she likes, and performs the duties assigned to her.
It is these people who help her when she is in trouble financially,
in need of accommodation or a job, in sickness or death.
Funerals—the obligation to bury and mourn—are one of the
major obligations of kinsfolk in Langa, as elsewhere, and our
informant would attend the funerals even of the relatives in
Kensington she dislikes. She occasionally visits her relatives
in the country—once in four or five years, and she stays for
four to six months. Some of her relatives from the country pay
her similar visits but stay for shorter periods, of a month or
two months.

Differences in category or class may complicate family
relationships. A fieldworker was present at the home of an
uscuse-me, a man with about nine years' education, when two of
his wife's brothers arrived, drunk, and ill-dressed. They did not
take their hats off on entering the house, and the *uscuse-me*,
annoyed, sharply told them to remove them, adding: 'What do
you think my house is, a beer hall?' They promptly took off
their hats, but the *uscuse-me* drove them out of the house. Then
he turned to his wife and said in English: 'Look here, I advise
you to warn your brothers that if they want to come to this
house they should come sober, otherwise they should not come.
This is not a house for drunkards and skollies.' His wife (a
woman of 31 with ten years' schooling) indignantly answered
back and said in Xhosa: 'Whatever they are they are my
mother's children, and above all when they come here they do
not come to you, but to see me, and when your friends or
brothers come I never interfere, and it's just unfortunate that we

[my people] are uneducated and come from an uneducated family.' The husband replied: 'Whatever you say makes no difference, the only relevant point is that I won't have drunkards in my house, no matter whether they are your brothers, my brothers, or anyone else.' This woman has five brothers, who are well known to be *tsotsis*, but she is devoted to them, and she identified herself with them against her husband and his family. In traditional Xhosa custom a woman's brothers would never have dreamt of going to a married sister's home when drunk, and thereby disgracing her in front of their brothers-in-law (*oosibali*), nor would her husband have driven his brothers-in-law away, no matter what they had done. In conversation the woman remarked that: 'The *ooscuse-me* are snobs and exhibitionists. They keep aloof from other people and think a lot of themselves and they are my husband's favourite type'—this though the wife has rather more education than her husband, and so might be expected to be more of the *scuse-me* type than he.

4. KINSHIP TERMINOLOGY

One of the features of the changing society is the change in kinship terminology. This is not quite recent—it was noted thirty years ago[11]—nor is it confined to Xhosa, for it occurs also in Sotho,[12] and I observed somewhat similar changes in Nyakyusa, where kinship terms were borrowed from Swahili.

The assimilation of English and Afrikaans words into Xhosa has been extensive, and hardly a sentence is spoken by townsmen without a foreign word in it, so the change may be viewed as part of a wider change in language, but there are certain peculiarities of interest to an anthropologist. Some terms have changed and not others. Why? One term—*usibali* (from the Afrikaans 'swaar') has ousted the old terms for brother-in-law, and sister-in-law, *umlanya* and *umlanyakazi*, even in the country,[13] so that young people do not even know the traditional term. Are the changes in usage, and the absence of change in some terms, related to change or absence of change in behaviour? This question is not yet fully answered, but it

---

[11] Monica Hunter, *Africa*, vol. VII (1934), p. 102; *Reaction to Conquest*, p. 460.

[12] I am indebted to my colleague Dr. D. P. Kunene for this information.

[13] Both terms were in use in Pondoland thirty years ago. Monica Hunter, *Reaction to Conquest*, p. 56.

seems appropriate to record what the change in usage is, and to indicate some possible connexions with changes in behaviour.

In town, father's sister, mother's sister, mother's brother's wife, and father's younger brother's wife are all lumped together by many people under one new term *uanti*, from the English auntie. Traditionally,[14] father's sister, *udadebobawo*, was distinguished from mother's sister, *umakazi*, and mother's brother's wife, *umkamalume*. Some informants still distinguished *udadebobawo*, but many did not. Furthermore, *uanti* tends to be extended to mother's contemporaries. This use is said to have begun in the boarding-schools of the eastern Cape where boys and girls addressed the middle-aged women servants as *anti*. It is not acceptable to conservatives, who reserve the term for a *relative:* 'How can I say *anti* to a person I am not related to ?'

uMama, on the other hand, is being restricted to the speaker's own mother, though in the country it is used in address to mother's sister, and also mother's contemporaries. Traditionally *ma*, rather than *mama*, was used in this extended way, but *ma* was also the formal address to mother. A town girl, in reply to a question on usage, said: 'I have only *one* mother, I have not got many mothers', and it is plain that townspeople are reluctant to extend the term they use for their own mother to anyone else.

Bawo[15] is now used by a man to his father, formally, and to no one else. A girl will use *tata*, the equivalent of the more familiar 'daddy', rather than 'father', and *tata* is used in the extended sense by both men and women, for father's brothers and senior men, but not *bawo* as it was traditionally.

uMalume is used consistently by everyone, in town and country, and both pagan and school people, for mother's brother, and mother's brother alone. The use of this term has not changed at all, and there is still an expectation of affection and familiarity between *malume* and *mtshana*. But *ompie* (from the Afrikaans 'oompie', little uncle) has appeared as a term for father's sister's husband, among school people, instead of *bawo* in address, and *umyeni kadade bobawo* in reference. It is felt to be a useful new term distinguishing a particular relative from own father in address. *Ompie* is also used by some in town

---

[14] Cf. Monica Hunter, *Reaction to Conquest*, pp. 53–7. Traditional terms were also checked with informants in town.

[15] In the vocative case there is no prefix.

for father's contemporaries: others use *tata*, whereas *bawo* used to be a common form of address to an elderly man. In short *bawo* is being restricted to own father much as *mama* is to own mother.

Udade wetu, still used by pagans and Christians alike in the country for sister, has been replaced in town by *usister wam*, which is applied in a more limited sense. 'Our sister' becomes 'my sister' and the stress is on the intimate tie between siblings alone. *Sisi* (from the Afrikaans 'sussie') without any possessive pronoun, is in general use as a polite form of address by a woman to a senior contemporary. It is used by a bride for all her sisters-in-law over puberty, replacing 'mother-of-so-and-so' in address,[16] and *indodakazi* in reference, and in the country it is used by all unmarried girls in addressing young married women, whereas traditionally, they would have used the clan name (*isiduko*), which is a polite form of address to a married woman.

But in town the stress tends to be on relative age, rather than on the difference in status of married and unmarried. A conservative says: 'How can I, a married woman with my own house, go about addressing unmarried girls as *sisi*?' But the more modern argue that 'marriage does not make them any older', and continue after marriage to use *sisi* to unmarried seniors. But, as has already been indicated, the cult of youth has appeared in Langa, and some townspeople, particularly women who have not married, have begun to resent any reference to their seniority. So a young woman who calls an older one *sisi* may be rebuffed. A young married woman of the *scuse-me* category was observed one day in Langa stopping another young woman, an *uMackazi*, unmarried, in the street to ask her something. She began: '*Uxolo sisi* [Pardon me, sister]', but was met with the angry reply: 'What are you saying? Since when have I been a sister to married women?' And she moved off indignantly, not waiting to hear the question that the married woman wished to ask. The *scuse-me* wife's comment was: 'These worthless bitches do not deserve any respect.'

It is not uncommon in a Langa street to hear an older girl saying to a younger one: 'Is your sister like me?' *Sisi* may, of

[16] The traditional form of address to a sister-in-law over puberty who was not yet married, or had not yet borne a child, is uncertain.

course, be used maliciously to an unmarried woman implying that she is an old maid, but a speaker intending merely to express deference may well be rebuffed by a *uMackazi*.

uButi (from the Afrikaans 'boetie', brother) has all but replaced the traditional *umkhuluwe* (elder brother, man speaking) and *umnakwethu* (brother, woman speaking) in town, and so sex and age differences, formerly stressed, are blurred. It is also used in an extended sense just as *usisi* is. In the country, among the Xhosa-speaking groups who circumcise,[17] uncircumcised boys address all those already circumcised as *buti*, irrespective of their relative ages. In town this is still usual though more regard is paid to age. Women also use *buti* to senior contemporaries. Brothers and men over 40 are addressed as *tata* by their juniors, and most do not object to that from a young man, but some protest when girls call them *tata*. A grey-haired man of 50 was observed arguing with a girl of 20, saying: 'How can you use *tata* to me, I am still young, don't you see?' And she replied in surprise: 'Honestly, *tata*, can't you see that you are grey?'

A change in the *extended* use of kinship terms indicating seniority therefore occurs, but there is, as yet, no parallel to the change in English usage that occurred between the wars, when in the upper classes, particularly among artists and intellectuals, kinship terms indicating seniority were largely dropped, and aunts and uncles, and even parents, were addressed directly by name. This was partly a revolt against the emphasis on seniority, and the authority exercised by the older generation, which had been so marked in the nineteenth century and even Edwardian England; it was the rejection of Mr. Barrett,[18] and all his ways; but it also sprang from the desire of the older people to be thought young.

A further complication in the use of *umama* and *usisi* appears in the families of migrants, and those town families who send their children to the country to be brought up by grandparents. The grandmother who has charge of the children may be called *mama*, and the real mother, who only sees them from time to time, *sisi*. The substitutions are a direct reflection of change in everyday behaviour.

---

[17] The Mpondo do not, or did not between about 1820 and 1935.
[18] Cf. Rudolph Bezier, *The Barretts of Wimpole Street*.

The use of terms in town is less consistent than it was
traditionally in the country, or even is today: usage is modified
by the personalities of the speaker and the person addressed.
This, of course, is but one manifestation of the greater diversity
in the changing and wider society. But the trend towards
separating own parents from their siblings or any other people,
of lumping together father's sister and mother's sister, and
resenting any suggestion of seniority in certain situations, is
plain enough. It is matched by the growing importance of the
elementary family, and the disappearance in town of the
homestead occupied by a lineage segment with their spouses.

Two absences of change should be noted: *umakhulu* is still
used by everyone living in town for *grandmother*; there is no
suggestion of its being ousted by *granny*; though children
brought up by a grandmother may use the more intimate *umama*
instead. *uMalume* is similarly resistant to change.

On the other hand, as has been shown, *usibali* has replaced
umlanya and *umlanyakazi* for brother-in-law and sister-in-law.
Most people limit *usibali* to brother-in-law or sister-in-law
and link the term with the passage of cattle. *uSibali zinkomo* —
the brother-in-law relationship *is* cattle—said one informant,
and another, *usibali ngusibali ngeenkomo kaloku*—a brother-in-
law is a brother-in-law because of cattle really. But youngsters
in town may be heard addressing their comrades as *sibali*,
and also *mtshana wam* (sister's son). Why *uMakhulu* and
umalume should remain constant and *umlanya* and *umlanyakazi*
change we do not know, but it is perhaps worth noting that
the relationships with grandmother and mother's brother were,
and are, both felt to be peculiarly warm and loving, whereas
the relationship between brothers-in-law was, and is, often one
of tension.

5 Churches, Schools & Traditional Rites

1. CHURCHES AS CORPORATE GROUPS

Corporate kin groups have disappeared in town, except for the elementary family, and corporate territorial groups are most marked among the migrants: they are somewhat shadowy among the townsmen. The vital corporations in town are associations based on common interest: churches, clubs, trade unions, and political parties. The nature of the church as an association, from the anthropologist's viewpoint, is very clear in a community with a pagan background: many people in Langa were not 'born into' a church, but have chosen whether or not to become church members.

Churches are the dominant type of association in Langa numerically, and in the influence they have exerted on the community. They have existed among the Xhosa for over a hundred years—four generations in some areas—and various informants spoke of the 'atmosphere of Langa' as 'Christian'. Between a quarter and a third of the inhabitants of Langa are actively connected with a church. Exact figures on the numbers of members and adherents of each denomination have been very difficult to collect, for the areas served by each denomination are not uniform, and figures for Langa separately are not always available. The approximate total in Langa, arrived at by adding together the number given by the leader of each church of substantial size, is 6,491, but figures for seven splinter groups, known to be very small in Langa, were not available. It is also possible that children of church members who have been baptized but are not old enough to be confirmed were sometimes omitted from the returns. The total population in 1959 (when figures were collected) was 24,932.

In a number of the long-established churches drawing their membership mainly from 'school' people, such as the Methodist Presbyterian, Congregational, and African Methodist Episcopal, women members considerably outnumber the men; but in those churches which draw mainly from the migrants, such as the Moravians, and (very different in other respects) the African Native Mission Church, and the Zionists, men predominate.

The Christian Church in Langa, is not one corporate body, but is splintered into thirty denominations, each organized independently of the other. Fifteen of the thirty owe their origin directly to missionaries from Europe or America or from 'white' congregations in South Africa; one is organized as a separate 'Bantu' church, but in communion with the mother church, and fourteen are independent offshoots organized and led by Africans. The splintering as it appears in Langa, therefore, is due as much to the splitting of the mother churches overseas as to what has been called 'the fissiparous tendencies' of African churches. This is not characteristic of South Africa as a whole where the independent African churches now number 2,300,[1] and form nearly a third (31 per cent) of the African professing Christians,[2] but it is true of Langa.

Churches in Langa owing their origin directly to missionaries	*Approximate membership in Langa.*[3]
Assemblies of God	40
African United National Baptist	60
African Methodist Episcopal	159
Baptist Union	200
Catholic (Roman)	630
Church of the Province of South Africa (Anglican) ..	1,000
Congregational Union	100
Dutch Reformed	100
Full Gospel	20
Jehovah's Witnesses (Watchtower)	?
Methodist	2,200
Moravian	120
Presbyterian Church of South Africa	500
Salvation Army	15
Seventh-day Adventist	69

One of these, the African United National Baptist Church, now has *only* African members, but it was begun by an Ameri-

[1] M. Horrell (ed.), *A Survey of Race Relations in South Africa* (1959–60), p. 129.
[2] *Union Statistics*, 1910–60.
[3] Figures by courtesy of the minister or priest in charge of each congregation.

can Negro missionary, Mr. East, who worked in the eastern Cape near Middledrift, and for a time it received support from the mother church in the United States. The African Methodist Episcopal, also begun by Negro missionaries, is a much larger and stronger organization and it still has close links with the mother body in the United States.

The Bantu Presbyterian Church is separately organized as a 'Bantu' church, but it still receives missionaries from Scotland, and it is in communion with the Presbyterian Church of South Africa; the Moderator of the Church is sometimes an African minister, and sometimes a Scottish missionary. Membership in Langa is 488.

The Order of Ethiopia has its own separate organization, but its members are members of the Church of the Province, and its Provincial is appointed by the Archbishop. It is therefore not a separate church, though many people speak as if it were one. Membership in Langa is 200, and it has its own building.

The independent African churches are:	Date of formation	Approximate membership in Langa
Presbyterian Church of Africa	1898	300
African Native Mission Church	1884	100
African Ethiopian Baptist Church ..	1946	very small
Ethiopian Church of South Africa ..	1892	30
Ethiopian Church of South Africa ..	1952	?
Bantu Methodist Church	1933	50
Africa Gospel	—	—
Church of Christ	1927	100
Holy Church of Christ	1946	—
African Holy Church of Christ	1947	20
Medium Zionist Church	—	20
Kenana Zionist Movement	—	—
Spiritual Zionist Church	—	—
Holy Apostolic Church	—	—

The churches with large memberships in Langa are therefore the Methodists, the Church of the Province, the Roman Catholics, the Presbyterian Church of South Africa, and the Bantu Presbyterians, in that order, the last two being about the same size. The independent African churches are all small, with the exception of the Presbyterian Church of Africa, which is, nevertheless, smaller than the other two Presbyterian churches.

The members and adherents of the independent churches probably do not exceed 750 out of a total of about 6,700 and they therefore form a much smaller proportion than the 31 per cent which the census returns give for South Africa as a whole. This discrepancy is doubtless partly due to a difference in classification of the churches, but it is also because there is no independent church in Langa with a large popular following.

Of the independent churches only four, the Presbyterian Church of Africa, the African Ethiopian Baptist Church, the Ethiopian Church of South Africa, and the Bantu Methodist Church, have buildings in Langa; the other congregations meet in private houses, or in some other township or suburb.

The causes of splits in the mother churches before they established missions in South Africa fall outside the scope of this inquiry, but we are concerned with the causes of fragmentation within the mission churches. Three main grounds of fission are apparent: race tension, disputes over church funds, and personal ambition. Often these three interlock, and they may be linked also with differences in tribal origin or class, tribe being of diminishing and class of increasing importance. Doctrinal differences have not once been found to be the cause of a split in the churches studied, but the differences between the original mission churches—for example in such matters as infant or adult baptism—continue to be reflected in the churches stemming from them.

The fact that race tensions are not the sole cause of secession is conclusively demonstrated by the way in which splits have repeatedly occurred within independent African churches. And certain individuals have moved from one church to another, sometimes after having been disciplined in their original church, and sometimes after a quarrel over leadership. There is also a marked tendency for a son to follow his father as leader of an independent church. Tensions within congregations, both of independent churches and those which grew out of 'mission' churches, constantly recur. During the period of fieldwork there was evidence of acute personal conflicts within four Langa churches; in one of them there was even a fracas during a service, and a subsequent court case.

The differences between churches are reflected in their clergy. Of the churches owing their origin directly to missionaries all have full-time ministers except the Assemblies of God, whereas of the independent churches only three of the fourteen—the Presbyterian Church of Africa, the Ethiopian Church of South Africa, and the Bantu Methodist Church—have full-time ministers. The clergy of the mission churches had all completed their primary school education except for the leader of the Assemblies of God, who had spent two years in a Bible School after passing standard IV. Ten of the fifteen had had some secondary education, or trained as teachers, before taking a theological course, and three or four of them had university degrees. Of the ministers of the independent churches only one— the minister of the Presbyterian Church of Africa—had attended a secondary school, and he and three others—the leaders of the African Native Mission Church, the Ethiopian Church of South Africa, and the Bantu Methodist Church—had attended theological courses extending over two or three years. The leaders of the various fragments of the Church of Christ, and the Zionist churches, had had no theological training at a recognized institution, and six of them had not completed the primary school course.

The people of Langa themselves distinguish between what they call 'real' and 'self-made' churches, and there is great unanimity in the classification of particular churches in one category or the other. The more recently established mission churches—which are also 'Sabbatarian' or 'Pentecostal'[4] in character—namely the Full Gospel, Assemblies of God, Jehovah's Witnesses, and Seventh-day Adventists, are in the second category; whereas the long established independent churches—the Presbyterian Church of Africa and the Ethiopian Church of South Africa—are included in the first. The date of establishment is not, however, the only factor, for the recent Bantu Methodist Church and the African Ethiopian Baptist Church are also included in the 'real' category. In the Zionist churches, and perhaps all the 'self-made' churches when African controlled, the form of ritual tends to approximate to traditional diviners' rituals and makes these churches particularly attractive to illiterate pagans coming to work in town.

The largest independent church in Langa, the Presbyterian

[4] Cf. B. A. Pauw, *Religion in a Tswana Chiefdom* (1960), p. 44.

Church of Africa, was formed in 1896 by the Rev. Mpambani Mzimba, an ordained minister of the Free Church of Scotland, who had been for twenty-two years in charge of the congregation in Lovedale. The precipitating cause of the split was that he claimed the right to dispose of funds which he had collected overseas, but which the presbytery held to be contributions made to the mission, and not to any individual.[5] It was also stated in evidence, however, that at the time of the split a cleavage was apparent between Mfengu and Xhosa, most of Mzimba's followers being Mfengu, as he was himself, and the mother church was built in an area occupied by Mfengu, but such a separation on tribal lines is no longer significant. The form of church order and discipline in the Presbyterian Church of Africa has remained very close to that of the mother church and, as in other Presbyterian churches, great stress is laid on education. The founder's son and grandson in turn became ministers, and their influence has been strong; members of other churches indeed criticize the 'personality cult' in the Presbyterian Church of Africa. Many of the members come from families of 'school people' of several generations' standing, and they tend to be middle class and conservative in their attitudes.

The African Native Mission Church also represents an early secession, this time from the Methodist Church. The Rev. Nehemiah Tile formed an independent 'Tembu Church' in 1884. The African Ethiopian Baptist Church is an offshoot of the African Native Mission Church, founded in 1946 by the Rev. P. Fasi. He had originally been a minister of the Bantu Presbyterian Church, which he left; he joined the African Native Mission Church, and left that in turn, taking a following with him. The present leader in Langa, who styles himself 'Bishop', is a son of the founder. The membership is very small.

The Ethiopian Church of South Africa is also split into two independent sections, one led in Langa by the Rev. H. Maya, the other by the Rev. Mr. Tshabalala. The church originated in 1892 when a Methodist, the Rev. W. Ngqayiya, broke away to form his own church. The split into two sections occurred in 1952, following a case in the Supreme Court concerning church funds.

[5] James Wells, *Stewart of Lovedale* (1902), pp. 295–6. *The South African Outlook*, June 1959, p. 82.

The Superintendent-General was charged with failing to account for church moneys. Mr. Tshabalala is a follower of the Magasela faction, which claims to represent the church formed in 1892, as opposed to three rebel groups. The Rev. A. Magasela had a quarrel with the son of the founder, the Rev. W. Ngqiyiya, also a minister, who controlled a church paper. One of the topics repeatedly referred to by the leader is a plan to establish an institution in Port Elizabeth for the training of candidates for the ministry.

The Bantu Methodist Church of South Africa is an offshoot of the Methodist Church; it broke away in 1933, after a dispute in the Methodist Conference over church dues, which were raised from 2s. to 2s. 6d. a quarter. 'Some members felt that the Methodist Church was demanding too much money from its members, and that such money was used only for the benefit of certain privileged church officials. . . . People felt that they were being exploited to provide their superiors with cars, and yet Jesus Christ himself used a donkey, and never indulged in any luxury. As always, the superiors are the whites and their type, so the first step was to form an all-African church which would not be dominated by whites.' A desire for 'greater freedom for African development' is admitted to have been at least as important an issue as the amount of the dues. Leading the secession was the Rev. J. Ramoshu. In doctrine and organization there has apparently been little modification. The church has had a regular congregation and ministers in Langa since 1955, the present incumbent having trained at the Lovedale Bible School. In outside opinion 'the Donkey Church', as it is popularly called, 'is becoming more and more respectable and one wonders if its leaders are still strong believers in donkey riding'. As in other countries, once-radical religious groups tend to become more conservative.

The Africa Gospel Church is a splinter group from the Full Gospel Church, which broke off in 1955 under the leadership of William Gciliza, who came from Durban. The reason given for the split is that the Full Gospel Church was 'white dominated and all the money the African leaders collected was squandered [ityiwa] by the whites'. It is also believed that Mr. Gciliza was a rival of Pastor Nzuzo, who was appointed pastor of the Full Gospel Church in Langa shortly before Mr. Gciliza broke away.

Two other grounds of cleavage which tend to increase the rivalry between Nzuzo and Gciliza are suggested: the former is Xhosa and the latter, with a number of his followers, is Zulu; secondly, the Full Gospel Church membership is more middle class while that of the Africa Gospel Church is among unskilled labourers. This is linked by an observer with the stress on *Africa* Gospel, 'There is always the complaint from the masses', he said, 'that the black educated middle class are the first people to betray the blacks by collaborating with the enemies of African nationalism, the whites.'

The Church of Christ is splintered into three independent groups, the best known being that led by 'Bishop' Limba, who has a large congregation in Port Elizabeth. Bishop Limba lived in Cape Town from 1914–27, and established his first following at Ndabeni, and he still visits Cape Town from time to time and keeps a tight control over the finances and activities of the Cape Town congregation, but his Cape Town following is now not very large. The leader in Langa is an old man, the Rev. Mr. Damane, who claims over 500 followers in the Cape Peninsula but was not explicit about the numbers in Langa itself. They have no site to erect a church building in Langa. All ministers of the church are instructed and ordained by Limba himself, and they visit him in Port Elizabeth from time to time for instruction; he alone conducts baptisms. As in most of the independent churches, the ministers earn their living by some secular job. Mr. Damane first came to Cape Town in 1918, and worked as a packer for one firm for thirty-five years, and is now retired on pension.

The Holy Church of Christ under 'Bishop' Dyantyi is a section of Limba's church[6] which broke away from him in 1946 after a dispute over the control of church property. The property was registered in Limba's own name, not that of the church, and there was a prolonged case in the Eastern Districts Court. Bishop Dyantyi acknowledges the leadership of the Rev. Thomas Matwana, who led the dissidents in Port Elizabeth, and still lives there, and is referred to by Dyantyi as their 'Arch-bishop'. The total following in the Cape is about 100 with 15 members in

---

[6] For an account of the origins and character of this church see L. Mqotsi and N. Mkele, 'A Separatist Church—Ibandla lika Christu', *African Studies*, vol. 5, no. 2, 1946, pp. 106–25.

Langa. As in Limba's church, the Jewish Sabbath is observed and baptism by total immersion is practised. Abstinence from shaving, smoking, and drinking is required, and members pay a fee of 5c (6d.) a week. A third section led by 'Bishop' Xibenye, called the African Holy Church of Christ, broke away from Sixabayi's church—the parent body from which Limba's church was formed—in 1947. Mr. Xibenye himself claims to have been baptized by Sixabayi in 1927. He broke away, he says, because Sixabayi was 'running the church as a business concern'. He is a Zulu by origin who has long lived in Langa as a trader. His *total* following in the Cape and at six country centres is said to be 'over 300'. The doctrine and ritual of the church are as they were under Sixabayi.

There are four Zionist churches in Langa. In 1956 Mzongozi Mnyaka formed the Medium Zionist Church incorporating some members of a defunct Zionist body which had previously been led by Mpongo. The twenty members are migrants, mainly illiterate, and they meet in one of the barrack-rooms. They wear a special uniform. In 1958 Sangota, formerly a member of the Medium Zionist Church, formed his own which he called the Kanana Zionist Movement, recalling Moses who led Israel to Canaan, the land of milk and honey. The same year Lalela, who was 'an archdeacon' of the Medium Zionists, clashed with Mnyaka over an administrative matter and broke off to form the Spiritual Zionist Church. Then in 1959 Matros, another member, formed his own Holy Apostolic Church.

Organization in those churches owing their origins to missionaries follows very closely the episcopal, presbyterian, and methodist models from which they derive, and in the independent churches these forms are usually maintained, but there is a tendency for many of the splinter groups to be personal followings in which constitutional forms are largely irrelevant, and an episcopal title is often taken by the leader.

Churches are primarily concerned with worship, administering sacraments, and religious instruction, but they have a variety of peripheral activities also, in general education. recreation, charity, and fund-raising. Far the most vigorous of the church associations are those for married women: all the larger churches have such associations (*manyano*) whose members hold weekly meetings for prayer and discussion. They

are the chief fund-raisers for each church, and their identity
and solidarity are emphasized by wearing a uniform. The leader
of each *manyano* is usually the minister's wife.

Most of the African ministers of churches classified as 'real'
belong to an African Ministers' Association which meets
regularly in Langa. Leaders of the 'self-made' churches are not
invited to join. The present secretary is Mr. Ndaliso of the
African United National Baptist Church, and before he took
office Mr. Maya of the Ethiopian Church of South Africa held
it for seven years. The association is important in co-ordinating
the activities of the many churches in a small township, and
ensuring that special meetings and fund-raising activities do
not clash. The members attend certain of each other's functions,
such as a farewell to a minister who is leaving. There is also
an association formed by the wives of members of the ministers'
association, each of whom is the leader in women's activities
in her own church. African ministers' associations are poten-
tially very influential bodies, as was demonstrated in 1957 when
their Federation convened a multi-racial conference to consider
'Human Relations in a Multi-Racial Society'; the church
leaders are keenly aware that they cannot disregard the political
ferment going on.

2. WHO ARE CHURCH MEMBERS?

For historical reasons, because particular missions established
themselves in one area rather than another, there are territorial
and tribal links with particular churches. For example, Scottish
missions were early established in the Ciskei, and many Ngqika
are Presbyterian; Anglican missions have been particularly
strong among the Mpondomise; Moravians among the Hlubi;
and the Paris mission in Basutoland. Adherents of the Paris
mission are directed to the Dutch Reformed Church when they
travel in South Africa, so the congregation of the Dutch
Reformed Church in Langa consists largely of Sotho. But these
connexions are in no sense exclusive, because no mission has
worked only in one area, and no country area is served by one
mission alone, and also because people may move from one
denomination to another. As has already been indicated, tribal
affiliations have been apparent in certain of the splinter groups
also: the African Native Mission Church was led by a Thembu,

7

and particularly favoured by Dyalindyebo, the Thembu
paramount chief; the Presbyterian Church of Africa was
dominantly Mfengu, the Order of Ethiopia dominantly Xhosa.
These local and tribal connexions appear to be growing less and
less important and numerous examples can be cited to show that
they do not operate consistently, but that every denomination
embraces various district and tribal groups.

In town *class* differences between the membership of different
denominations are more apparent. Educated middle-class
people are most often members of the Anglican, Presbyterian,
African Methodist Episcopal, or Methodist churches, whereas
the Zionists are mostly uneducated country people, often of
pagan families, and most members of the Moravian congregation are simple countrymen, and migrants, but from Christian
families. The Church of Christ (Limba's) is referred to as 'a
business church' and it includes many townsmen of the less
educated sort—*amaTopi* rather than *ooscuse-me*. Its offshoots
are of the same type.

The 'decent people' in town are mostly churchgoers, and
some of the migrants: the *ikhaba*, *ooMac*, and *iibari* are not.
In a bus one day an elderly African was discussing the scriptures
with the man sitting next to him. An *uMac* remarked to a
fieldworker:

'It is amazing that such old men fail to see a simple thing. These
people are for ever making a noise about the wonderful Jesus Christ
who walked on the seas. Who saw him? It's amazing the way people
swallow all the stories they are told by the whites.' 'Why do you
regard the scriptures as stories?' Rather surprised at the question,
the *uMac* asked, 'If this religion was that good, do you think that
its originators, the whites, would have abandoned it? How many
whites go to church on Sunday?'

What at first was a small argument developed into a regular
polemic. The following points were made:

'We have never known whites to be so kind as to be interested
in the welfare of the black man. Why are they so keen in offering us
religion and yet when it comes to other things, they are not prepared
to move even an inch? They would rather die. Every Sunday at
Langa we cannot be at ease, we are being pestered by Stellenbosch
boys to buy bibles. Where do they think we get all that much money?

We are constantly reminded of the torture and misery in hell. Aren't the whites also scared of hell-fire, seeing that they are determined to perpetrate cruelty in this world? Or is hell meant only for the black races? What happened to the people before the whites came with their religion? Did they all go to hell? It seems that the whites are the very people who brought hell for us. We cannot be deceived any more, we have seen through the fraud of Christian religion. For years Christians have been teaching us equality and mutual love amongst all people of the world. But who is the first person to practise inequality? It is none other than the Christian himself.'

The same arguments are constantly met in Langa and express the attitude of an average young man in the flats or the married quarters. Many of the younger generation consciously associate Christianity with white supremacy and see Christianity as a form of exploitation. They refer to ministers as 'shrewd business men who live off the blood of poor widows'. Many *ikhaba*, *ooMac* and *iibari* are supporters of nationalist organizations, and as the nationalist movement becomes more radical it implies to some the rejection of Christianity. The older nationalist leaders are mostly Christians—Chief Luthuli and Professor Matthews are outstanding examples—but for many of the younger ones political action and Christianity are felt to be irreconcilable. As one put it: 'I cannot go to church in the morning and address a political meeting in the afternoon; the Gospel tells me to turn the other cheek.'

The opposition of the *ikhaba* and *ooMac* to churches and to the 'decent people' explains why church buildings are so often set alight in a riot. The *tsotsis* are the rioters: they attack government property first, and 'then they go for the things the educated people would defend'; they 'feel that the middle class are protecting their positions'. In the Langa riot three churches were burned, those belonging to the Order of Ethiopia, the Bantu Methodist, and the Dutch Reformed, also a tent used by the New Apostolic Church. Of these the first two are essentially non-white organizations (see above, pp. 93, 97), therefore the burning must be regarded as anti-church, rather than simply anti-white. Other churches were attacked but were saved by members of their congregations. At the same time the municipal library was set alight and some educated people who protested were told by the toughs: 'You educated people are the first to sell out', i.e. to betray the Africans to the whites.

The race cleavage is apparent even in those denominations in which white and non-white members of the same church join on equal terms in one synod or assembly. It is forced on churches partly by the compulsory territorial segregation which prevents white priests from living in Langa, but it appears also in a difference in salaries paid to white and non-white priests and lay workers, in the composition of congregations, and admission to private schools which certain churches control or influence. The idea of racial segregation is explicitly rejected by almost all the churches, but it penetrates everyday action, both individual and corporate.

Rejection of the churches does not necessarily imply atheism, or abandoning the idea of a moral order: there is a deep-rooted conviction, expressed by both pagan and Christian, when discussing the political situation in South Africa, that 'God watches over things all the time', and that ultimately retribution will fall on those who oppress their fellow men.

3. SCHOOLS

A very close link has existed in South Africa for a hundred years between the churches and schools for Africans. Until the passing of the Bantu Education Act in 1954 all the schools in Langa were mission schools, aided by government grants: since that date all, except the Roman Catholic school, have been government schools, controlled by the Department of Bantu Education. The change met with great opposition, and those who consented to serve on the newly formed school committees were bitterly criticized. Each school has a committee to which four members are elected and six nominated by the government; and the various committees elect four members to a school board, on which the other members are nominated. The school board controls the appointment of teachers. Those who serve on the committees and board are mostly clergy and ex-teachers: apparently only a small number of people take part in the elections, and office does not carry prestige—rather it is accepted by some as an unavoidable duty. No one expressed approval of the new system.

Most of the children between 7 and 16 attend school, and

compulsory education has been repeatedly asked for, as at the 1952 conference of the National Council of African Women which met in Langa (cf. plate 12). Of 4,314 children under 16 living in Langa in 1961, 2,818 were attending school, 2,421 in the five primary and 397 in the secondary school. Children start school only at 7,[7] but some remain on after 16, and the high school takes pupils from other townships. The infant mortality under one year is 191 per 1,000 live births, so we estimate the 7–16 age-group to number well under 2,600. No child from Langa has been excluded because of lack of accommodation,[8] but in the two lowest classes the teachers take two shifts of children, each for two hours in the morning. One primary school with 160 children has two staff members, but the usual ratio in primary schools is one teacher to 55–65 children. In the high school it is 1 : 26.

Standards, as reflected in the proportion of passes in public examinations, have dropped very sharply throughout the schools controlled by the Bantu Education Department since the new system came into operation. In 1935, 47·3 per cent of the pupils entering for the senior certificate examination passed, 90 of them with matriculation exemption, and by 1960 only 17·9 per cent passed,[9] 28 with matriculation exemption. In Langa in 1960 there were 11 matriculation candidates of whom 1 passed. The comment in Langa is that teachers generally have lost interest in their work. A considerable number who were politically active or outspoken in their views lost their appointments in different parts of the country, and others have taken posts farther north in Africa.

The boys at school play rugby and soccer, and the girls netball, and an inter-school athletic competition is held each year. There are also school choirs, and choir competitions, and annual school picnics, but beyond this there are few activities associated with the schools outside their curriculum.

A night school, run by a voluntary organization, and mainly staffed by voluntary teachers—whites—long existed in Langa, and had an enrolment of 300 to 400. There illiterates were taught to read and write and some pupils continued to secondary

[7] Seventy infants and young children are cared for in a day nursery.

[8] Children from outside the Cape Peninsula are not admitted without a special permit.

[9] *House of Assembly Debates*, 14 February 1961, col. 1256.

education. In 1957 it was forced by the Administration to discontinue, but a night school working under the school board was permitted. It employs eleven African teachers (paid out of the voluntary association's funds), and has an enrolment fluctuating between 60 and 120. It takes pupils only as far as standard VI. This school is now used mainly by migrants. The importance of the night schools in helping enterprising individuals to educate themselves is apparent in many of the case histories collected.

4. INITIATION RITES

Attendance at school is generally accepted by townsmen as proper and necessary for children, but it is still felt by the majority that some form of the traditional initiation for boys is essential *in addition*. The notion that a youth is not an adult until he has been circumcised, and that the physical operation should be accompanied by something of the traditional ritual, is still very widely held among Xhosa-speaking people. A few parents send their sons to hospital for the operation, but to acquiesce in this is regarded by many men as somewhat soft and unmanly: the great majority of boys growing up in town either go to relatives in the country for their initiation, or a ritual is celebrated for them on the outskirts of Langa itself.

In town no corporate group of those initiated together is formed, and there is no long period of seclusion during which the boys may be trained in certain attitudes; instead one individual or, at most, two or three boys, the sons of men who happen to be friends, are treated together, and the emphasis is on the physical operation and certain attendant ritual acts, rather than on the formation of an age-group with a defined status and responsibilities. No chief or headman is concerned, but the father of a boy, alone or in consultation with other fathers, may decide to celebrate the ritual. The migrants from the barracks are asked to assist, for it is they who are held to be acquainted with traditional custom, and there is insistence all through that *traditional* forms should be followed. 'The boys themselves insist on conformity, though the parents might prefer circumcision in hospital for safety.'

The essential acts, as followed in the initiation of one young man in Langa early in 1961, and commented on by others, are

(i) purification and sacrifice at the induction (*umngeno*); (ii) seclusion and circumcision in a *boma* built 'in the bush'; (iii) the burning of the *boma*, purification, feasting, and admonition at the 'coming out' (*ukusoka*). The ritual is geared to the regular working week and begins on a Friday afternoon. A goat, preferably white in colour, is killed in an enclosure built for the purpose in the backyard of the boy's home. This enclosure represents the cattle-kraal, and it is there that the initiate is then shaved, all his hair being removed. He is given the ritual cut, the *intsonyama*, from the right fore-leg of the goat, and he must taste of it before anyone else eats the meat. Pieces of skin are also cut from the goat to tie around his wrists and ankles; these are 'protective knots'; and hairs may even be taken from the tail of a European-owned cow to provide him with the traditional protective necklace of cow hair.[10] All who choose come to dance and sing and feast on the meat, as well as on beer, soft drinks, bread, and cakes, which are provided. The goat's flesh must be finished that night and the bones burned in the morning, as in a traditional sacrifice.

An initiate's hut, a *boma*, is built beforehand 'in the bush' outside Langa, and there the initiate is taken very early on the Saturday morning. He is accompanied by a party of initiated men, singing a traditional song, *somagwaza*, and sparring with sticks, in the traditional fashion. Countrymen remark with amusement that 'the town boys'—*ikhaba* and *ooMac*—'keep at the back with the old men', for they are afraid of the young migrants with their sticks, since town boys do not learn to fight with sticks as country boys do. On the way, the initiate runs through the cold showers at the barracks, to chill himself thoroughly, and the party avoids roads as far as possible since they are contaminated with *umlaza*, the ritual impurity associated particularly with women and sex activity.[11] At the *boma*, the circumcisor, 'the ogre [*isigebenga*] from the bush' is called upon to operate, and in dressing the wound some conces-

[10] Here form, not substance, survives, for the cow was important traditionally as a symbol of the family shades. In town it is said the hairs are taken from a cow 'belonging to people who have no customs' (*amasiko*); cf. Monica Hunter, *Reaction to Conquest*, pp. 234 ff.

For an account of initiation in the country cf. Wilson *et al.*, *Social Structure, Keiskammahoek Rural Survey*, vol. III, appendix B.

[11] Hunter, *Reaction to Conquest*, pp. 46–7.

sion is made to modern ideas by the use of a disinfectant, but this initiates prefer to conceal; all the emphasis is on following tradition exactly. The initiate is smeared with white clay, and remains in seclusion, attended by a man appointed as 'nurse'.

Within a month or so—as soon as the wound is healed—the initiate 'comes out'. Again very early on a Saturday, a party of men come to burn the *boma*, and the initiate, stark naked, flees from it without looking back, and races for the showers, leaving the blanket he has worn, and the utensils he has used, to burn. 'Everything is left behind.' He washes off the white clay and is wrapped in a new blanket, and taken home—again to the enclosure representing the cattle-kraal—for the admonition.[12] The older men address him on the duties of a man and the change of behaviour expected of him. Their speeches were summarized as follows:

Today, my boy, you are a man, and a man is not a man just by circumcision, but by his actions. A man fears to do anything bad or disgraceful; he refrains from using obscene language and indulging in unbecoming behaviour. From henceforth we should see no more of you at street corners, nor should we see you hanging on bus decks, or whistling and running up the street in the evenings. On your return from work you should come straight home and you should sleep at home every night. Look after your parents and obey them, remembering that to them you are not a man and will remain a boy. Look after your younger brothers and sisters; they should never starve while you live.' 'Don't squander your money on drink! Don't buy a car! If a boy once has a car he will sleep away from home.'

Each man, after admonishing the initiate, gives him a small present.

It will be noted that although the obligation to look after his parents and brothers and sisters is stressed there is no reference to building up the cattle herd as in the country, and the adolescent behaviour castigated is peculiar to the city.

All through the ritual, manliness (*ubudoda*) and enduring hardship with fortitude are stressed. Candidates must not show fear or cry out at the operation, or complain of the rough treatment, lack of drinking-water, poor food, and cold, to which,

[12] In theory *all* circumcised men and *only* circumcised men may attend, but when the question was pressed it was agreed that a Zulu man might be made welcome, though the Zulu do not circumcise, whereas a Jew or other circumcised European might be excluded.

traditionally, they were subjected. In Cape Town the winter is too wet for camping, so boys are circumcised during the summer, and escape the ordeal by cold, but they are reminded of what is required. During the ten days after 'coming out' the initiate must behave very humbly 'exactly like a bride'. He sits in an obscure corner with his eyes cast down and a handkerchief tied low over his forehead like a bride. He must smear himself with red ochre, go barefoot, dress in khaki shorts and shirt, and carry a ritual stick. The use of ochre and such countrified dress is felt very embarrassing by a young man in town, but 'it must be seen that he has been initiated'. He is in a vulnerable state and should not go about to parties and public gatherings any more than a bride does, nevertheless 'he must be seen by people', he cannot hide indoors at home. There is a notion that on the initiate's behaviour now will depend his future character. 'If he cannot abstain now and goes about to parties he will become a dissipated man, quite uncontrollable.' The association between an initiate and a bride is constantly made; however it is modesty and respect (*ukuhlonipa*), not femininity, which are emphasized. The dress remains that of a man, not of a woman, the initiate carries sticks, whereas a woman does not, and manliness (*ubudoda*) is the quality required above all others.

What disturbs the older men is that manliness, as they understand it, is not achieved in town; in their eyes the ritual is no longer efficacious. Traditionally it was expected to produce a change in behaviour, and informants are of the opinion that young men in the country do in fact behave differently after it, but there is a general complaint in town that it is ineffective: 'There is no difference', said one mature informant on urban initiation, 'between the circumcised and the uncircumcised. They are all alike'; and his view was endorsed by many. The symbols of a break with the past—separation, purification, isolation, burning of the old clothes and the seclusion hut without a backward glance—remain, yet practice does not follow. That is judged to be bad.

5. THE ACCOMMODATION OF CHRISTIAN AND PAGAN BELIEFS

The discrepancy between the account of churches and schools and that of initiation will not have escaped the reader: the one stresses the structural organization, the other the cultural activities. There are two reasons for this: first, in a familiar society cultural activities can largely be taken for granted—most people who read English have some idea of worship in a church or instruction in school—and therefore it is possible to concentrate directly on the structural aspect with which this book is primarily concerned. The second reason is that pagan rituals celebrated in town are scarcely reflected in the urban structure at all: the lineages, clans, and chiefdoms which celebrated them traditionally have little coherence in Langa, where circumcision or sacrifice depends upon the action of an elementary family, or a narrow network of friends or kinsmen, and with migrants drawn in as 'men knowing the customs'. No corporate group is formed of those initiated together. What remains is an assertion of the solidarity of those circumcised by Xhosa, Thembu, Mfengu, or Sotho rites, on the continuity of custom, and so on the identification of the initiates with their forebears. In fact the contrast between the account of churches and modern schools and the traditional ritual of initiation reflects a reality: in town organized groups exist for Christian worship and modern literary education, but not to celebrate circumcision and sacrifice. If, however, these activities were ignored this account of town life would be distorted.

The influence of Christian doctrine spreads far beyond the churches. Almost everyone believes in the existence of God, though the traditional idea of God was shadowy,[13] but belief in God is combined with a lively belief in the shades. The two are not felt to be incompatible.[14] The shades are thought of as a source of blessing, and young men are urged to 'visit home', 'not to stay in town too long'. Even if their parents are in town they ought to visit 'old people' at home. Something more is implied than the return of members of an English landed family to the family seat, or of the Darwins to Down, for 'home' is inextricably bound up with the blessing of the shades.

Reverence for the shades, and a sense of dependence upon them, are occasionally expressed in sacrifice. In the circumcision ritual just described the killing of the goat was traditionally an

[13] Cf. Monica Hunter, *Reaction to Conquest*, pp. 269–70.
[14] Cf. Rev. S. P. Lediga, 'The Disciple of Christ Facing African Religions', *Ministry*, 1962. Mr. Lediga was minister in charge of a Langa congregation for twelve years.

offering to the shades, and wearing a cow-hair necklace was also an appeal for their protection. A 'commemoration dinner' is often celebrated about a year after the death of a senior member of the family—father or mother—when the tombstone is erected, and this occasion is the modern substitute for the traditional *ukubuyisa ekhaya*, the 'bringing home' of the shade to the family hearth. A goat may also be killed if a child is ailing—a white goat was sacrificed traditionally for every child. This happened even in a middle-class family, in which the wife had grown up in town. She had had a serious quarrel with her husband, and her youngest child, not yet weaned, was ailing. He was said to be 'asking for' a goat, so, when she and her husband were reconciled, a goat was killed in the backyard and she and her child were given the ritual portion to taste before anyone else ate. There was no prayer to the shades, but the implication of appeal to them was surely in the minds of the participants. The mother concerned was a regular church-goer. For many people no contradiction is felt between belief in God and appeal to the shades.

Nowhere are men's deep-seated attitudes to their universe more clearly revealed than in their reaction to misfortune. Perhaps the most fundamental differences between societies are between those which interpret misfortune in personal terms, and see all sickness and death as due to the machinations of an enemy, and those which think in terms of impersonal causation on the one hand and either divine Providence or chance, on the other. The difference was epitomized in the question of an Mpondo teacher, put many years ago. He accepted that typhus (then raging in eastern Pondoland) was carried by lice, but he wanted to know, 'Who sent the louse? Why did the infected louse bite one man and not another?' Many people in Langa are still, in effect, asking, 'Who sent the louse?' and when serious illness or accident occurs they seek to know *who* has caused it. For this reason, diviners still practise in Langa: they are consulted most readily by migrants (p. 161) but townsmen also, including some middle-class families, apply to a diviner when misfortune follows misfortune, or an illness proves incurable. However, the townsmen, and more particularly the middle class, go to diviners secretly; it is felt by many to be 'uncivilized', besides being contrary to the teaching of most of the churches. Furthermore, the stress is no longer on discovering the exact identity of the witch but on 'treating the patient', that is on providing protective medicines against the jealousy or envy of persons not precisely identified. The ill will of others is still thought of as a cause of misfortune but, partly no doubt because allegation of witchcraft is a criminal offence, the diviner is expected merely to indicate the 'direction' from which misfortune comes and protect the patient against assaults from that direction. This may be viewed as a first step towards the acceptance of impersonal causation. It is true that, traditionally, categories of persons responsible were indicated before the individual was named, but the diviner was expected to particularize so that the witch or sorcerer might be publicly accused and tried; whereas today he stops short after indicating categories.

The sort of situation in which a middle-class family may consult a diviner is typified by the case of an elderly woman, who came from a family of school people and had had six or eight years' schooling herself. She was a church member, active in the women's *manyano*, and had represented her *manyano* for ten years or more at conferences. First she was ill for some time and in hospital, then a little later she fell and broke her thigh. She called in a diviner, who attributed her accident to two things: (*a*) the new house she had moved into was 'dirty' (i.e. contaminated by a witch); and (*b*) fellow church members were jealous of her, in particular they were angry over some dispute about money. She 'did not know whether to believe the diviner or not' but accepted the treatment prescribed. Another case is cited on p. 167.

There can be little doubt that the fear of witchcraft and sorcery presses hard on many church members. One clergyman drew attention to the fact that he had found a packet of medicines over the doorway of his house, which he assumed had been left by his predecessor who had just vacated the house. Another spoke of the talk among members of his own congregation that the prolonged illness of one of his children was due to witchcraft. The fear is real because envy and anger and lust are real, and men still think of them materializing as familiars. As one of the diviner's songs sung in Langa puts it: 'You can roam the world, and find no place free of back-biters speaking against you.' And back-biters are felt to have power to injure.

Belief in personal causation of misfortune, and the power of the shades, is nourished by diviners. They practise in town—a fieldworker attended a seance in Langa at which there were ten *amagqira*, four men and six women—but they are rooted in the country. One diviner explained how 'wise and thoughtful people always go home for their apprenticeship'—'in town the rites are just fakes'—and at the seance referred to, the congregation was composed almost exclusively of migrants. They had a heated argument with one townee present who refused to remove his hat.

The traditional religion was rooted in a pastoral economy and expressed itself in animal sacrifice and libations of home-brewed beer; the worshipping groups were lineages of larger or smaller span and they, also, were inextricably bound up with pastoralism; so it is no accident that the model, the ideal, to a pagan is a rural and never an urban one.

But a link is emerging between respect for the ancestors, expressed in celebration of *amasiko* (traditional custom) and modern nationalism. The leaders of the Pan-African Congress, when on trial after the riots in Sharpeville and Langa, spoke of 'the old gods of Africa', and 'the spirits of the dead' who would 'take vengeance' on those who disobeyed them.

6 Clubs

1. TYPES AND RANGE OF MEMBERSHIP

Clubs are nothing new in Langa; they have existed since the inception of the township in 1923, and before that in Ndabeni[1] They are numerous and probably include a substantial proportion of the people living in Langa.

In a useful study of voluntary organizations operating among Africans in the Cape, made in 1954 under the auspices of the School of Social Science in the University of Cape Town, Father Botto found the total membership of the various clubs and societies to be just over 11,000 out of a total African population of 44,300.[2] Probably many individuals belong to more than one club, and the number of persons participating in the clubs listed is smaller than this, but on the other hand numerous small clubs which exist in Langa—home-boy choirs and the like—were not recorded. Moreover Langa, the oldest surviving African township and the one in which many middle-class people live, possibly has a higher proportion of 'club men' than other areas, so an estimate of a quarter of the population participating in clubs may be on the conservative side. This, it must be emphasized, is no more than an informed guess.

The clubs having the largest number of members are sports clubs, mostly for rugby football, soccer, and cricket, but also for tennis, golf, boxing and weight-lifting, with netball for schoolgirls. The 22 rugby clubs, 13 soccer and 9 cricket clubs listed by Father Botto had 2,095 members, and the others only

[1] Evidence given by the City of Cape Town to the Native Economic Commission, 1931.

[2] R. Botto, Some Aspects of the Leisure Occupations of the African Population in Cape Town. Unpublished M. Soc. Sci. thesis. University of Cape Town, 1954, p. 168.

This excluded the members of churches and pupils in day schools, but included the associations of men and of women organized by churches, and night schools and first-aid classes. I am indebted to the Director of the School, Professor Batson, and to Father Botto for permission to quote from this useful thesis.

394 between them. Spectators at a match might number up to 700, with an average of over 10,000 attendances at the various matches of the year between African teams, but many men doubtless attended a number of matches, so the persons involved would be much fewer. Many African men also watch international and other matches played by white teams.

There are also numerous bands, choirs, and dance clubs, and the *umgalelo* clubs which combine saving with 'parties'. There are 'casino' clubs for cards, a vaudeville and two drama clubs, three social clubs organized by educated people, a branch of the National Council of African Women with professional women as its nucleus, and, it is alleged, dagga-smoking and drinking clubs patronized by the *tsotsis*. The membership of the music, dance, and drama clubs is given by Father Botto as 834.

To the anthropologist, the most interesting questions are: Who joins what clubs and how are they organized? It is with these that this chapter is primarily concerned.

2. SPORTS CLUBS

The sports clubs may be divided into those patronized by townsmen and those by countrymen; most country clubs have a home-boy basis. This is immediately apparent from their names. Among the rugby and soccer clubs in the Cape, for example, there are, or have been, the Transkeian Lions, Zulu Royals, Natal Wanderers, Basutoland Happy Lads, and Bechuanaland Swallows. As numbers in a club increase, it tends to split, again on a home-boy and urban-rural basis. For example, splits have occurred between those coming from the larger towns of the eastern Cape—King William's Town, East London, and Grahamstown—those from villages in the reserves, and those from the country towns (dorps) of Fort Beaufort, Bedford, and Adelaide, whose connexions are mostly with farm people. The following account of the growth of rugby clubs in Cape Town illustrates this very clearly:

'The first non-white group to be interested in rugby in Cape Town were the Coloured people. The strongest Coloured club was the Busy Bees; it was open to all non-whites, and included a few African members. As the African membership increased they formed their own section, still constitutionally linked with the original club. This was in 1923. As the African section began to assert itself conflicts developed. Some Africans sided with the Coloured members, whose superior knowledge of rugby they acknowledged; others were totally opposed to Coloured domination. A split occurred, and about 1928 the present Bantu club was formed by those Africans who rejected Coloured leadership. The Bantu was an exclusively African club and it welcomed every African interested in rugby. The policy of the club is still to accept any African, and it is not representative of any particular category. Those Africans who remained in the Coloured club drifted away from the Coloured members as they learnt more about rugby and felt able to stand on their own, but they retained the name Busy Bees and eventually formed an African Busy Bees club independent of the Coloured club of the same name.'

Most of the members of the African Busy Bees came from the King William's Town area. The Border was, in fact, the first area in which Africans began to be interested in rugby and cricket, doubtless because three large and famous boarding-schools, and the University College of Fort Hare, were established there. So the Busy Bees club, unlike the Bantu, consisted of members from the same area, the Border; and it is still largely composed of home-boys.

As the membership of the Busy Bees increased, those from King William's Town and East London, who knew more about rugby than those from smaller centres such as Peddie, Mount Coke, and Alice, controlled the club, and when selecting players for the first XV, they tended to choose from among themselves and their friends, to the exclusion of 'the pagans' (*amaqaba*) from country villages 'who know nothing about rugby'. When the group which felt itself discriminated against had enough members to form a club, it withdrew from the Busy Bees and formed the Harlequins. Most members of this club come from villages and country towns on the Border, and they live in Langa in the barracks and zones, whereas the majority of the Busy Bees come from the larger towns of King William's Town, East London, and Grahamstown, and they live in Salt River, Woodstock, and District Six, so rural-urban differences and home-boy loyalties are both expressed in these two clubs. The Busy Bees are townspeople (*abantu basedolophini*) and the Harlequins 'ignorant pagans' (*amaqaba angazinto*).

However, each group is, in a sense, one of home-boys to the

other. When there are matches at Langa between various teams, the Busy Bees members always cheer the Harlequins, and the Harlequins reciprocate. If a fight breaks out the boys from these two teams rally to each other's help, as happened when a fight broke out during a match between a Kensington team and the Harlequins. The Border boys watching, some of them members of the Busy Bees, were the first to rush on to the field to help their home-boys. And a member of the Bantu club, who also came from the Border, was restrained by his fellows on the ground that the fight did not concern him. He protested: 'You can't say that, those are my home-boys, those are my fellow small boys.'

As the number of home-boys increases, the more narrowly are areas defined. The King William's Town, East London, and Grahamstown boys would never have discriminated against the others had their numbers not been sufficient to form a reasonably large club, and the country boys would not have broken away had they not also been numerous enough to form a club. The process is continuous. As the Harlequins increased in numbers they too split, this time on the basis of reserve versus farm people, a cleavage which is old and familiar.[3] The Red Lions who broke away from the Harlequins mostly came from the Fort Beaufort and Adelaide area. Though they knew more about rugby than the other Harlequin members, who came from villages in reserves, the villagers 'would not be commanded by squatters and vagrants [amaranuga] who had lost their traditional customs'. The amaranuga, for their part, 'could not waste their time trying to teach unteachable sheep from the villages', and so the split occurred.

At first the boys born and brought up in Cape Town did not have any particular club of their own. Either they were not interested in rugby or else they joined the Busy Bees or the Bantu. About 1947, when the first generation born and brought up in Langa was old enough to form and control a club, and when rugby had become popular, the city-born boys asserted their difference from the migrants by forming their own club called the Mother City. One of the conditions of membership is that the recruit should give evidence of having been in Cape

---

[3] Monica Hunter, *Reaction to Conquest*, pp. 506–7. Wilson *et al.*, *Social Structure*, p. 6.

8

PLATE 7   A trader and dance studio manager typical middle class

PLATE 8 Flats with 'Nylon' in the fore-ground

PLATE 9 A barber at work outside the flats

Town for a continuous period of at least five years. The aim
was to keep out people not permanently settled in town. It was
an expression of the opposition between the *iibari* in the flats,
and the *ikhaba* and *ooMac*. An *ibari* informant, speaking of the
Mother City, said contemptuously, 'Mother City is the team of
landless wanderers [*amarumsha*], ooclever'; and another,
assimilated as a townsman but one of the decent people, said,
'Mother City is the skollies' team'. The team is criticized by
others for its foul play 'and yet when it comes to the election
of the Western Province Rugby Board officials, and the selection of the Western Province team, the Mother City carries
most weight'.

The first rugby club to be formed by men from the north-east
Cape, and the Transkei, was the Thembu, for those who came
from Thembuland. The dominant group in this club were boys
from Queenstown. They had a better knowledge of rugby than
those from the Transkei and Burgersdorp, and as numbers
increased, the Queenstown boys, as 'townsmen', felt that 'they
could not be bothered with pagans from the country who had
never seen rugby before'. So the Transkei and Burgersdorp boys
formed their own club, the Bush Buck. Most of them live in
the flats, and the club is well organized and disciplined; 'They
had to be to prove that they are as good as anybody else. They
are at the bottom of the social scale, and the least mistake would
lead to their expulsion from the Langa Union. Of course they
do not cringe and pander to their betters [here a Thembu
speaks], on the contrary they are most aggressive when need be.
In fact they are the only group the Mother City does not take
chances on. The Mother City players are pugnacious and rude;
the Bush Bucks can be equally aggressive and rude. During 1958,
each time they played against the Mother City, they carried
sticks to the field, determined to "Fix up those skollies". "Who
are they?" the Bush Bucks said. "Things which live by picking
up orange peel in the street." The Bush Bucks have not much to
lose socially, and if they assert themselves enough, they stand
a chance of improving their position.'

The splitting of clubs has been described. We have no evidence
of any compensating process of fusion between clubs as such,
but certain clubs are known to have disintegrated, and their
members have joined other clubs. For example, the Bechuana-

land Swallows, a club of Tswana home-boys which was one of
the foundation members of the Western Province Union formed
in 1935, was defeated some years ago by the Busy Bees by
89 points to nil, and 'thereafter no more was heard of them'.
No doubt they were already disintegrating, before this defeat.
The Morning Stars, made up of Port Elizabeth and Albany
men, existed for a number of years but eventually dissolved
'because all its members knew too much and no one man would
listen to another'. The Port Elizabeth men were both experienced
players and townsmen, socially acceptable in Langa, therefore
they were welcome in the town clubs; furthermore their home-
boy loyalty was much less than among countrymen. As one
man explained: 'They could afford to let their club disintegrate
for they could join certain other teams without meeting any
opposition or being criticized by their own home-boys.' The
more conservative of the disbanded Morning Stars joined the
Red Lions 'who are in a sense their home-boys because they
come from the eastern Cape' (Fort Beaufort and Adelaide
districts are contiguous with Albany); the less conservative
joined the town clubs, the Bantu and the Mother City.

The Black Lions, and they, too, disintegrated, some
members joining the Red Lions and others the Bantu. An East
End club 'declined due to atrophy of leadership', and the
Universal Rugby Football Club lasted only one season, that
of 1951.

The clubs are affiliated to local rugby unions, a Western
Province Rugby Football Board, and a South African Board
which has its headquarters in Johannesburg. All of these are
exclusively African organizations. In the Peninsula there are
four African rugby unions: Langa, Nyanga, Kensington, and
Retreat. (The last is sometimes referred to as the Midlands
Union.) Each club is represented by three members in its union,
and each union by three members on the board. In recent years
the Langa Union alone has included eight or nine clubs,
among them the Langa High School club, and each club
normally enters A and B teams for the weekly competitions,
but in 1956 three clubs had three teams each, and two only
one each.

The Langa Union holds weekly meetings in the board-room

of the Municipal Offices, and minutes are kept in English. It is responsible for arranging fixtures for the weekly competitions between clubs, registering players, appointing referees from nominations made by the clubs, and ruling on disputes which arise. The De Kock manual is used as the authority on rules, but there are numerous disputes over the rulings of referees, and the status of individual players. Often one club complains that another is fielding a player not registered with them, and the union has commented caustically on the 'dishonesty' among players, and the difficulties incurred by their using aliases, and urged clubs to be wary about whom they register. Clubs are fined for fielding players who are not registered. Occasionally there are reports of assaults on referees, and some allege that in an important match the referee is careful to be near the edge of the field and the exit, before he blows the final whistle! With much business to discuss and many arguments, union meetings may last for six hours.

The unions compete for a board trophy awarded on a points system, and the board also sends a team annually to the inter-provincial tournament, and arranges fixtures with the Cape Coloured Board.

The finances of clubs, unions, and board are complicated and often a source of friction. Clubs pay R6 a season for affiliation to the union, but when it is in difficulties the union sometimes orders a levy of as much as R16 on each club, and each club is required to sell a given number of tickets for union and board fund-raising functions. Boots, jerseys, and stockings are expensive in terms of African wages, and a player may be ordered off the field if he is not correctly dressed. Team members are commonly required to buy their own togs, but the club, or in tournaments the union or board, must provide balls and referee's whistles, and pay for the hire or upkeep of a field. Until 1960 the only enclosed field in Langa was the High School field, and there gate-money was charged, but elsewhere there was no possibility of charging an entrance fee to spectators. Now there is a new stadium and spectators at matches there must also pay to get in.

The largest expenditure in the unions and board is in organizing tournaments, and in paying travelling expenses for teams. In 1952 the South African Board requested contributions of £100 from each regional board for the expenses of a touring team; the Western Province Board promised £100. There have been many complaints of the inadequacy of accounts kept by the various bodies, and of corruption. It is alleged that over £1,000 collected at various rugby tournaments in 1959 cannot be traced. A number of trophies for rugby and other sports have been presented for competition by interested outsiders, mainly whites, and there are reports of cups being damaged, or disappearing altogether.

The history of the growth and splitting of soccer clubs is very similar to that of the rugby clubs. The first soccer club in Langa was the Transkei Lions, and the leading members in it came from the eastern part of the Transkei, between Umzimkulu, Kokstad, and Umtata. Many men in the eastern districts go to Durban for employment, and soccer is popular in Durban, so the men from the eastern districts were, at first, the best players, but the club included members from all over the Transkei. As numbers increased, those from the west felt that they were being 'discriminated against'; the men from the east were said always to choose their own home-boys for the teams, 'even if they were not very good', and a split occurred. The splinter group was headed by Tsomo boys (from the western Transkei); they were regarded as the second best group of footballers in the original team. Engcobo boys supported the Tsomo group, and some from Ngqamakhwe joined them, to form the African Rovers. Then, after a time, Tsomo and Engcobo boys were said to be discriminating against Ngqamakhwe, and the latter formed their own club, the Bombers. Besides the three Transkeian teams there are the Zulu Bombers, the Basutoland Happy Lads, a town team called the Langa Blues (or Blue Birds), and the Police Soccer Team.

Each of these teams, except for the police team, has a clearly recognized home-boy basis, but individuals are not absolutely bound by home-boy ties. The Transkei Lions still include some Tsolo, Engcobo, and Ngqamakhwe members who remained in it either because they themselves were favourites, or because they had in it special friends who had gone to the same school, or worked in the same firm. The Lions also include a Sotho from Matatiele on the border between the Transkei and

Basutoland. He was known to be an excellent footballer and the Lions, aware of this, welcomed him warmly, and organized a pass for him. He then felt indebted to them and he still plays for the Lions rather than the Basutoland Lads, even against the Sotho team. As he put it: 'The Sotho boys want me, but I cannot just leave the Lions. They have been very helpful and have done great things for me—the Sotho boys have done nothing for me. Much as I like them, the Sotho know nothing' (i.e. about town ways). But when it comes to the Mshweshwe Day celebrations he celebrates as a Sotho. 'Remember that I am also Sotho, and when the Sotho show themselves on their day it behoves me to show myself also.' He is nicknamed 'Sputnik' because he is so fast, and supporters of the team cheer him shouting: 'Scoring machine, turn the ball to the goal, O Sotho!'

Furthermore, the Lions' goalkeeper, and one of their full-backs, are Coloured men. It is suggested that the tension between Coloured and African is greater with townsmen than country folk, for the town African resents working under a Coloured foreman, feeling that he knows as much as he, and it is only racial discrimination that puts the Coloured man in a position of authority, whereas the less sophisticated country Africans are more willing to take orders from a Coloured townsman. Certainly in Langa there is more tension between the Langa townsmen and the Coloured community in Bridge-town than between the men in barracks and flats in Langa and Bridgetown. The foreman who plays for the Lions explained that, 'I work with some of these boys . . . they are very good and I like them. It is pleasant to work with them; if you tell them to do something they do it, without argument. I do not like people who argue. These boys are simple . . . country people are like that, they are not full of nonsense and trouble-makers.' Asked if he would join the Langa Blues, he replied: 'I don't like those boys, they are rough, and like fighting. Their minds are full of nonsense . . . they know too much and won't listen to anyone, whereas the Transkei boys are prepared to listen and learn. That is why I came to help them. . . .'

A somewhat similar situation was noted in one of the rugby clubs, the Olympics, based in Windermere. It consisted mainly of home-boys from the eastern Cape, but included a Coloured man who played in all the matches, though he did not attend club meetings.

Other ties may also override the Sotho–Nguni cleavage. 'Sputnik' played with a Transkei team, and in the Langa Blues there was another Sotho. His parents have been in town for over twenty years, and he grew up in Langa, so there was no question of his joining the Basutoland lads even though he is Sotho by origin. *His* home-boys are the townsmen.

Whether or not a split takes place in a team depends, first, on size. The critical number is thirty-five to forty-five playing members, for as soon as there is the possibility of both the original and the seceding group fielding full teams, then the need to overcome differences is less urgent. Practice games are arranged with another club, but splits may be delayed by calculations as to the possibility of beating rivals. The numbers of Engcobo boys have now increased to the point that they feel strong enough to form their own club, but they are asking themselves whether or not they will be strong enough to beat the Langa Blues. 'Langa must be beaten at all costs.' One of the Engcobo men said: 'Though there are enough of us to form our own club we don't wish to weaken the Transkeian Lions, and if we formed an Engcobo club our boys who are members of the Lions would have to resign and join us. But the Langa team is becoming stronger and stronger and the only one that can beat it is the Transkeian Lions.' In reply to a question he explained that: 'It is a general feeling amongst all the other clubs that the Langa boys must be beaten because they think too much of themselves, and think they know everything.' This man does not play for the Lions, though he has been pressed to do so, he plays for the Rovers, and he explained when asked that: 'As soon as they got a better player or a player as good as I am they would push me out, but no one can ever push me out of the Rovers'; i.e. he feels more secure with his own home-boys and prefers to play for them rather than for the stronger team. He had also been invited to play for the Langa Blues, and to do so would have greatly increased his social prestige—he lives in the flats, and is on the fringe of the town group. When asked about this he replied: 'I take more pride in my home neighbourhood than anything else, and besides I would never dream of playing for them because they are conceited, and, above all, they are drunkards.'

It is clear, then, that each club does not consist solely of home-boys and even the colour cleavage is sometimes ignored, but the rivalry between town and country is so keen that at least one man living in the flats would not consider playing for the town team, and the desire to beat the town boys may prevent a split in the leading country team. Similarly, a boy who has grown up in town does not join the club of his family's place of origin; town loyalty even overrides a difference in home language.

The country clubs all wish to beat the townsmen of the Langa Blues, but town and country alike are united in their determination to beat the police team. Most members of the Langa police force are town residents, and therefore the townsmen are their home-boys, but the migrants can abuse the police as much as they like, and the townsmen will not come to the aid of the police, but join the attackers. When the police team plays, the onlookers all support their opponents and jeer at the police; indeed a game against the police team commonly develops into a fight, and the spectators make no objection to deliberate assaults on police players, whereas in any other match they would protest at such foul play. Small boys will shout sarcastically: 'Arrest them when they trounce you so.' The tension has increased very considerably during the last five years, for in 1955 a fieldworker was told that 'there is no stigma on the police team, owing to the fact that the feeling between police and Africans is much better at the Cape than in other South African towns'. The attitude towards the police team now is comparable to that of non-whites towards the Springboks when they play a visiting team from overseas; nowadays the non-whites always support the visitors, whoever they may be.

Besides the clubs at present playing in Langa there are, or have been, a number of other soccer clubs in the Cape, in other townships or suburbs. Like the Langa clubs, most of them have, or have had, a home-boy basis: there are records of the Bechuanaland Swallows, Zulu Royals, O.F.S. Callies, Natal Wanderers, and Griqualand East, but two clubs were specifically linked with occupation; the Railway Tigers was primarily for railway workers, and all the members of the United Pioneers were domestic servants. Neither of these clubs has survived, nor has Griqualand East, Eastern Rangers, or Hot Spurs. Some of them apparently lasted only a few months; they missed fixtures and other engagements and finally disintegrated.

The soccer clubs, like the rugby clubs, are members of local unions which include a Langa Union, and a Western Province African Football Association, which is linked to the South Africa African Football Association,[4] and competes with other provincial teams and Rhodesia. An earlier association, begun in 1927, broke down owing to the dishonesty of a former office-bearer, who is said to have absconded with £100. A new association was formed in which three Sotho men played a leading part. Soccer is less popular than rugby among the townsmen, and in the eastern Cape, but it is *the* game in Basutoland, and there are at least two other clubs of Sotho home-boys in the Cape, besides the Happy Lads, namely Dinare and Matlama. Criticism of the earlier association was couched by the later regime in chauvinistic terms: 'The Xhosa are incapable of managing any organization amicably', and once the Basutoland Happy Lads asked the union to appoint referees who could speak English, as they had had one who spoke neither Sotho nor English. However, as we have seen, the main cleavage in the club nowadays is between town and country, rather than between Sotho and Nguni.

Rugby and soccer clubs have not only playing members but supporters, older men who nominally join the club and take a lively interest in it, attending matches, and sometimes representing their clubs on the rugby union or board. These supporters have not generally been included in the numbers given for each club, which refer to playing members. The supporters are also home-boys where the club has a home-boy basis.

Participation of large numbers of migrants in the rugby and, more especially, the soccer clubs is possible, because so many migrants in Cape Town have attended village schools and learnt the rudiments of football as boys.

The number of Africans playing cricket is smaller than that playing rugby and soccer; however, ten clubs (including one at

---

[4] 'South Africa African' used of a football association is a fit partner for 'foreign native' used in numerous government reports.

Langa High School) were recorded in the Peninsula,[5] and they are organized in a Western Province Union, which arranges fixtures with other centres and with Coloured and Indian unions. There are not sufficient clubs to form unions in Langa and other townships or suburbs as with rugby and soccer. The clubs are organized again on a home-boy basis, with the urban-rural cleavage strongly marked. In Langa there is the Try Again composed of the town boys, the Far East and Ocean Sweepers, both from Peddie, the King's Sons from King William's Town, the Thembu from the Transkei, and Home-Boys Midlands, from Adelaide and Fort Beaufort. Enthusiasm for cricket is considerably less than for rugby, and the game carries less social prestige. Some of the best players from Langa (notably Ben Malamba) have abandoned the Langa clubs altogether and sought admission to Coloured clubs where the standard of play is higher. It is suggested that splits have been fewer in cricket than in rugby clubs just because there is less enthusiasm about it and less competition for leadership. The only club which did split—that from Peddie—was one in which the players were noticeably keen and the cause of the split was again the complaint that one group was 'discriminated against'. There was also competition for leadership.

Tennis is a game of the *ooscuse-me* and the numbers involved are small. At one time there were clubs in Ndabeni and Cape Town, and three in Langa, which together formed the Cape Peninsula Bantu Lawn Tennis Union, but in 1948 there were financial disputes and the union disintegrated. Part of the difficulty was the cost of the dues; in the Transkeian club (one of the three in Langa) dues were 25s. a season, per player, and some members failed to pay. In 1951 a single club was resuscitated in Langa, and there is another in Nyanga.

Sport for Africans in the Cape has been very seriously hampered by lack of playing-fields. According to Father Botto not more than 30 acres were available for fields in 1954, for 44,300 Africans, whereas by the standards of the United States and Germany 220 acres would be required. He concluded that: 'Only a fraction of the demand for sports facilities is being met.' During the years 1954 to 1959 matches were played on the few available fields from 1 p.m. on Saturdays until the light failed,

[5] One in addition to those listed by Father Botto.

and throughout the day on Sundays. In 1960 an enclosed stadium, paid for by the municipality, was opened in Langa, with a rugby and a soccer field, changing-rooms, and seating accommodation for about 10,000 spectators. For a time it was boycotted by the football clubs because the municipality claimed two-thirds of the gate-money, but gradually the various clubs have begun to use it. Elsewhere in Langa three all-weather tennis courts have been built.

3. MUSIC AND DANCE CLUBS

In Langa there are a number of bands and choirs which draw their membership from different social groups. The cleavages are again between townsmen and countrymen, between different age-groups and classes in town, and between countrymen from different neighbourhoods. The best known of the town bands is the Merry Macs. Its members are all *ooMac*, and their ages range between 28 and 36. They are a steady group and command respect among the townsmen of Langa. They are competent in reading music and have a considerable range, playing jazz, calypso, and samba, as well as the more old-fashioned ballroom dances. They are the only band favoured by the *ooscuse-me*, and they are popular with the *ooMac* also, and are engaged for all the respectable dances in Langa. Their only critics are the *ikhaba*, who admit that they play well but complain that they are too fond of '*idance*', i.e. old-fashioned ballroom dances, as opposed to jazz. The *ooMac*, for their part, find the *ikhaba* bands altogether too exhausting. 'These small boys are tiring, they play hot numbers throughout the night.' Although the Merry Macs are approved of by the *ooscuse-me* for parties, no *uscuse-me* would join such a band—to do so would be beneath his dignity. However, membership carries great prestige for an *uMac* and, as we shall see, a number of country men sought membership and were excluded, as being *iibari*.

Another band, the Tuxedo Slickers, existed in Athlone five years ago, but it disintegrated because it failed to secure engagements and make money. It lost at least one of its leading members to the Merry Macs. There were also two junior bands, the Hop Skippers and the Honolulu Swingsters which were linked with the Tuxedo Slickers. The first has disappeared and the Honolulu Swingsters are moribund. Occasionally, however, they are called upon to play when other bands are engaged. A band in Cape Town itself, the City Jazz Kings, together with the Merry Macs, and various other clubs scattered through the Peninsula, make up the Western Province African Musicians' Association. For a time the Langa and Peninsula bands were fierce rivals, each trying to grab promising players from the others, but in 1951 at an annual musicians' picnic to Buffels Bay, the idea of a combined organization was first mooted. Picnics—the typical townsman's recreation—are popular among the more sophisticated people in Cape Town; among the musicians the charge is R1.50 (15s.) a head, and they hire a bus for the day. So, encouraged by the euphory of a picnic, an association was formed, but outside it there is an independent group called Die aBafana (The Young Men—Afrikaans and Xhosa are typically mixed in the title). Their leader had left the Merry Macs after a quarrel; he was temperamental and sometimes refused to play, so at the reception for the Commonwealth champion boxer, Jake Tuli, another pianist was engaged by the Merry Macs to play for them. In the music clubs personal rivalries appear to be particularly acute.

The *ikhaba* bands which play such hot numbers and exhaust their seniors are also composed of Langa residents—youngsters. The Cordettes and Disciples are two competing bands, both new, both trained by the same man, and both have their headquarters in the same street. The Cordettes call themselves 'the small cords'—meaning musical chords—and the Disciples are twelve in number, hence their name. The present Disciples are the former Die City with some new members. A certain rivalry exists between the Cordettes and Disciples, but it is not yet acute. Members of the two clubs are to be seen lounging about together in Langa streets, and at the 1961 New Year picnic of the Peninsula African Social Club (see below, p. 131) when a fight broke out between Langa and Nyanga boys the Cordettes and Disciples stood together.

There is also a choir called the Jig Aces which is closely linked with the Cordettes, and a second choir of the *ikhaba* category, the Saints. Besides these there is, or was until recently when the leader left Langa, an *ooscuse-me* type of choir, the Langa Choristers, with twenty-four members, which sang traditional music, both European and African, not the 'hot numbers' of the *ikhaba*.

In the flats there is a well-known jazz band, the Statelytes, with fifteen members, which is rather more than most bands. It was formed in 1956 by a group of young men who had been refused entry into the town bands on the ground that they were merely 'raw' people (*iibari*), pagans (*amaqaba*) from the Transkei. In fact, they were better educated than the townsmen who rejected them; most of them had matriculated and one was a university graduate; but they were from the country. Their band was well organized and they became popular with the townsmen, except for the *ikhaba* with whom they were in competition. They shared rooms in the flats, messing together in small groups, and around the town they were commonly seen together. The basis of association was a double one: a common interest in jazz, and a common origin 'across the Kei'—in the backveld. In fact they came from different magisterial districts in the Transkei—Willowvale, Idutywa, Centane, and Engcobo. Now, after five years or more in town, they are of the same age group as *ooMac* and are being assimilated to them. None are yet married, but they spend more of the time visiting friends in the township than in their rooms in the flats, and they mix with *ooMackazi* girls; their strong feeling of identity as 'boys from beyond the Kei' is dying fast, and they are less close-knit as a group. Few people still regard them as *iibari*, and there is little doubt that the process of absorption was hastened by their creation of a successful band. Significantly, their name— Statelytes—referred not to home origin but to aspiration: it is interpreted as meaning 'United States Boys'.

When they started playing as a group the Statelytes 'did not like the idea of having a leader' and so they formed an 'executive' responsible for the band, 'but in actual practice it was obvious who their leader was'. He was considerably more skilled as a musician than the others, and taught and led them.

In the flats there are also more than twenty choirs with a home-boy basis: thirteen were listed with the districts from which they came:

Transkeian Singers	..	..	Transkei
Happy Lilies	..	..	..	Tsomo, Cofimvaba

Springbok	..	..	Libode, Qumbu, Flagstaff
Happy Brothers	..	..	Mount Frere
Sweet Melody ..	..	..	Mount Frere
Havana Swingsters	..	..	Qumbu
Church Choir	..	..	Qumbu
Humming Bees	..	..	Qumbu
Happy Boys	..	..	King William's Town
M.T.D.	..	..	King William's Town
A.M.B.	..	..	Matatiele
Harmonizers	..	..	Alice
Never Give Up	..	..	Ngqamakhwe

The original Transkeian choir was the Transkeian Singers, but as it increased in numbers it split, and those from Tsomo and Cofimvaba formed the Happy Lilies, and those from Libode and Flagstaff the Springboks. A.M.B., Harmonizers, and Never Give Ups are on a district basis, and the others from Mount Frere, Qumbu, and King William's Town on a village basis. But the home-boys' divisions are not rigid. So long as his district has not got an organized choir a man is free to join another from the Transkei. Among the Happy Brothers from Mount Frere is an Engcobo man, a magnificent singer, see above, pp. 40–1. When asked why he was a member of the Mount Frere choir he replied that: 'This Engcobo gang is not serious about anything, and in any case people who know one another well at home always quarrel in general social activities. They know each other too well and do not respect each other, whereas people whom one does not know so well treat one with respect and courtesy.' The Happy Brothers is the best choir in the flats — it is invited to sing at school concerts, and sometimes has engagements as far afield as Worcester—and the music lover from Engcobo felt free to join them. In fact he is a personal friend of the leader of the Happy Brothers, and shares a room with him, for rooms in the flats are not occupied strictly on a home-boy basis as they are in the barracks. In the flats personal friendships have greater play.

Divergence of interest begins to be very important in town and a basis of association that competes with home-boy loyalties. A comment on the Engcobo man's statement was this: 'When my friend says that people from the same place often quarrel, what he means is that people from the same place do not necessarily have common interests, and their differences at home may show even here in town. When he speaks of mutual respect among "strangers" he means the harmony which prevails among people whose interests converge.' As in rugby, a good club may attract a man other than an immediate home-boy.

Each choir usually has from fifteen to thirty members: if it grows larger it is difficult to get members to attend regularly. There is always a recognized leader or choir-master. The members of the choirs formed by men living in the flats mostly belong to the 'respectable' section in the flats, rather than to the *iibari*, and they sing the country school songs, not jazz music. According to the leader of the Happy Brothers, 'Many of the chaps here in the flats regard our music as "migrant's music"'.

A club much patronized by Transkei men from the flats, but quite different in its structure from either the Statelytes band or home-boys' choirs is a Ballroom Dancing Club. It is open to all non-whites, and includes Coloured people, 'Nyasa', and other town Africans, as well as many men from the flats. The members from various districts in the Transkei—Umtata, Qumbu, Tsomo, Lusikisiki, etc.—address one another as *mkhaya* (home-boy); in this situation they form a 'home' group.

The *ikhaba* and *ooMac* mostly prefer jive or *umsakazo* to traditional ballroom dances, but in the Transkei ballroom dancing is popular—'Jive is a dance for wild *tsotsis*', the Transkei men say. So in this club the main competing groups are Transkeians, 'Nyasa', and Coloured. And all the Africans regard themselves as a group in competition with the Coloured members, despite the opposition in Cape Town between Republic Africans and 'Nyasa' from the north. According to one informant: 'We prefer a Nyasa to win rather than a Coloured man. The Coloureds are very conceited and they think that they are better than the Africans.' The Western Province champion is said to be an African, married to a Coloured woman, and he lives among Coloured people, but when there are no Coloured people present he speaks Xhosa and tells his African friends that they must 'concentrate and beat the Coloured people at dancing'. The story may well be apocryphal, but it reveals the latent tension.

All the dance clubs are hampered by the disproportion of the sexes in town and by the fact that only some of the married men who dance take their wives with them. Those wives who do go to dances are selective about which they will attend.

A Peninsula African Socialite Association (PASA) was begun in 1952. It was organized by the *ooscuse-me* category, but *ooMac* and *ikhaba* men and women joined it also, and a start was made with collecting funds to build a community centre. In 1954 there came a split, the *ooMac* and *ikhaba* breaking away to form their own Peninsula African Social Club (PASC) for PASA did not really cater for them. An African social worker, employed at that time by the municipality, was active in organizing the boisterous youngsters in boxing clubs, and Scout troops, and he was also concerned in the formation of PASC. He drew up a formal constitution which prohibited drinking and gambling, and got the club going. However, he left Langa in 1957, and his successor was nothing like so efficient; also the members of PASC grew older, becoming *ooMac* rather than *ikhaba*, and they no longer included the youngest age-set. Some of the young teachers are now, in March 1961, organizing a new young people's club, the Langa African Social and Cultural Association (LASCA) for the group younger than that in PASC. The divisions, it will be noted, are on the basis of class and age, the original PASA being primarily for the intelligentsia—*ooscuse-me*, mostly over 30; PASA beginning with *ooMac* and *ikhaba*, and then ceasing to cater for the youngest age-set; and the new club being formed for the youngest group, the new *ikhaba* set. The present cleavage was exhibited at the New Year, 1961, when both PASA and PASC organized picnics on the same day (2 January), the *ooscuse-me* (PASA) going to Hermanus, and the *ooMac* and older *ikhaba* (PASC) to Platboom. One of the objects of the organizers of the newest group is to maintain a link between all three clubs so that the funds already collected and held by PASA may be used for a community centre which will be open to all of them.

4. RAISING FUNDS

Fund-raising is one of the most important common activities of any association, and one which both binds members together in a common effort and affords innumerable causes of conflict. In the white community its importance is perhaps particularly clear to middle- and upper-class women who are involved in organizing innumerable fêtes, balls, bazaars, jumble-sales, cake-stalls, and the like, to aid churches, charities, schools, and political parties.

In Langa all the clubs, as well as the churches and schools, must raise funds if they are to function at all—they can never balance their budgets on membership fees or subscriptions alone—and groups of friends also try to collect money in the same sort of way for their own benefit.

Three principles are dominant. Entertainment is offered and people pay for it; this, rather than the sale of goods, is the main means of collecting money. And secondly, conspicuous and competitive giving is contrived in the most public manner possible. Few, in their charity, follow the injunction 'Let not thy left hand know what thy right hand doeth',[6] and fund-raisers, like their counterparts in professionally organized fund-raising campaigns in the white community, depend on exploiting the desire for prestige by publicizing the gifts made. Thirdly, groups and individuals form unions in which it is agreed that each member should attend functions organized by the others and contribute a specified sum; each member takes it in turn to organize a function and benefit from the pool. Exact reciprocity is required and it seems that obligations are, in fact, normally fulfilled.

The simplest form of collecting money for a club is that employed by bands and choirs: they undertake engagements and are paid for their services. The Merry Macs are by far the most successful in this, being engaged for all the 'decent shows' in Langa, both dances and concerts, and also playing at dances all round the Peninsula. Choirs also organize concerts in Langa or Kensington, each acting independently in hiring a hall and collecting the fees.

Commonly refreshments are provided, and anything up to R100 may be netted, though if attendance is poor there may be a deficit. Some music clubs form unions, with the obligation to attend each other's concerts, and make an agreed donation as a club, or as individual members. Each club may pay R10,

[6] Mark vi. 3.

PLATE 10 Mother City plays Moroka Swallows from Johannesburg

PLATE 11 Lunch-hour game in a Cape Town street

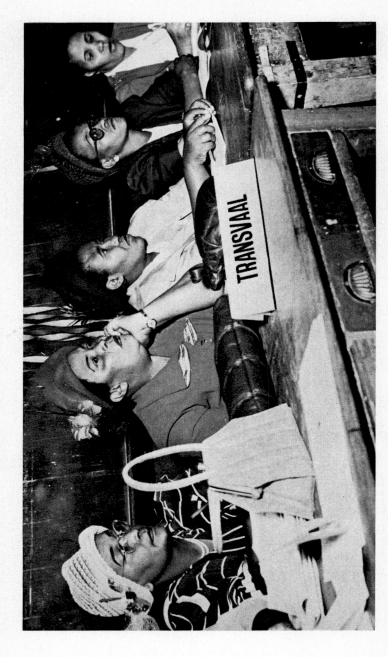

PLATE 12   Annual Conference of the National Council of African Women—Transvaal delegates

at a concert organized by another member of their union, or the members may each be required to pay anything between R2.50 and R4, and concerts must be held in rotation; no club may hold two before each other member has had its turn.

At these concerts ordinary people pay at the door to enter, but they also pay for particular items to be sung, and it is expected that men should bid against one another. This is half the fun. The pattern is exactly that of the school 'concert' in the country,[7] and the pagan *itimiti*,[8] and it apparently dates from the beginning of mission education. It appears in its most elaborate form at an 'afternoon spend' and is described below.

Benefit concerts are also given for individual members of a choir or band, again in rotation. 'These clubs are very useful to the members because it means that when a man is in financial difficulties he can arrange a concert, if it is his turn, and individuals occasionally get lump sums which makes it possible for them to buy things they could not otherwise afford.' Here is the typical reason given for the menage or savings club, so widely found among people with a money economy who live in poverty. Occasionally individuals cheat and abscond after having received their benefit; that is accepted as being unavoidable, but it does not appear to happen frequently.

In the choirs making music is at least as important as raising funds and, with twenty members each, individual 'benefits' can come round only about once a year. However, there are other clubs which are primarily concerned with mutual aid in accumulating money. These are *umgalelo* clubs—'pouring' clubs—whose business it is to 'pour out money' at a friend's party. No *umgalelo* club ever has more than eight members, and the average is five or six. Ten such clubs were noted among the townsmen (mostly living outside Langa) and they have names much like those of the choirs—Happy Lilies, Harmonizers, Heavy Bombers, Night Walkers. The Night Walkers have three full members and two associate members, called *abanxusi* (from *ukunxusa*, to hang on temporarily). The *abanxusi* cannot afford to pay the set fee of R9 for each party or 'afternoon spend', as it is called. They pay only R3, and when their benefit comes round, full members pay only R3, so a strict

---

[7] Wilson *et al.*, *Social Structure*, p. 140.
[8] Monica Hunter, *Reaction to Conquest*, p. 361.

reciprocity is maintained. The club has a chairman, a secretary who records the sums each member 'plays', and parties are held in rotation for the benefit of each member.

The five Night Walkers are not home-boys. The two women members come from Port Elizabeth and Graaff-Reinet; the three men from East London, Umtata, and Queenstown. All five of them live in Woodstock or Salt River, but only two in the same street, and only two work for the same employer; their ages range from 26 to 48. According to the chairman, the basis of association is personal friendship; friends who are *trustworthy* were invited to join.

Each member in turn arranges an 'afternoon spend'. The club must provide suitable accommodation, paying for it if necessary, and the secretary sends out invitations to all the individual patrons and friends of the club. Other clubs are also invited as clubs. The Night Walkers each pay their usual contribution; other people pay an admission fee, and when members of another club come as a group they pool the money and it is offered with a polite speech by their chairman or secretary, who expresses their delight at being invited to such a gathering and says how much honoured they feel that their hosts should show them so much respect, and hopes that such an attitude may continue.

On the request of individuals, who offer to pay for the privilege, the various clubs or individuals attending perform. For example 'a man stands up and says: "I request that the Harmonizers give us some food for the ear, and I am saying that with 20c." If he is lucky the Harmonizers take the stage, but usually such a request is met with opposition. Another man stands up and says: "Whose children are those who are willing to sing for a mere 20c? They are *not* going to sing on the strength of my 50c." Other people join in and before you know where you are you will hear the chairman announcing: "R11.20 for those who are in favour, and R9.70 for those who are against." ' The Harmonizers then sing and R20.90 goes into the kitty. 'People poke fun at others by asking them to do inappropriate things. For example at one party a man of 48 was requested "to sing a jazz piece and jive to his own music because nobody else could jive to such expert music". He tried to buy himself off but everyone clubbed against him, and he had to perform.'

The 'afternoon spend' continues from about 2 p.m. until
10 p.m. when it is formally closed. Refreshments are served at
intervals, during the eight hours, but not everyone stays for the
whole period. Alcohol is usually banned on the ground that if
it is allowed people get drunk and fight. The secretary records
not only the sums 'played' by members of the host club but
the names of visiting 'players', and on a later day a statement
is made to the host club together with representatives of other
clubs who have attended. It is absolutely necessary that, when
a club which has patronized you has an 'afternoon spend' you
should return what it 'scored' or gave. Certain clubs patronize
one another regularly though they are not formally linked.

Savings clubs in the Cape occur among the poorest people,
as this type of club does in other countries,[9] and none were
found in the middle class, but they are said to exist among
African nurses in Johannesburg who, though not poor by
African standards, are seeking to live above their means and
find the savings club a useful method of accumulating money
to buy some expensive item of furniture or clothing which they
particularly want.

In Langa, besides the club functions, there are parties
organized by individuals for their own benefit, and it is these
which are popular among the more well-to-do and sophisticated.
The only people formally invited are the host's home-boys
and personal friends. He will have ground for feeling annoyed if
they fail to come, without good reason, and if a man repeatedly
neglects his home-boys in this way he cannot expect them to
come when he gives a party. The sanction is reciprocity. Other
people come just for entertainment. The organizer must arrange
for accommodation, music, and refreshments. A piano or
piano-accordion is hired, jazz and dance tunes are played, and
people make requests and pay for whatever 'number' they wish.
Others oppose them and the takings mount up. In the 'zones'
there is a common room and the men bring their 'girl-friends',
drawn from among the *ikhaba* and *ooMac* girls living in Langa
and domestic servants in the city. Such parties are held only at

[9] Savings clubs organized on a similar principle to the *umgalelo* have been
reported from India (where they receive government recognition), Nigeria,
Tanganyika, Northern Rhodesia, and Britain. According to Dr. W. Watson
they increased their activities in Scotland during unemployment (personal
communication). Cf. Bascom in bibliography.

the week-end and they may continue all night. Each person pays a fixed admission fee of 20c or 25c, and a record is kept of those admitted, and the amount they have paid at the gate, and for entertainment. A man who is generous in his spending can expect his friends to reciprocate when they come to his 'party', but the exact balancing of payments is not as rigidly enforced as when the guests are fellow members of his club, or of a co-operating club.

Sometimes a function (whether for a club or an individual) is a flop. For example, on a Sunday afternoon in 1956 a certain rugby club organized an 'afternoon spend' to raise funds towards the R70 needed for a fresh set of togs. The club was disintegrating—some members were drinking heavily and the team had lost its last match 40–0. Very few people turned up for the 'spend' and they made less than R10. They had hoped for anything from R60–R120. At a party in the 'zones', given by an individual in December 1961, R30 was collected, and this was regarded as satisfactory, but not conspicuously good.

7 Classes & Leaders

1. CATEGORY AND CLASS

Everyone in Langa classifies people, and there is a general consistency in the classification described in chapter 2, and elaborated in later chapters. No one questions the differentiation between migrants, the partly urbanized in the flats, and townsmen, or between the 'decent people' and *tsotsis*, or between age-groups like *ooMac* and *ikhaba*. But what is the relationship between *category* and *class*? The existence of social classes implies a stratification, a distinction between inferior and superior.

The emergence of a middle class—the *ooscuse-me*—in Langa is plain. The nucleus is the small group of professional men and women—teachers, nurses, lawyers, doctors, ministers of religion; but to these may be added the relatively well-to-do whose manners and way of life permit them to qualify as 'decent people'. Education, occupation, and wealth tend to go together, but they can vary independently, and it was instructive to hear Langa residents discuss the relative importance of each in determining social position.

A 19-year-old factory worker, brought up in town, and with only eight years' schooling himself, rated education higher than wealth, since wealth might be lost, whereas education remained, and moreover an uneducated man could not handle his own wealth. And a hawker of soft goods, 28 years old with ten years' schooling, who grew up in the Transkei, also regarded wealth as of secondary importance. He said: 'There are people who are not wealthy, but who are very polite and well behaved. I would prefer to have such people at my celebrations rather than the rich and uncultivated [*indlavini zezityebi*].'

But a shopworker of 25, of the same educational level, who has become absorbed as a townsman said: 'Education means nothing if you are starved.' And a countrywoman with eight

137

years' schooling, who has been living as a housewife in town for some years, took the same view: 'What is the use of education if you have not got money?'

Occupations are graded according to the pay and hours— dairy work ranks low because it is poorly paid and allows no week-ends off—but also according to its nature. Work in the brickfields and in building, and in the docks, is disliked because it is heavy, and therefore townsmen shun it and leave it to the migrants. As already noted, factory work is favoured by the townees because of the opportunity it offers of pilfering. Excellence at sport, or success in the world of entertainment, carries great prestige, and also, of course, it often carries wealth. Jake Tuli, one-time Empire boxing champion, who was a Zulu, received a tremendous ovation from the African population when he visited Cape Town, and visiting artists, like the stars in *King Kong*, are received in something the same way.

The *ooscuse-me* hold themselves somewhat aloof. They are glad to engage the Merry Macs to play at their dances, but an *uscuse-me* would not consider being a member of the band: to do so would be beneath his dignity. And a middle-class woman explained that she no longer visited an aunt and her family in Kensington because 'they had become real townees'. She went to them only if she had to, as in the case of a family funeral. Women like this are battling to maintain standards of cleanliness, honesty, sobriety, and the like, and to bring up their children as responsible citizens, and not *ikhaba*. However, ordinary folk call the *ooscuse-me* snobs.

Townsmen look down on the migrants and the partly assimilated: 'They are ignorant pagans [*amaqaba*]', 'barbarians', 'country bumpkins' (*oonolali*), and so on. The migrants for their part, despise the townsmen in general for their wickedness and lack of discipline, but if one probes a bit further it emerges that it is really the *tsotsi* section which is despised. The attitude of those who remain incapsulated in groups of home-boys is 'thank God we are not as those townees are', and the migrants would never admit themselves to be lower in status than the *tsotsis*, though they show a reluctant respect for their 'cleverness' in making money and evading the police.

The *tsotsis* regard the migrants as lower, and the fact that many migrants seek to be absorbed into the ranks of townsmen, but no townsman ever wishes to become a migrant, suggests that there are, at least, the beginnings of a class distinction in the urban environment. Gay young men from the country aspire to be accepted as 'bright boys' by the *ooMac*, and many more countrymen gradually merge with the 'decent people' of the town. They show respect for 'those who have been here a long time', and seek to copy their behaviour. As often happens, priority of occupation is claimed as a ground of status. One informant remarked that 'people who had lived in Ndabeni', and then moved to Langa when it was first established, 'always wanted the last word'. Those who were in Ndabeni in fact claim precedence as do the Voortrekkers and Settlers, and their claim to 'the last word' is respected by some, but 'many people resent it'. 'School people' are more readily absorbed in town than the uneducated, and professional men and women—teachers, nurses, lawyers, doctors—are accepted immediately into the *ooscuse-me* group.

Certain clubs have a distinct class status and social climbers proceed by the familiar method of trying to join the 'right' clubs, but some individuals prefer to stick to their own sort and others are rejected by the clubs of their choice. As noted above, a countryman, living in the flats, was invited to join the Mother City rugby club and 'would have increased his social status very much if he had accepted', but he refused on the ground that he did not like the manners and morals of townees (see above, p. 122). Several well-educated young men living in the flats were refused admission to the town bands; they were told: 'You are *amaqaba* [pagans] from the Transkei.' So they formed their own band, and only when it had proved successful did they begin to be accepted as individuals into the ranks of the *ooMac*.

Townsmen gain prestige by being members of a successful sports club or band, the younger men as players, the older men as members of the rugby and soccer committees or board, or as band leaders. And the members of the town clubs are said to carry much more weight on the board than other people.

The *ooscuse-me* have clubs which they particularly patronize. Tennis is exclusively a middle-class game, and the Peninsula African Socialite Association is a *scuse-me* organization to enable townsmen 'to devote leisure time to the best advantage'.

Its constitution prohibits gambling, or the consumption of intoxicating liquor on the premises, or the admission of drunken persons. However, its dances became so popular that *ikhaba* boys even put on ties to get in. They object on principle to wearing ties but, finding themselves refused admission if they did not wear them, they devised a technique whereby *one* tie served for a group of friends. It was passed through the window to each in turn that he might enter!

Besides the churches, and the more formally organized clubs, there are in Langa groups of friends who interact frequently with people of similar interests. Such cliques exist among church people, sportsmen, musicians, 'socialites' (the American word is used), and political leaders, and are comparable, in some sense, to the groups of home-boys whose common interest lies in their village of origin. Often those who interact as members of a clique are members of the same church or club, but not invariably so, and there may be a number of cliques within organized groups. Visiting—dropping in to see one's friends—occupies a very large part of the leisure time of both men and women, and the visiting is mostly between intimates of one clique. What clique a man or woman belongs to is much more important than membership of a church in determining status.

Tribal affiliations have little to do with class status in town. There is a Xhosa stereotype that 'Sotho know nothing about town ways', quoted by the Sotho rugby player from Matatiele who was indebted to Xhosa members of the team he joined for obtaining him a pass (see above, p. 121), but there is a parallel stereotype used by Sotho of all Nguni in Johannesburg. They say: 'Clickers [*isiqhaza*] are country bumpkins', *isiqhaza* being a recently coined word alluding to the clicks in Xhosa, Zulu, and Swazi. In Cape Town it is also said that 'Transkeians are the most despised, as being backward and uncivilized'. The countryman is constantly derided as being *iqaba*, one who smears himself with red clay; as has been noted already, the word is used in the country for heathen in contrast to Christian, but in town for an uncouth countryman, and therefore it is very close to the original meaning of pagan. For three hundred years the white immigrants have disparaged the indigenous peoples of South Africa as being 'heathen' and 'uncivilized', and these are the terms used by Africans today to express class differences among themselves.

Status in town and in the country are by no means identical, but there is some correspondence between them. Wealth and professional qualifications carry prestige everywhere, and membership of a middle-class family; but the status of hereditary chiefs is ambiguous. The members of the Chiefs' Reception Committee in Cape Town are middle-class men, and formal receptions are arranged, but the organizers are themselves embarrassed by the arrival of the chiefs, and many people expressed the wish that they would not come to town. The man said to have invited the Zulu chief to Cape Town took care to be away during his visit! Although the social prestige of the hereditary line is still considerable, Bantu Authorities are so unpopular that anything connected with chieftainship is suspect. Migrants are conscious of the difference between 'landless wanderers' from the farms and those from the reserves (see above, pp. 116–17), but this distinction does not carry on to those rooted in town.

Diviners, who were accorded so much respect in the traditional society, and who are still feared by conservative pagans, are not highly regarded by townsmen, whether of the educated middle class or *ooMac* and *ikhaba*. Their clientele in town is mainly among the migrants and semi-urbanized.

The surprising fact to a white South African (and still more to an American) is the quite open differentiation between various categories of guests at weddings and other ceremonies. Even at a country wedding middle-class guests will be invited to sit down at table, and given rather different food from the crowd of villagers feasting on meat outside, but the whole bridal party is treated in the same way—often at a separate sitting; they are among the honoured guests of the day. In town the *ooscuse-me*, the 'gentle and respectable', and the 'common vulgar people' (an informant's phrases) are entertained as three separate categories. This differentiation is linked with the fact that ceremonies—feasts—are open to any who care to attend. Kinsmen, special friends, and middle-class people will be specially invited, but there is also presumed to be a general invitation to all who care to come. And traditionally there was differentiation according to sex and age, some groups being given considerably more of the fine food provided than others, and the chief and certain kinsmen having perquisites.[1]

The effect of colour bar on class stratification is complex. On the one hand, the mobility of Africans in South African society as a whole is rigidly limited, and the growth of a middle-class among Africans is impeded by the restriction of opportunity in industry through the conventional colour bar and job reservation; by the restriction of entry to town and choice of employment; by the difficulty in acquiring skill since an African can rarely be apprenticed and technical colleges are not open to him; and by the restriction on investment in land or a house. Where freehold land may be bought by Africans (as, for example, in the old Mfengu village in Grahamstown) families save every possible penny to buy a site and a house—a family home—but, as already noted, an African in Cape Town cannot now buy land or a house, or build a permanent home for his family, and the main stimulus to the growth of a property-owning class is absent.

On the other hand, the very fact of a colour barrier tends towards an emphasis on stratification within the subordinate castes. Professor Frazier has described the struggle for status among Negroes in the United States and argued that the stress they lay on 'society' is linked to their exclusion from American life. They struggle to become 'socialites' and achieve status through conspicuous consumption in clothes, cars, and lavish parties partly because they feel excluded as Negroes.[2] A similar interpretation might be applied in Langa: there is a lively consciousness of differentiation within the African group and a struggle to achieve recognition as 'civilized' as opposed to 'barbarian', partly because so many whites do not accept any Africans as civilized. The white attitude, in its extreme form, is expressed in the familiar phrase: 'You may have a B.A. but you still remain a Kaffir with me.'

As will already be evident, classes are not sharply defined, and there is considerable upward mobility through sojourning in town, the acquisition of wealth, and the education of children. Cases are known in which a Christian minister, with a university training, comes of a pagan family with an illiterate father.

---

[1] Monica Hunter, *Reaction to Conquest*, pp. 359, 364–6.
[2] E. Franklin Frazier, *Black Bourgeoisie*, 1957.

Nevertheless those families which first seized the opportunity of education, and which have had sons and daughters in professional posts for three generations, form an *élite*. They tend to intermarry; their kinship connexions form a country-wide network, cross the Nguni–Sotho division, and today are extending up Africa. They have been very closely linked with certain schools; notably Lovedale, Healdtown, and St. Matthew's, in the Ciskei, St. Peter's in Johannesburg, and Adams in Natal, and with the University College of Fort Hare. Their quality is best understood in some of the autobiographies by members of this *élite*, which are now appearing.[3]

2. THE CHOICE OF LEADERS

Now we turn to the question of who in fact leads the various groups that have been defined. Is it members of this *élite* or some other type of person?

Within each group of home-boys there is, as we have noted, a recognized leader, usually the senior man of the group, but he must also be someone with personal weight. He has recognized deputies who act for him during his absence, and his authority derives entirely from acceptance by his group. He is himself a migrant, and one who has rejected absorption in town, so he is the antithesis both of the professional man and of the 'bright boy' who has made money in town by dubious means.

Leadership in the churches varies with the form of church government, and whether it is part of a multi-racial organization or an exclusively African one (see above, pp. 92–9). In all the churches, however, the priest or minister is the initiator of most activities, and he is expected to be, and usually is, better educated than the bulk of his congregation. He is a member of the group—the church—but holds his position by virtue of a divine call and specialist training and dedication. The *manyano*, or women's associations linked with the churches, offer the greatest scope for leadership among women.

In the sports clubs, and choirs, and bands there are leaders who emerge by reason of their skill in the particular activity — rugby or hot music as the case may be. They tend to collect a group round them and form a club, often one of their own home-boys splitting off some larger unit. It appears—though

---

[3] Ezekiel Mphahlele, *Down Second Avenue*, 1959; Noni Jabavu, *Drawn in Colour*, 1960.

the evidence of this is not yet substantial—that splits in the music clubs tend to be essentially personal followings whereas in the rugby and soccer clubs the cleavage is more one between rival sections, competing for places in the team. In the football clubs there are also the wealthy men, no longer players, who are elected to the unions and boards, and who are viewed with some suspicion by young players from the country. Their power derives from their position as townsmen (as opposed to country-cousins), from their wealth—they subscribe to club funds—and their offers of transport when required, for men of this sort always own a car. It is said that 'higher class people— townsmen—carry much more weight in the "Rugby Union" than the representatives from the country-boys' clubs.' The rugby clubs also invite as 'patrons' (the English word is used) middle-class people such as an advocate living in Langa, or a minister of religion. Responsibility, honesty, and education, are looked for in leaders in sport as in other things. The most respected sportsman in Langa, Ben Malamba, was not only an excellent rugby player and cricketer, and a table tennis champion, but he was also matriculated and a senior clerk in the Administrative Office. Even the leader of a team or choir of countrymen is expected to have at least as good an education as anyone else in the group.

In the economic field initiative lies very largely with whites and the number of African employers is few. There are a number of men and women who are self-employed, working as craftsmen or traders, but the *dux* in the economic field who initiates an activity, and rallies a group of followers, is almost always white.

The general leaders in Langa are the political leaders, because politics touch on all the immediate problems of every-day life: a pass, a job, wages, accommodation, the right to have a wife and children in town, education for the children, the right to visit one's friends in another town, or even in Nyanga, and so forth. For reasons already referred to, neither trade unions nor political associations were studied, and therefore the question whether middle-class people are in fact the leaders in Langa cannot be adequately answered.[4] The indications are

[4] The following books discuss political movements and leaders but the first two are banned in South Africa: Leo Kuper, *Passive Resistance in South Africa*, 1956; Charles Hooper, *Brief Authority*, 1960; Anthony Sampson, *The Treason Cage*, 1958; Albert Luthuli, *Let My People Go*, 1962.

that many of the general leaders are members of the middle class but detailed evidence to prove or disprove this was not collected. To accept leadership in a trade union or political party is dangerous, for such a man or woman is likely to be regarded by the authorities, and many employers, as an 'agitator', and may lose both his job and permit to live in the area. Thirteen active members of one trade union are said to have been 'endorsed out' of the Cape.

In churches and clubs generally, however, there is keen competition for office. Scope for leadership among Africans is very limited, and office in almost any sort of organization is a source of social prestige. Whereas, for a white man or woman, there are many alternative opportunities of exercising leadership in work, in politics, in local government, as well as in church, or social clubs or sport, the opportunities for an African are few. To the white man the secretaryship of a rugby club may indeed be a burden, not willingly undertaken, but to most Africans office in almost any organization carries prestige—far more than in a corresponding white club—and it is sought for that reason. 'People in Langa cling to positions as tenaciously as if they were careers.' This is one of the reasons why personal conflicts leading to splits are so common.

Those with highest status in Langa are those who have absorbed most of Western culture. For the *ooscuse-me* the reference group whom they seek to resemble is the white middle class. The comment is often made: 'Whites don't do that'; 'Educated people don't do that'. And the *ooscuse-me* prefer Cape Town to any other city, for in Langa, at least, they have tended to set the tone. In Johannesburg they find little security; an African who wears a collar and tie and speaks English is particularly liable to attack by *tsotsis*, and no one can move about freely in the townships at night unless protected by a gang.

The 'ideal type' for this middle class is the respectable man who is skilled in some fashion and is earning a high wage, or is making a good income from his profession; who drives a car and lives in a Western style of house, furnished exactly like a middle-class white home, and whose dress and food are indistinguishable from that of the white community. In his games and dancing, and music, his tastes are very close to those of whites of the same generation, and though he will probably speak Xhosa at home his language is 'refined', purged of the somewhat earthy metaphors of the pagan countryman, and he must be fluent in English. He will use English in many public situations, including his own sports committees and music clubs, as well as in relations with whites and others who do not speak Xhosa. English carries status rather than Afrikaans, and the educated people think of it as the life-line linking Langa with the outside world. The only link with the traditional culture still insisted upon is circumcision.

The *ikhaba* and *ooMac* are very different. They find their patterns in Johannesburg among the *tsotsis* there. From Johannesburg come fashions in music, dress, speech, manners, and way of life. An *ikhaba* or *ooMac* on holiday tries, at all costs, to visit Johannesburg, where he hopes to taste the joys of driving around in a fast car, smuggling, and stealing. Germiston, Springs, and the other towns of the Reef share the glamour of Johannesburg itself, then, in descending order of status, come Cape Town, Durban and Port Elizabeth. And the Johannesburg *tsotsis*, in their turn, look to America—the United States—as it is depicted in Hollywood films. Crooks and smart guys, and crooners, commanding big money, provide their ideal. Except in sport, where the greater experience and better organization of the Coloured clubs, particularly in cricket, have been admitted in the past (cf. pp. 114, 125), the Coloured people are not openly acknowledged as a reference group, but in practice there is some evidence to suggest that would-be 'socialites' measure themselves against the Coloured group.

For country people, the migrants, and those in process of being absorbed as 'decent people' in town, Cape Town is preferable to Johannesburg, partly because wages are higher than elsewhere and partly because the *tsotsis* are fewer and security greater. In Rhodesia and Nyasaland, as well as in the Transkei and Ciskei, men speak of going to work in Cape Town as the city of their choice. For the true migrants the reference group is still in the home village; they are concerned *not* to be absorbed in town, but to remain loyal to traditional ideals. They are the only exception to the rule that status is linked with a Western way of life. But even though the leader of each group of home-boys is a countryman and a conservative, he may, nevertheless, be a Christian, and a man with some schooling, and he is unlikely to favour the institution of chieftainship.

Absorption of Western culture does not imply support of white domination and, indeed, the man of high status normally expresses opposition to white authority in more or less guarded terms. His status partly depends upon his doing so for con-formists—'Uncle Toms'—are despised, and suspect as 'quislings', or 'sell-outs'.

Most Africans who are in any position of authority have conflicting obligations, to the blacks they control and to the whites who are in authority over them. They are in an inter-calary position, i.e. one linking opposing groups in an authoritarian system. The position is closely analogous to that of foreman in any industrial concern, or of a trade union official under the Coal Board.[5] The contradictions involved in it increase with the degree of opposition between the groups concerned, and as tension between black and white in South Africa mounts, the difficulties of African clerks, and foremen, and headmasters become greater and greater.

Clerks in government or municipal offices administering the pass laws are required to enforce a law which no African accepts as right or just. They are expected by the Africans to be lenient and sympathetic because they understand how hardly the law applies, and if they are 'harsh' they may be ostracized; but if they fail to apply the law strictly they are in danger of losing their jobs. Many in fact accept bribes and are praised by Africans as being 'sympathetic'; those who are discovered are charged in the courts with corruption. An air of authority, which is assumed by some, is particularly detested. 'They behave and speak as if they were whites' is the damning criticism.

In a private firm the clerk's position is much easier: it is possible for him consciously to identify himself with the other workers and to make this clear in the transmission of any orders. 'They [the whites, or the bosses] say' . . . he instructs, rather than giving a direct order himself. The tension is much less because the private firm is not directly involved in administering a totally unacceptable legal system. The clerk can satisfy both his employers and his fellow workers, whereas a clerk in a government or municipal office cannot.

[5] N. Dennis, F. Henriques and C. Slaughter, *Coal is Our Life*, pp. 90–116.

Foremen in factories, and the crews of buses plying to Langa and Nyanga, are also sandwiched between their employers and the people to whom they belong. The foreman holds the typical intercalary office in an industrialized society, and his position is exacerbated when employers and workers are of different colours and even more rigidly separated in all fields of activity than coal-miners and 'the bosses' were in England before 1914.[6] Bus-crews are men in relatively well-paid jobs, anxious to retain their positions, but, when fares are raised or transport inadequate (as it usually is to African townships), the crews are liable to be treated as scapegoats.[7] The crews who were instructed to drop passengers outside Langa during the 1960 'emergency' were the butt of bitter criticism.

Nowadays the headmaster of a school has conflicting loyalties. Many of the regulations governing schools under the new system of 'Bantu Education' are extremely unpopular, but the headmaster's tenure depends upon his applying them. For instance, one headmaster was bitterly criticized by the community for expelling five boys in the matriculation class who had absented themselves from the unpopular 'handwork' classes to continue work on other subjects. 'The general feeling was that he should not have gone to the extent of expelling the boys. After all, they were right, and above all, being an African, his action was considered indefensible. . . .' 'Since X became a headmaster he has forgotten what he is [i.e. a black man], he seems to think he is an earthly God.' African sub-inspectors of schools, who are obliged to enforce the system of Bantu Education, are in a similarly difficult situation.

For an African sister in a hospital the position is not so acute, for though hospital discipline is strict, it is not resented in the way in which pass laws or certain of the regulations of Bantu Education are. Nevertheless, 'The nurses expect the black sisters to be lenient to them and turn a blind eye to all their little misdeeds, and protect them even in such serious cases as theft or abortion. They are *expected* to do this because they are also black. The sister, on the other hand, knows that she is closely watched by the white staff and that a failure on her

---

[6] Dennis, Henriques and Slaughter, op. cit.

[7] However, during a bus-strike in Port Elizabeth in 1961, the African crews had the support of most location dwellers.

part will be a confirmation of the stereotype that "Africans have no sense of responsibility and are untrustworthy". If she succeeds she does so not only for herself but for her group as well. At the same time she has to consider the feelings of the nurses, otherwise they will feel that she is betraying them.' The sister who is successful is one who is considerate to her nurses and has their support, but maintains high professional standards. One was described who 'did not jump on the nurses for every little mistake they made. Instead she used to take wrong-doers to her office and speak to them, not in English, which is the official language, but in Xhosa or Sotho'; and she concluded her admonition with this phrase: 'Don't do such things because if I act as I should then you complain that I am betraying you to the whites.' When she was in charge the nurses 'saw to it that everything was in order' because she commanded great respect. In contrast to her, another sister was described who maintained strictly formal relations with the probationers and found herself friendless. 'She was so unpopular that the nurses used to organize passive boycotts against her. . . .'

Techniques of the successful exercise of authority probably do not vary greatly in different colour groups, but in South Africa anyone who exercises authority is open to the charge of 'siding with the whites'. Many of those in intercalary positions are middle-class men and women; and the middle class as a whole is somewhat suspect and sometimes accused of 'timidity, belly-crawling, cringing, and pandering to the feelings of their white superiors'. Unless they directly support a radical movement through providing funds, food, or transport, middle-class people are liable to lose all their property in a riot, for then the *ikhaba*, to whom they are always opposed, take the opportunity to attack them. The burning in riots of churches, schools, and libraries (as opposed to the administrative office where passes are issued and taxes collected) is, in part, an expression of the conflict between the townees and the middle class; it is something whole-heartedly condemned by most of the middle class and other 'decent people'.

The African police are not included among those in intercalary positions for they are regarded by Africans as being 'on the other side'—the white side—and they do not form any link between opposing groups. Their duty is to administer laws which are bitterly resented. A middle-class man, a school-teacher, summed up the general view: 'Every state needs a police force to maintain peace and order, but any black who serves in the police force cannot be regarded as anything else than a traitor. . . . The police in South Africa are not used to protect the people but to oppress them.'

The police are aware of the hatred against them and 'even when they could do something for the people they seem unwilling to act. . . . When a case is reported at the Langa Police Station [which is commanded by an African] the police show little interest. . . .' On Fridays the police raid buses going into Langa for liquor. 'The way they carry out this task makes one feel that the raid is more in revenge than to maintain law. The people resist, and are extremely rude to the police, and they in turn grow more brutal.' 'The relationship between police and people is altogether irreconcilable, and explosive.'

The attitude towards the police in a well-to-do suburb is very different from what it is in the slums in any society; the peculiarity of South Africa lies in the fact that all the 'decent people' of Langa, including the middle class, are in conflict with the police in only a slightly less degree than the *tsotsis*. This is not new—it was noted in East London thirty years ago[8]—but the degree of tension between police and people has increased considerably in Cape Town in recent years, particularly since March 1960. If a law, or a system of laws, is not accepted it is irrelevant whether it is administered directly by whites or through African intermediaries. The existing social system is generally felt to be bitterly unjust. It is maintained by white authority, and therefore any exercise of authority tends to be identified with whites and white 'persecution'. Unjust laws bring law as a whole into disrepute. This rebellion against authority, because it is identified with its unjust exercise by whites, is often commented on by African parents. It is a major difficulty in bringing up children, and one of the reasons why the *ikhaba* in town are so undisciplined.

Whites as a group are suspect, why then are individuals often called upon by clubs to act as adjudicators, or even initiators in some activity? For example, in a beauty contest organized in Langa by the African Music Society, white judges were held to

[8] Monica Hunter, *Reaction to Conquest*, p. 470.

be indispensable, because the decision of an African panel would be questioned. 'Whatever decision they gave they would be said to have been biased.' And whites are sought as referees for boxing contests, as well as the more important rugby and soccer matches. Whites are found useful, also, to make and enforce unpopular decisions in a school or church, and Africans employ a white attorney to collect a debt, in preference to employing a fellow African.

Recent sociological investigations have shown that the outsider, the foreigner, is often acceptable as a leader when a member of the group is not.[9] The keenest rivalry is between equals, and the member of another class, or tribe, or nation may be aloof from local conflicts and therefore acceptable. The greater jealousy of the equal sometimes outweighs the greater distrust of the outsider. Moreover, the evidence shows that a leader is often dropped when a conflict becomes too intense, and the outsider is much easier to drop than a member of the in-group. Whites are sometimes brought in as 'outside-leaders' to an African club, in the way in which a member of the upper class is brought in as a leader in a village club on the Welsh Border. It is possible also that in Cape Town, which is so dominantly Xhosa-speaking, Sotho are occasionally accepted in the same way. In a group of home-boys from Centane, working as fishermen at Cape Point, there was found a Sotho, a man of some education, who wrote letters for the Centane men and did other services for them and was in some sense a leader. They referred to him affectionately as *umSuthwana*— 'our little Sotho'.

The outsider as a *leader* is to be distinguished from the outsider who is sought as a *patron* because he is useful. The extent of white patronage in South Africa today is a measure of how far privilege depends upon colour. Not only are there financial advantages in links with the more wealthy white community—advantages which often accrue to sports and music and other social clubs as well as to churches—but a white patron, personally interested in you, is extremely useful in many practical situations from securing a job, a railway

[9] R. Frankenburg, *Village on the Border*, pp. 3–6; M. Gluckman, 'How Foreign are You', *The Listener*, 15 January 1959. According to Dr. L. S. B. Leakey the Masai laibons were invariably of Kikuyu extraction (personal communication). The most famous doctors in many African groups are outsiders.

ticket, accommodation, and a pass to live and move in South Africa, or rescue from prison, to obtaining a scholarship, or a place in a school or training hospital, or a passport to travel abroad. The remark of an illiterate countryman, newly circumcised, was revealing. He said to a white contemporary, familiar from childhood, in a hopeful sort of voice, '*Ndiya mfun' umlungu ngoku*' —'I need a European [i.e. a patron] now'.

Class distinctions plainly exist in Langa but they are flattened by the cleavage between the colour groups which, in a technical sociological sense, form castes. Differentiation within each is limited because mobility between them is prohibited; thus an African in Cape Town cannot become a skilled mechanic employed as such in a garage, or a bank clerk; nor can a white man become a dock labourer. Differentiation within Langa is also limited by the absence of opportunity for the middle class to own or build their own houses, or even to live in a different quarter from the *tsotsis*. Racial ideology puts all blacks in one undifferentiated group, and all whites in another, equally undifferentiated. This is as far from reality as the notion that differences in culture are determined by biological differences in racial type.

8 Arbitration in Disputes

Class differences in Langa, and the selection and function of
leaders, are clearly reflected in the settlement of disputes. For
arbitration to be possible the people involved must hold certain
ideas and values in common, and the arbitrator must embody
these. There is little ideological compatibility between migrants
and *ooMac*, or *ooMac* and *ooscuse-me*, therefore an *uMac*
cannot arbitrate in a case between migrants, or vice versa, nor
can an *uscuse-me* and *uMac* arbitrate for one another; but
between *ikhaba*, *ooMac* and *amatopi* there is a certain compatibility, and the senior may arbitrate for the junior, though
not the other way round.

1. DISPUTES AMONG MIGRANTS

The most elaborate system of arbitration in Langa is that
among the migrants. As has already been explained, they
normally live in the barracks and zones as groups of home-boys.
Each group numbers between ten and twenty-five, and is in
contact with other groups of home-boys living elsewhere in
Langa, or in another township of the Peninsula. The members
of the group occupying the same room are closely tied together
by common activities and interests. Among them arbitration
is institutionalized. 'In each room in the barracks there are
arbitrators who are known and acceptable to all the members.
Where they come from the same village [*ilali*] or village section
[*isiphaluka*] the man who is most senior at home is accepted
without question as arbitrator. Where room-mates come from
different *ilali* or *iziphaluka*, the situation is slightly different.
A formal meeting is called and members from the various *ilali*
or *iziphaluka* announce the names of the men they wish to be
recognized as their custodians of law and order [*abantu abagcina
umthetho*]. Those so nominated enjoy unchallenged prestige and
authority. Seniority by age is invariably one of the qualities

153

members look for in electing their "peace-makers"—in the barracks grey hairs are still associated with experience and wisdom. Other considerations such as intelligence, fluency in speech, and good behaviour also count, but only when accompanied by age. In other words, an intelligent, fluent, and well-behaved young man cannot be one of the arbitrators, whereas a stupid and inarticulate but old man may be nominated. In such a case the other arbitrators make decisions for their dull contemporary. One factor that cuts across this rigid principle of gerontocracy is bad behaviour. No matter how old a man is, if his behaviour violates the norms of the group, he cannot be an arbitrator, and he may even be excluded from the group. Such cases among migrants are rare—none was recorded—but the migrants argue: "How can a criminal teach other criminals not to be criminals?" '

The room or 'block' arbitrators are sometimes held responsible to a committee that consists of two arbitrators from each of a number of rooms. This occurs when the number of home-boys is so large that they cannot be accommodated in one room or one block, or when the functional group consists of men from different but adjacent villages, or home-boys have to live with men from elsewhere. Though the policy of the Administration is to allow home-boys to live together, in some cases this is impossible. Even if they come from different districts room-mates still interact as a close-knit group, but the pull of their village home-boys on them is greater than that of the room-mates. So whenever there is a dispute, their home-boys are automatically involved; but it is not everybody who can intervene, and hence the need for a representative committee to handle such matters.

If the committee fails to resolve the conflict then it is referred to the Langa Superintendent, and if his decision is considered unsatisfactory and the case is serious, it is taken to a court of law. In practice, very few cases ever go beyond the committee stage: for an individual to refuse to accept the decision of the arbitrators is in itself a rejection of the values of his group.

Another form of arbitration that is often resorted to by migrants is divination; it is used in cases of suspicion, when the evidence is inconclusive; and in certain circumstances the diviner's verdict is accepted.

(i) *The overworked fag*

This case shows arbitration in its simplest form. The conflict was between a newly circumcised young man (*ikrwala*) and another young but more senior man (*umfana*). The *ikrwala* refused to co-operate with his room-mates because he felt that he was being overworked. For two days he would not cook. The *umfana* reported the matter to one of the older men. On this occasion the senior man did not bring the matter to the notice of all the men in the room: he simply called the two young men concerned to his sleeping-place and asked the *ikrwala*, 'What is wrong? Who has exempted you from cooking?' The *ikrwala* replied, 'Nobody has, but I am weary of it because nobody is prepared to help me, and yet I also come tired from work'. 'Who knows about this state of affairs? Have you reported it to anybody here, and if not, why? What is the good of letting me know now, when you are already reported as a trouble-maker? Don't you know that it is a usual thing for juniors to be taken advantage of by their seniors? Please stop looking for trouble.' After this speech the old man turned to the *umfana* and said, 'Listen here, you; this is always the trouble with you young men. Whenever you are granted privileges, you abuse them. Why should you be so heartless? What reason have you to overwork these children so much? Do you think that they are immune to fatigue? Or have they committed a crime by being obedient? When these children start being disobedient or disrespect-ful, you are the first to complain, forgetting that you are responsible for that sort of thing. Be reasonable. Go and do your work, and refrain from causing us to talk and talk all the time. Hard words are not good for young people.' The senior man fell on his back and relaxed. He had completed his task, and everybody had silently watched him administer justice on behalf of the group.

(ii) *Insulting a man's mother*

A fieldworker found migrants in the barracks discussing the land problem. There were two opposing views; some members maintained that 'white farmers are so prosperous because they own acres and acres of fertile land, and that the black peasants are so poor because they have very little land, and have no money to buy the necessary implements'. The other side granted this, but contended that it was was not the sole reason for the poverty of the African peasant. 'Even more important than the reason suggested', they argued, 'is the African's ignorance and laziness.' A speaker from the first group, obviously heated, said, 'What do you mean by laziness when we toil every day, working, not for ourselves, but for other men?' His opponent, X, replied, 'Even so, how much land did your forefathers use for cultivation? And yet they had plenty of grain and millet, and we, up there on the escarpment, still get plenty of grain because, unlike you, we are prepared to work hard.'

The first man, Y, lost his temper. 'I am not surprised', he said, 'that you can make such a statement. You are an irredeemable moron. You inherited all the stupidity of your mother's people.' (It is a great insult to refer to a man's mother in such a way.) 'In fact, you can very well say what you have just said because you and your group, through your unparalleled witchcraft, every year blight our crops. You are such incorrigible witches.' X took great offence at this. 'If that is the way you are going to speak', he said, 'we had better stop arguing.' Y replied, 'I agree, because if there is anything I hate in a man, it is stupidity'. That was the end of the argument, but not the end of the heat it generated.

The following day, in the evening, the fieldworker revisited his friends. Though they exchanged a few words with one another it was apparent that there was tension in the group. The argument on the previous night had almost developed into a fight, but some members were quick enough to prevent it. Immediately after supper, one of the senior men asked for attention from all the men. 'Silence in the house please!' He went on, 'X has a complaint and he would very much like the house to look into it.' Another senior man replied, 'Let him speak so that we may hear'. The complainant proceeded: 'Honoured Sirs, I have not much to say except that I should very much like you to find out for me from Y what he means by so insulting me. I know of no occasion on which he has found me practising witchcraft. Or has my stupidity, as he says, made a witch of me? I will stop there meantime.' 'You all hear, men', said the first senior man. Referring to the defendant, he said, 'There you are, Y, what have you to say in your defence?' The defendant replied, 'Sirs, I have nothing to say except to apologize to X for insulting him. It was only out of temper that I used the words I used in speaking to him yesterday.' The first senior man again spoke,'Mh-m-m! we see. That is what he says, men.' The second senior proceeded with the actual settlement of the case and said, speaking to Y, 'You are understood, but it is not enough to apologize without punishing yourself by offering something to appease these men for the trouble you have caused them. The words you used to X are really shocking, and I think to cleanse his name, you must provide two paraffin tins of beer for the house. That is my verdict, men.' A third senior man took up the issue and said, 'I agree with Mbinca [clan name], but he seems to forget one thing—that X himself is not altogether innocent. In fact, his crime is even worse, because if it were not for the alertness of these men, blood would have flowed in this house.

He was the first to take up a stick to fight Y without having first put his complaint in front of us. This he did despite the regulations of this house that nobody, under any circumstances, should ever dare to raise his arm against one of his room-mates. I therefore think that two tins of beer is too much, one tin, in my opinion, will do just as well.' Without further discussion, the men agreed on one tin. The first senior man concluded the meeting in the following words: 'I am glad you are both sorry for the bad thing you nearly did. We know that you, as young men, are still quarrelsome, but you must always try to restrain yourself. Self-restraint is the best of all virtues. As I say, I am particularly pleased to learn that you are still prepared to accept discipline from us, your fathers. This is finished now, and we do not wish to hear anything more about it.'

(iii) *The thieving room-mate*

This case involved the disappearance of R60 from a suitcase belonging to one of the men in a migrants' group. When he came back from work, he found his suitcase forced open. He immediately reported the matter to the senior man of the group and invited him to examine the suitcase himself. The senior man dramatically drew the attention of the other men to himself by saying: 'Dead silence please, here is something.' Most of the men were really startled because they had not noticed anything wrong. The senior man asked the complainant to state his case.

He proceeded very carefully and said, 'Fellowmen, some money is missing from my suitcase. Before I went to work this morning I locked my suitcase and took my key with me, as I usually do; when I came back from work I noticed that my suitcase was forced open, whereupon I immediately checked to see if my money was still there. It was gone. I immediately reported the matter to father Z, and I showed him my suitcase.' One of the senior men took up the issue and said meditatively, 'I see'. Speaking to Z, he went on: 'Is it true that this young man reported the matter to you and showed you his suitcase?' 'Yes, that is quite true', said Z. The second senior man, P, said to the complainant, 'Where do you usually keep your suitcase?' 'Under my bed', was the reply. 'If so, how did you notice so quickly that it was forced open?' was the next question from P. 'I was looking for something else I needed', replied the complainant. 'How much money was there?' asked P. 'R60', said the complainant. 'Yhu!' exclaimed the man, alarmed by the magnitude of the figure. 'Where is the suitcase now, let us see it', went on P. The suitcase was brought out and everybody took a good look at it. P said, 'Gentlemen, I am satisfied for the moment, and any other man who has questions to ask may do so'. A younger man was the next speaker. He wanted to know if there was anybody in the room during the day. It appeared that there was nobody. The next thing he wanted to know was whether everybody was present. It was established that one man was missing. Then Z, the chairman, quickly said: 'In that case, the meeting cannot continue until everybody is present.'

The meeting was discontinued, but discussion amongst individuals went on. All the men were trying to work out who the culprit could be. By the time the missing member returned everybody's suspicion centred on him. This was after three days. These were the lines along which the men reasoned:

1. D, the suspect, is an habitual thief.
2. He disappeared for three days without telling anybody where he was going to.
3. For three days he did not report at work and yet he was not on leave.
4. The day the money disappeared he was the only one who could have been in the room during the day, because he did not go to work.
5. He was the only one who could have known that the complainant, C, kept his money in the suitcase that was forced open, as he slept next to C.

The meeting was resumed shortly after D had returned. It was a Saturday afternoon and everybody was lounging around after a week's hard work. Before the meeting started several men asked D one or two seemingly innocent questions such as, 'Where do you come from, my comrade D? Where have you been all these three days? You are really an impossible fellow.' D, flattered, smilingly told the inquirer that he 'had been to Paarl on business'. This casual conversation was brought to an end by the senior man's announcement, 'Silence in the house, men, please'. Every man sat down in perfect silence and the atmosphere was completely changed. The senior man opened the meeting. 'I am glad you are back, D [using a clan name]. While you were away we have been spending sleepless nights trying to solve an insoluble case. As a resourceful man, you might be able to save us trouble. To give you some light: on Wednesday, the day we first noticed that you were missing, there was a mysterious happening. R60 was missing from C's suitcase, which was forced open. None of the men here could trace the money. Could you perhaps help us if you have some clue to its disappearance?'

D, rather nervous, stood up and said: 'Thank you father S, for informing me about this matter. I should very much like to help you, but, as you also know, I have been away for the last three days, and so I cannot possibly tell you anything about what happened in my absence.' S said: 'By the way, where have you been?' 'In Paarl', replied D. 'Did you tell anybody about your trip before you left?' 'No', said D. 'Is that the usual practice in this room?' 'Don't you think that by so doing you have made us suffer unnecessary anxiety, as we were bound to do not knowing what had happened to you?' said the senior man, clearing the ground for his charge. D, fully aware of what he was up against, replied, 'Indeed, what you have said is true. I admit I was wrong, but I could not help it, as I only decided to go to Paarl when I was already at work.' 'In view of your behaviour since Wednesday, would you blame us if we held you responsible for the disappearance of the R60?' The senior man laid his charge.

The same young man who wanted to know if everybody was in when the case came up for the first time said: 'Did you really go to work on Wednesday, D?' 'Yes, yes, what do you think I am, a liar or a thief?' said D. The young man calmly pursued the point, 'If so, could you please let us see your contract card?' D indignantly turned away to his suitcase. He took about twenty minutes turning his clothes upside down innumerable times. The young man, realizing what was happening, offered to help him. They quickly collected all the cards, and went through them one by one until they came across the latest one. 'This is the one, isn't that so?' said the young man, asking D to confirm the statement. 'I think so', said D, with sweat pouring down his face.

The card was examined and it showed a blank for Wednesday, Thursday, and Friday. It was accordingly put to D that he never reported at work on Wednesday, otherwise his card would have been signed even if for two hours' work. D maintained that he was at work on Wednesday and that his foreman must have made a mistake by not signing his card. Immediately D said this, a young man was sent to call a fellow worker of D's from one of the neighbours' rooms. He came and took a seat. The senior man, S, addressed him and said: 'There is nothing serious, Hlubi [clan name], except that we cannot agree on a very small point. Could you please tell us, was D at work this Wednesday or not?' The reply was that he had not been to work on Wednesday. This one point was cleared, and the man from the other room was thanked and allowed to go back to his room.

A second senior man now spoke. He said: 'D, you are making things rather difficult for us. Besides your unusual behaviour since Wednesday, you are now deliberately telling lies. You know that you did not go to work on Wednesday. Why should you tell lies?

Under the circumstances what else do you expect us to do other than ask you to give C back his money.' The decision was made. D had now stopped arguing logically. All he did was to deny having stolen the money. This being the case, the men asked C what step he wished them to take next. He suggested that all the suitcases be taken out and searched. This was done, though most of the men felt that it was not a particularly bright suggestion, as D could easily have left the money in Paarl. Quite unexpectedly R6 was found in D's suitcase. He was asked where he got the money as he was so out of pocket that he borrowed R1 from one of the men earlier in the week. D replied that he got the money in Paarl.

The case still remained unsolved. The next thing to do was to refer it to the committee. After the committee had gone into the matter thoroughly they decided to call a meeting of all the home-boy groups they represented. The meeting was called for a Sunday, but it had to be postponed to another date because one of the leading men could not be present. On the appointed day the members met and the same evidence was heard, and the same decision was reached. D was still not prepared to pay the money. One of the senior men concluded the meeting in the following words, 'You all see, men, what is happening. We cannot do anything about the situation because the country no longer belongs to us, it belongs to the white man, and nobody is prepared to listen to us. We Africans are a degenerate nation. We have abandoned all our customs and traditions. We have lost our sense of humanity, and we lack a sense of shame. What has happened today is really an unbearable shame, but as I say, we cannot do anything about it. C, we offer our humblest apologies to you for failing to help you. We only hope that you will appreciate our difficulty, and we hope that you won't, out of disappointment, stop bringing your complaints to these grey-headed men who are your fathers. As far as this particular case is concerned, we grant you the choice of action.' The meeting was closed with everybody highly incensed against D.

C decided to take the case to the Langa Superintendent, who dismissed it on the grounds of lack of conclusive evidence, and further pointed out that suspicion, legally speaking, is not grounds enough for convicting a man. In the meantime D's immediate home-boys, out of a sense of shame and the conviction that D had stolen the money, offered to repay it because 'they wanted to stay in peace with their district home-boys, and so that their district home-boys should not point an accusing finger at them'. The in-group, accepting joint responsibility, was prepared to pay the money, but at the same time they were bent on getting it out of their mate, even if this meant a physical clash.

On the other hand, C, though he wanted to have his money back, wanted D to confess first. He therefore suggested that they go to a diviner. D also agreed. They went to a diviner in Nyanga. The diviner, as often happens, pointed out the person suspected, D. D was told that he had no reason not to admit his crime. D was still not satisfied, and said that he wanted to go to a diviner of his own choice. The other men agreed. They went to D's diviner and got the same result. At long last D was prepared to pay the money 'if the diviners say so', yet he would not admit having stolen it. He paid the money and still lives with his friends, but he is no longer fully accepted by the group.

2. DISPUTES AMONG TOWNSMEN

Arbitration among *ikhaba, iibari*, and young *ooMac* is much less formal, and also less effective, than among the migrants. Conflict among them more often than not expresses itself in physical violence and it usually leads to social separation. Once they have clashed, *ikhaba* boys constantly attack each other without warning, using knives; *iibari* and *ooMac* do so also if they are drunk; so separation is the only solution.

(iv) *The insolent 'ikhaba'*

A group of *ikhaba* boys were lying on the grass bordering a Langa street; some *ikhaba* girls passed, giggling and laughing. One of the boys, rising, asked, 'What are you laughing at, you kids?' 'Is that your business?' answered one of the girls. The boy, pretending to be annoyed, charged the girls. He got hold of the one who had answered back and slapped her face saying, 'What business have you to speak like that to me?' One of the boys sharply reprimanded his comrade and said, 'T, leave the girls alone. What has that one done that you hit her?' T answered indignantly, 'What has the whole thing to do with you? Is it because you have an eye on that girl?' The intervener was growing annoyed and said: 'You are speaking through your neck now and the next thing I will do is to kick you.' T, also getting heated, said: 'You are assuming rather too much. Aren't you?' The other boy, without saying anything further, stood up and rushed T, who was standing ready for a counter-attack. They exchanged a few blows with their fists then, as usually happens, T reached for his back pocket and whipped out a knife. The other boys quickly intervened and told T not to use a knife because his opponent had none. T would not listen and still wanted to stab his opponent. The other boys threatened T. They told him that they would either give his opponent a knife or all hit him. T seemed to have understood what this meant, for he laid off. The fight was over and the boys went back to the patch of grass. The atmosphere was still tense, and it was obvious that the two who had quarrelled were not at all reconciled. By the time the fight started the girls had already left.

(v) *An 'ikhaba' boy insults another's sister*

A group of *ikhaba* boys were kicking a tennis ball at a street corner. A young *ikhaba* girl passed by. After she had gone, the boys started discussing her character. Most of them did not have anything pleasant to say about her. One boy, G, was particularly unpleasant and abusive in his comments. Another boy, A, jokingly said, 'Anyway, G does not have to be so abusive because his sister is just as bad, if not worse'. G took the joke too hard, and said to A, 'I have been always watching you; you have absolutely no regard for me. What do you mean by insulting my sister in front of me?' A, still treating the matter very lightly, said, 'I am not being insulting, I am stating a fact. This is no news to you. Or is it?' The other boys were laughing and having fun at the expense of G.

G sulkily went away. In a few minutes he reappeared. Behind him walked an *uMac*, who apparently had seen G tucking a knife under his shirt, for he asked G, 'Hey! boy [*kwedini*], where are you going to?' 'There', said G, pointing at the other boys. 'What are you going to do there?' asked *uMac*. G did not answer. Instead he went straight to A, who, not knowing quite what was happening, stood up quickly, and met G's descending knife. The knife tore open A's jacket and shirt and made a small cut below his shoulder blade.

The *uMac* who was following G was already on the spot. He took the knife from G and chased him away, then came back and ordered the rest of the boys to disperse immediately. At the same time he remarked that the whole group did not know how to behave and that they did not know what to fight about.

In the two following cases there was no effective arbitration, and the onlookers who tried to stop the fights failed to do so.

(vi) *The bilking 'uMac'*

Five *ooMac* had been drinking in a shebeen. On their way home they began arguing over money. One of them, M, had paid for the drink of his friend R, on the understanding that R would stand him a drink later. R failed to fulfil his promise and thereupon M demanded his money back. R rudely told him that he would get it near the sun (meaning that he will never get it). In reply to this M hit R on the jaw. A fight started with the other *ooMac* watching instead of intervening. The fight went on for some time, and R was obviously losing. He rushed home. Everybody knew that he had gone to fetch a knife; he is notorious in Langa for stabbing people. Coming back, he went straight for M. When he was just a few feet away M said contemptuously: 'Tell me, R, what is the sense of your travelling all the way to your place to fetch a knife knowing full well that I have no knife on me?' This did not deter R from attacking with the knife. M managed to ward off the first few blows, but soon he was lying bleeding, with his stomach cut open. R was still kicking him when an elderly man, an *itopi*, appeared and said, with an air of despair, 'Do you think we will ever be a nation like other nations when we are still capable of butchering one another in the streets like this? Why are you killing the other child, my child? What is this great atrocity he has committed that justifies his being murdered?' R was, for a moment, overcome with shame. He walked away in silence with his head down. An ambulance was called to come and pick up M, who was kept a month in hospital. He is back in the township now and is bent on having his revenge. He is still seen hanging about with the same *ooMac* who left him fighting with R. Their explanation for not intervening is that they were not aware that the fight could be as serious as it turned out to be. Now they feel that R carried things a bit too far and that therefore he also deserves to be stabbed.

(viii) *The excluded 'ibari'*

A young man living in the flats was due to go home to get married. His friends organized a combined farewell and presentation party for him, which was held in one of the houses in Langa. The hosts were drinking freely, dancing and donating money, when a group of *iibari* came in already tipsy. They had their own private supply of liquor, and at regular intervals they helped themselves to it rather too generously. In doing so they excluded one of their friends on the ground that he wanted to drink without paying. All the time they were drinking he was watching them, and when nobody was looking he stole one bottle of brandy and hid it outside. After some time his friends discovered that a bottle was missing. He was the immediate suspect. One of the men came to him to ask if he had seen anyone taking the bottle. He said, 'No! Anyway, why should you come and ask me after stinting me your liquor?' The other man demanded the bottle. The culprit became aggressive and warned his accuser that 'if you are looking for trouble, you will soon get it'. Another man from the same group interrupted them by calling the alleged thief outside. The reply he got was 'What for? Voertsak, I am not coming.' They dragged him off, but before they could get him out of the house he freed himself and quickly drew his knife. This was the beginning of a big knife battle that spread to the street. The owner of the house stopped the party and sent a youngster to go and call the police. On seeing the police van, the fighters scattered. That was the end of the fight and the end of the group, because after it the group split.

Disputes between married people who are neighbours in the township are much more readily settled than those between *ikhaba* boys, and bachelor *ooMac*. The arbitrators called in are usually other neighbours, or senior relatives, as is illustrated in the following cases.

(viii) *The disputed toolshed*

One afternoon I visited a friend in the location. The friend is a young married woman (*umfazana*) of about 30 years of age, and a former *uMackazi*. We were talking when we heard a noise made by someone striking wooden poles with an axe. My friend quickly peeped through the window and saw her next-door neighbour pulling down a little 'pondokkie' she and her husband had built in the backyard for keeping their garden tools. The backyard is common to both houses, and up to then nobody had bothered about partitioning it.

She went out and asked: 'What do you mean by pulling down this "pondokkie" without even consulting us?' Her neighbour answered, 'I have no time for that. All I am interested in is getting enough space to plant my vegetables.' 'But this part of the yard belongs to us', said my friend. 'Says who?' asked the neighbour. 'If that is your attitude, then I will leave the matter to you and my husband to settle.'

As soon as my friend's husband heard about the matter, he went to see his neighbour. He was in such a rage that he would not listen to any explanation. He gave his neighbour an ultimatum either to build and finish the 'pondokkie' within three days, or face him personally. When the neighbour tried to argue, he threatened to hit him. At this stage another neighbour, who heard the row that was going on, intervened. He asked both men to come inside and discuss the matter.

After the discussion the man who had pulled down the 'pondokkie' was proved wrong. He was asked to apologize to his neighbours and pay them some compensation for the 'pondokkie' he had destroyed, or make arrangements to rebuild it. He paid compensation.

(ix) *The jealous town wife*

A fieldworker was present when two friends—neighbours—had a quarrel. They were both *abafazana* and former *ooMackazi*. About

11

11 p.m. one of the two women knocked at her friend's door, and found, amongst other people in the house, her husband. She immediately accused her friend of keeping her husband until late in the night. The friend, somewhat taken aback, said, 'What do you really mean by that? Do I ever ask your husband to stay at my place until late?' 'Why don't you tell him to go home when it is time for him to do so? You can see yourself that he hasn't any common sense', said the angry friend. 'I am sorry, N, I really can't do that. I have not got the courage to turn your husband out of my house. If you do not want him to come here, tell him yourself. Another thing, I do not like what you imply by saying that I keep your husband in my house. S has been visiting here for so long, often in your company. Why now, all of a sudden, do you come and accuse me of keeping him? I am afraid! I am convinced that you mean much more than you have just said. Just imagine what my husband would think of me when he hears that I am being accused by my best friend of keeping her husband!'

By this time the woman and her husband were on their feet ready to go. Before the husband walked out, he said to his hostess, trying to console her: 'Do not worry about this one, she does not know what she is talking about.' Soon afterwards everybody departed, leaving the hostess, T, quite upset. A day or two later T went to report her friend, N, to N's mother, who called both of them and admonished them (*ukuyala*). They were reconciled and they are still good friends.

(x) *Spanking another's child*

Two neighbours, young mothers, quarrelled over children. It all started when one mother spanked her neighbour's little son for being naughty when playing with other children. The child cried, and the mother came out when she heard his voice. She inquired, 'What is the matter Z? Who is beating you?' 'L's mother', replied the child. L's mother came out and confirmed the statement. She explained why she spanked the child. The mother of Z, obviously dissatisfied, asked, 'Why did you not bring him to me instead of hitting him yourself? Why do you find it so easy to hit other people's children, and yet nobody ever hits your children?' L's mother replied, 'Any parent is free to put my children right when she finds them doing wrong. That is how I was trained by my parents, and up to this day I do not hesitate to punish a child for doing wrong. I do this irrespective of the parentage of the child. However, I apologize for punishing your child without your permission, if that is what you mean by remonstrating with me in front of the children.'

The mother of Z flared up and said, 'You seem to think a world of yourself, you bitch. Do you think that I give birth to children for you to beat?' Before the unpleasant exchange of words could go any further, a third young married woman (*umfazana*) came out and said, 'For the sake of us all [all *abafazana*] please stop this. What are the people going to think of us, *bafazana* of this street?' The quarrelling women quickly disappeared into their houses. The woman who intervened, though also an *umfazana*, is senior to the other two and they 'respect her because she is well behaved [*unesimilo*]'.

(xi) *The insulted mothers*

An *itopikazi* went to complain to a mother of three naughty sons about their behaviour. She alleged that they were in the habit of interfering with her young daughters. The defendant, also an *itopikazi*, tired of hearing the same story, said, 'It is all very well coming to complain to me about my sons, but it is surprising that none of you ever tries to find out how your daughters get mixed up with undesirable types like my sons. Without defending my sons, I may tell you one thing: namely, that these little bitches are also not as innocent as you, their mother, might think.' The first *itopikazi* did not like the idea of her daughters being referred to as 'little bitches'. She, therefore, turned away and went home without saying a word more. She reported the matter to her husband, who was annoyed by the lack of manners of the mother of the three boys. He quickly sent for his next-door neighbour, also an *itopi*, and told him the whole story. He asked him 'What does one do about a matter like this?' The neighbour suggested that the mother of the three sons be called in so that she could explain what she meant by calling somebody else's daughters bitches.

By the time she arrived two or three additional people were there. The fieldworker was politely requested to wait in the other room while the old folks had their discussion privately.[1] The neighbour who had been called in began: 'There is nothing much except that a few minutes ago I saw a child coming in to tell me that his father wanted to see me. I came to find out what the matter was and I was told what you had to say when my neighbour's wife came to complain about your children's behaviour. In my opinion, your reply sounded a bit odd. For that reason we considered it fair to call you in to come and explain what you meant, in case she misunderstood you. The offender, rather bashful, said, 'Yes, it is true that I spoke rudely to M [using a clan name]. I have heard so many complaints about my sons that I have become extremely sensitive about the whole thing, and I genuinely wish that people could please tell their daughters to stop mixing with my sons.' The neigh-

[1] In the barracks any man (circumcised), provided he was not a stranger, would have been allowed to stay while the discussion took place.

bour: 'I think that is what you should have said instead of using
unpalatable words when speaking to M. I will, therefore, suggest that
you apologize to her, and that in future you try to avoid using bad
language when speaking to people, no matter how upset you are.
It has to be like that because we, as old people, should set an example
to our sons and daughters. The offender apologized, and equilibrium
was thus restored. Tea was made and the old people began chatting,
discussing the behaviour of children in general.

(xii) *The tale-bearer bewitched*

A man quarrelled with his friend's wife because he had told his
friend that she had a lover. The woman went to create a commotion
about it at the tale-bearer's house. Several friends who were present
when this happened intervened and tried to stop the quarrel.
Though things were talked over by the couples concerned with the
help of their friends, the man, who was supposed to have made the
accusation, was perpetually having nightmares. He was convinced
that his friend's wife was bewitching him. He therefore approached
a diviner and got himself treated so that he would be immune to his
friend's wife's witchcraft. After this, he claims, his sleep was undis-
turbed. This man had passed the junior certificate examination
(ten years' schooling), and had been in town for nearly fifteen years.
He was an *uscuse-me* in every way, but still he was prepared to spend
R20 on a diviner for treatment.

(xiii) *The unfaithful husband*

A man, a rather violent type of *uscuse-me*, lived with his wife,
children, and a younger brother. He fell in love with a nurse. She
could not telephone him because his wife might answer the phone
or might listen to their conversation. They decided that she (the
nurse) should write to tell him whenever she was free to see him. In
case his wife should notice the unfamiliar handwriting he asked her
to address the letters to his brother.

The plan worked well until one day the wife, when sending clothes
to the cleaners, found in her husband's jacket a couple of letters,
addressed to his brother. She read the letters. In the evening the
younger brother innocently walked in, and after greeting his silent
sister-in-law, he sat down. She threw a potful of hot water at him.
He jumped up in agony and before he could say anything a pile of
letters was flung at him. He knew what had happened and ran out.
He was dripping wet but he could not go into the house to change.
He got a friend to take him to the hospital for treatment of his
burns.

The husband, later in the evening, found his brother sitting outside the gate. His brother told him what had happened. They both went in, and the elder brother was raging. After a heated argument with his wife, he hit her 'for brutally attacking his brother', as he put it. The following day the wife went to report the matter to her husband's two best friends. In the evening the two friends came in and the matter was discussed. The husband's action was deplored. His friends emphasized that 'it is a bad thing for any man to beat his wife'. Virtually nothing was said about his adulterous behaviour. The wife also was criticized for her violent behaviour. It was pointed out to her that it is a disgrace for a woman to use physical violence. The matter was settled and peace was made.

Some time later the same man fell in love again. He began to spend nights out, and to make things worse, he ill-treated his wife, hitting her almost every time he came home. She went to report the matter to his father's brother, who told the other senior men of his clan. On an appointed day they gathered at the quarrelling couple's house. The man's father's brother introduced the discussion in the following words: 'M, your wife has some complaints against you. She tells us that you never sleep at home and that on top of that you have made a habit of hitting her on the few occasions you do come home. Is this true or not?' M answered, 'It is not true, uncle. The only occasions I don't come home are when we are busy at the business. As for beating her, I only beat her because, lately, she has been so cheeky that she never pays any attention to what I say.' 'I thought you said that the allegation was untrue. In any case, what right have you to beat your wife? Who beats you for your countless transgressions? If you are still interested in what goes on in the street, why did you get married at all? We know of no married man who sleeps out. As a matter of fact, it is only the uncircumcised boys [amakhwenkwe] who do that sort of thing. As for hitting this child, remember one thing, and that is, this is your wife in name. In reality, this is the wife of the Dontsas [Dontsa clan]. You are old enough now, you ought to know this. For how long can we go on telling you the same thing? Do be careful, lest a curse fall upon you.' After this admonishment the husband's behaviour was greatly improved for a time, but a few months later he not only hit his wife again but drove her away. This was a serious case and the senior members of both husband's and wife's families came to arbitrate. M was fined R20 and his wife was brought back ceremoniously.

3. THE ARBITRATOR

Arbitration implies the coercion of some members of the community by others. People exert pressure in proportion to the respect they command, and they cannot exert it, except by force, unless there is a community of values. Men are respected in so far as they embody the values of a group. As has already been shown, the values of the migrants and the ordinary towns-men differ from each other and from those of the middle class, and arbitration by members of another category whose values are different is not acceptable; but between the different age-groups of townsmen—*ikhaba*, *ooMac* and *itopi*—there is a measure of understanding, and the senior may arbitrate for the junior. In case (v) an *uMac* intervened between *ikhaba*, and in case (vi) an *itopi* reproved *ooMac* who were fighting.

Church people refrain from approaching non-church mem-bers when the conflict has something to do with church affairs. If the case is directly connected with the church the matter is taken to the minister or elder, or a respected lay-preacher. For instance when an elder failed to announce the date of the funeral of a member's wife in a church gathering, because of his personal differences with the husband, the latter complained to the minister. Where the connexion with the church is more indirect the matter is taken to the senior members of the same social clique belonging to the church. For example, a certain *manyano* member, out of jealousy, was continually attacking the *manyano* president, and spreading scandal about her, outside the church. After some time the president reported the matter to the more senior of her friends—also *manyano* members—and they called in the scandalmonger and remonstrated with her.

Neighbours occasionally arbitrate for one another irrespective of class, but generally *ooscuse-me* 'keep out of affairs that do not concern them', and ordinary people prefer to 'leave stuck-ups alone', so most of the arbitration by neighbours is within the same class.

Seniority and conformity with the norms of the group are the two essential qualifications in an arbitrator. In the barracks an arbitrator should himself be a migrant, senior, and well behaved. And among the townspeople in the married quarters the neighbour called in to arbitrate is a senior man or woman, again judged to be well behaved. A close friend, or kinsman, is expected to exert more influence than a stranger, so the plaintiff often appeals to the friend or kinsman of the defendant.

The duty of the arbitrator is to find an acceptable solution and, as is clear from the cases quoted, *both* parties are commonly criticized. 'In most cases the arbitrator has something to say for or against both parties. Where one party is completely wrong he is not condemned outright, but helped to retreat gracefully.' Those who accept the arbitrator's decision are approved by the group: those who reject it are disapproved and may eventually be excluded (*vide* case (iii)). But no amount of arbitration can stop a young man who has accepted urban ways from being in constant conflict with his home-boys in the barracks, or a *scuse-me* man clashing with his *Mackazi* wife, because they reject each other's values. The most arbitration can do for them is to bring about a temporary settlement.

Divination is used as a form of arbitration. The diviner commonly confirms suspicion and settles any lingering doubts if the evidence is not conclusive. His supposed supernatural powers give him considerable prestige and he may compel an admission of guilt, or at least provide the accused with an excuse for accepting the decision '. . . if the diviner says so' (see above, p. 161).

Migrants show a lively sense of responsibility for their home-boys, and townsmen an appreciable, though lesser, responsibility for their neighbours. The idea that those who occupy one neighbourhood are 'members of one another' is tenacious even though the young townees knife one another so readily, and are reluctant to accept arbitration. Cases (iv)–(vii) illustrate the difficulty of compelling *ikhaba*, *ooMac* and *iibari* to accept any sort of arbitration. Among them the more aggressive and violent a man is the more respect he commands, but there are no organized gangs, with a recognized leadership, as in Johannesburg, where township gangs are organized on a territorial basis and the security of a boy or young man depends on his membership of the local gang, and submitting to the leader. The older generation of townsmen in Langa try desperately to exercise some sort of control over the younger ones: they succeed in part with the girls, and with boys at school, but there is a lawless residue.

Among the middle class, arbitration occurs as cases (xii) and (xiii) illustrate, but middle-class families generally like to settle disputes in private. '*Ooscuse-me* believe that what goes on in their families and among them is their own affair, and it has nothing to do with outsiders.' Serious cases of theft, assault, adultery and seduction are commonly taken to a magistrate's court without first going for arbitration to neighbours. This change in attitude to arbitration among *ooscuse-me* is important since they tend to establish a pattern which others copy. One African attorney practises in the western Cape but the bulk of cases brought to him, and to the many white attorneys, are between black and white, or involve the government.

9 Conclusion

South Africa is not immune to general social processes and urbanization is one of them. We find in Langa that a community has emerged with characteristics very similar to those of urban communities in other countries, and radically different from the traditional tribal societies of the Nguni peoples. In Langa there is differentiation of occupation; and diversity in language, custom, religion, and forms of artistic expression; just as in any other city. In the structural aspect[1] the diversity appears as a multiplicity of corporations and associations formed by people with interests in common, whether it be profit from the production or exchange of some commodity, mutual aid in saving, insurance, or the improvement of working conditions, political action, the enjoyment of a game, instruction, or the worship of God. From the point of view of the individual the diversity allows of choice, some opportunity to select what sort of people he will co-operate with, what sort of associations he will join. The exercise of choice is apparent even among some migrants, as in the case of the musician quoted on p. 129. Social position is not as strictly determined by kinship and age, as it is in a small-scale society, instead it is fixed by colour classification (as legally determined),[2] by education, wealth, and the degree of sophistication in urban living. Traditional differences in language and custom and status are disappearing, but new differences in speech and manner of life and a new class system are emerging. What strikes townsmen is the difference in speech and manner between migrants and *ooMac*, or *ooMac* and *ooscuse-me*, not the difference between Xhosa and Thembu, and Pondo and Zulu. The relationship in Langa between *ikhaba* and *ooMac* on the one hand, and *ooscuse-me* on the

[1] For the theoretical implications cf. Godfrey and Monica Wilson, *The Analysis of Social Change*, 1945.

[2] In theory this coincides with biological category: in fact it does not always do so.

other, is directly parallel to that between 'corner boys' and 'college boys' in Chicago[3]: it epitomizes *urban* class differences.

In a city, relationships are often anonymous and impersonal in a way in which they can never be in a primitive or peasant community; the impersonality and anonymity are functions of the size of the group; not everyone can know everyone else, and those who wish to can disappear easily. Such impersonality in relationships brings to many a sense of loneliness and isolation,[4] the *anomie* of which Durkheim spoke,[5] which implies the slackening of control over its members, by the group, as well as sometimes a disintegration of personalities. Among the migrants in Langa isolation scarcely appears—each individual finds a warm refuge in his group of home-boys—but there are indications of it among the *ikhaba* and *ooMac*, particularly in the apparent imperviousness of many individuals to pressure from their fellows.

Partly, no doubt, because of the spectre of loneliness, slum-dwellers, as well as the more affluent, often cling tenaciously to a known neighbourhood, finding security in their 'personal space'. The feeling of belonging, and the security of moving around in a well-known territory, are important to men,[6] as they are to birds and animals. It is apparent in Langa in the extreme aversion shown by many residents to the idea of having to move elsewhere.

The high rates of illegitimacy, drunkenness, and crime profoundly shock the migrants from the country. These disorders recur when industrialization is proceeding very fast and country folk pour into a city. Nowhere have they been more apparent than in the English slums of the eighteenth century.[7]

[3] W. F. Whyte, *Street Corner Society, passim.*
[4] Cf. D. Riesman, N. Glaser, R. Denney, *The Lonely Crowd.*
[5] E. Durkheim, *Le Suicide.*
[6] This is brought out vividly in a recent study of a Liverpool slum: Madeleine Kerr, *Ship Street.*
[7] G. M. Trevelyan, *English Social History*, pp. 331, 343, 345. Trevelyan writes: 'The lower strata of the population of the capital, the dockers and unskilled casual labour of a great mart and port lived under the most filthy conditions of overcrowding, without sanitation, police or doctors, and far beyond the range of philanthropy, education and religion. Such was their state both in the City proper and in the liberties beyond, in the days of Defoe. The death-rate among them was appalling, and was still going up because they were learning to drink spirits instead of ale. The privileged sanctuary of outlaws in "Alsatia", so

(*Continued overleaf*)

And the fact that so disturbs the Langa residents, that the bulk of the crimes of violence are committed by teenagers, is also characteristic of cities elsewhere.

Certain local peculiarities in Langa are linked to colour bar, and to the limitation on Africans, particularly women, entering Cape Town and living there. Attempts are now being made to prevent the permanent settlement of Africans in the western Cape, but they are wholly unacceptable to the African population, to white employers, and to the considerable body of white and Coloured people who believe that citizenship of a country should include the right to move about freely in it. A settled African population without roots in the country is already an accomplished fact in Langa. Only a portion of the migrants remain 'incapsulated' indefinitely. There is a continual seepage of men from the tight-knit groups of home-boys living in the barracks to the ranks of townsmen. Some men remain, throughout their lives, more part of a home village and its outlier in town—the home-boys' group—than of the urban community; these are generally the least educated, and the more schooling they have had the less likely they are to do so.

Elementary families are important in town but the wider kinship groups are of negligible importance as corporations, and even the network of kinship relationships is modified by the need for a job, or the desire to associate with others of like interests. The very fact that kinsmen are so scattered proves that kinship is no longer dominant. Most families in Cape Town have kin not only in the country, but in other towns of the Republic, and it is very common to find members of one lineage scattered in Johannesburg, Port Elizabeth, East London, and Cape Town. Kinship connexions do not ensure that kinsmen, even siblings, congregate in one town: rather they look for

(*Note* 7 *Continued*)

outrageous to the dignity of the neighbouring lawyers at the Temple, had indeed been abolished a few years before Anne came to the throne, but the fraternity of thieves, highwaymen and harlots had only been scattered thence to spread themselves more thickly over the whole metropolitan area.'

Burials in London between 1740 and 1742 were 'twice as many as baptisms' and Hogarth's 'Gin Lane' depicted an everyday scene. There was an 'appalling infant mortality among the poor and especially among deserted bastard children'. All this roused the 'stormy pity' which led to the establishment of hospitals, schools, and orphanages, and a body of legislation which eventually created the welfare state. (*English Social History*, Longmans, Green & Co. Ltd.)

work wherever it is to be found. For the townsman, as opposed to the migrant, the transformation from a society based primarily on kinship to one based on association is complete.

There is a rumbustious quality about the townees, a swaggering truculence, that is reminiscent of the first Elizabethans, and the complexity and vitality of the new social groups are indisputable. Langa townsmen are no amorphous mass of persons but are linked in a network of families, churches, and clubs which unite those with a common interest, whether it be sport, music, dancing, politics, or merely smoking dagga.

Churches and clubs are so numerous partly because they have split repeatedly; they have done so more frequently in the African than in the white community in South Africa. Why? This question is one manifestation of the fundamental problem of social anthropology: what holds groups together and what causes them to disintegrate? Do the same general principles apply in all types of social groups? Can we, for example, compare a church or a club in Langa with a clan, tribe, or village in one of the traditional societies of Africa, as well as with the churches and clubs of Europe and America? Can we discover what are the general social conditions under which groups cohere or split?

In the most general terms the coherence of a group depends upon a balance between the strength of the common purpose and the intensity of conflicts within it. The conflicts may be conflicts of end—purpose—or the method of achieving it, or rivalries for leadership. If a common end is passionately desired disagreements over method and rivalries for leadership are submerged. For example, in the Transkeian Lions soccer club in Langa a split threatens but has been prevented, or at least delayed, by the consideration that this is the *only* country club likely to beat the 'town boys' in the Langa Blues, and rivalry between countrymen and townsmen is such that the dissidents in the country club are prepared to sink their differences in order to challenge successfully the town boys' dominance in soccer (see above, p. 122).

In churches in which the doctrine of the church, as opposed to a worshipping group of Christians, is emphasized, the common purpose necessary to resist fission is strengthened. The fact that the Order of Ethiopia remained within the Anglican fold, as part of the Church of the Province, is evidence that the members of that Order accepted the authority of the church in spite of a strong desire for independence.

In churches and recreation clubs alike, ownership of property discourages fragmentation. If a dissident group stands to lose nothing it splits off more readily than when, by becoming independent, it loses a building in which to worship, or a playing-field and club-house. Enjoyment of property is a buttress of coherence in associations, as it is in lineages.

Success or failure in the common purpose also affects the integration of a group. A flourishing sports club, or church, or political party attracts members, whereas an association that continually fails to achieve its ends loses members. The Bechuanaland Swallows rugby club disintegrated after a conspicuous defeat: it was already crumbling before this game, but the defeat contributed to its final dissolution. And the rugby club formed by domestic servants did not survive because its members could not attend practices regularly, and it could not therefore achieve its end: regular fixtures, and success in them. Splinter churches have multiplied in South Africa and Kenya, in the Pacific, in Brazil, and in China when communities are struggling to adjust to conditions that overwhelm them. Dr. de Vries speaks of these splinter churches as 'expressions of despair'.

Any comparison of groups to discover the basis of cohesion is complicated by the fact that different people may seek different ends, or the same individual several ends, in the same association, whatever its ostensible purpose, and the same type of group may serve different ends in different communities. For example, one man may join a rugby club in Langa primarily to enjoy a game, whereas, to another, prestige—the prestige associated with office, or at least of playing in the first or only team—is at least as important. The evidence suggests that in sports clubs in Rondebosch, recreation, the enjoyment of a game, is the chief draw for members, whereas in Langa opportunity for leadership is relatively more important because it is so circumscribed in other fields. In Langa, office in sports clubs is sought, whereas in Rondebosch it is often felt to be a burden. Where outlets for leadership are limited, rivalries are likely to be more intense, and this in turn will tend towards the splitting of associations. In churches, music clubs, and sports clubs in Langa personal rivalries have clearly contributed to splits, though less so in sport than in music, for the team captain is relatively less important in his group than the band leader.

From the Langa evidence it appears that the size of the group which coheres is directly related to its function; if it grows larger than the efficient minimum then splits are tolerated; if it grows larger than the efficient maximum then splits are essential. In the savings clubs three to five members is considered ideal; if they grow larger then the danger of one member absconding is greater, and each member's turn to take the pool comes round too infrequently; if they are smaller than three then the advantages of pooling resources are lost. In the rugby clubs the minimum necessary for a team is fifteen playing members. A club will have more chance of success in tournaments if it has a considerably larger body to draw from, but if the members exceed sixty then more than half the members cannot play in either first or second teams, and have little chance of playing in matches. Commonly they prefer to form another club of their own and, as the statements quoted on pp. 115–16, 120 indicate, the usual reason for members withdrawing from one club and forming another is the feeling that their talents were overlooked when teams were picked. Father Botto's investigations show that the rugby clubs range in size from 15 to 75 with an average of 37 members. Soccer clubs averaged 45 members, and cricket clubs 80. Sports clubs in the white community in Cape Town are often considerably larger than this—rugby clubs may have five to eight teams and 150 members—therefore function is not the only factor. In the white clubs the enjoyment of a good game, and the prestige of belonging to a well-known club, outweigh the feeling that a member should be in the first or second team, and large and old-established clubs enjoy the ownership of fields and club-houses which seceding groups cannot hope to equal. A Langa club owns no property at all, except a ball, or a cricket bat.

Some of the rugby and soccer clubs in Langa have survived for thirty-five years or more, though, as has been shown, new clubs have split off from them; others have existed only for a season or two. Our hypothesis is that those which survive are those with a strong home-boy or local urban loyalty, which unifies them in opposition to other like groups. Once the separate identity of a group diminishes its association is liable to disintegrate. For example, the Morning Stars rugby club dissolved partly because its members were welcome in the local town clubs; their identity as Port Elizabeth men was not maintained (see above, p. 118). And again, the Statelyte band of Transkeians living in the flats (see above, p. 128) which has been strong for five years, is said to be disintegrating now as its members are becoming absorbed in town. It was formed as a group of *iibari* in opposition to the townees who would not admit 'country bumpkins' into their bands, but as the individual members merge into the town population their unity and identity as Statelytes are disappearing.

All co-operation implies some subordination of the individual to the group, and co-operation ceases when individuals cease to submit to the authority of the group. Quarrels of greater or less severity may be regarded as part of the co-operation—they imply continued interaction—but they may culminate in the dissolution or fragmentation of the group. In a community in which order is maintained by force, any exercise of authority tends to be resented; all authority is identified with power,[8] and resisted as 'persecution' or 'discrimination'. The resentment at any exercise of authority in schools or universities in Africa or India during and after the struggle for political freedom illustrates this, and in the Langa context it is instructive to find that the Statelytes, a group of educated young men, refused to choose a leader 'though in fact it was obvious who their leader was'. They followed a pattern prevalent for a time at Fort Hare, when teams refused to elect a captain.

Experience of organization—of leading and of following, and the actual techniques of working in committee, of accounting for and administering moneys collected by the group—increases coherence. Quarrels over funds have repeatedly led to splits in churches and the disintegration of all types of clubs. By the standards of Europe or America the book-keeping and

---

[8] Cf. Bertrand de Jouvenel, *Sovereignty*, p. 32: 'Power is something very different from authority. The distinguishing mark of the latter is that it is exercised only by those who voluntarily accept it: if the rulers have authority over only a part of their subjects, they may receive from that part a strength sufficient to subject the others to their power.'

auditing are generally inadequate and there are numerous reports of club funds being misappropriated: theft of club funds seems to be easier, and to occur a good deal more often than in the white community. However, the fact that it occurs does not preclude the creation of numerous savings clubs of one sort or another whose members trust one another.

The innumerable associations of the modern African townships may, indeed, be seen as a school of civilization. In managing churches and clubs a great many men and women are gaining experience in the organization of groups which are no longer based on kinship and which are part of a money economy. The savings clubs, and choirs, all keep written records of the contributions paid by members and contributions received when each takes the pool. Reciprocity is insisted upon, and though the 'accounts' might not satisfy an auditor they are felt to be an essential part of the system. In the sports clubs there are chairmen and secretaries, subscriptions are paid, and rules are enforced. Clubs are fined a shilling or two if their representatives do not turn up to union meetings or match reports are not submitted, or if the referees they provide for matches are late, and there is constant pressure to make players attend regularly and punctually. In the club committees minutes are kept, usually in English which is vivid if ungrammatical—we read of 'sport . . . literally crawling on its stomach', and 'deliberations' which 'bristled'. As has been indicated, the churches are the organizations of longest standing and largest membership, and it is in them that the older generation has served an apprenticeship as office-bearers—elders, deacons, leaders of the women's *manyano*, and as fund-raisers.

The coherence of a group is related also to the prestige and personality of its leaders. Limba's church—of which there is a branch in Langa—is the creation of a born leader, and its size and wealth in Port Elizabeth are directly due to his personality. The same is true of Bhengu's church in East London and Shembe's near Durban, and it was, in a less degree, true of the Industrial and Commercial Workers' Union under Clements Kadalie. No comparable leader has emerged in Cape Town partly, perhaps, because a charismatic leader of that type is less likely to attract the more sophisticated community of the Cape than the people of the areas in which they have succeeded. Both Limba and Kadalie worked for a time in Cape Town but both failed to gain any mass following there, and they moved elsewhere.

The revolution in social structure which occurs when illiterate countrymen become urban workers involves, as we have seen, a change in the effective social groups; the society is transformed from one based on kinship to one based on association. As the groups change the positions of leadership change, and Langa is characterized by uncertainty as to what the positions of leadership are to be, as well as who are to hold them. The uncertainty is most clearly reflected in the attitude towards chiefs who visit town. This sort of uncertainty reduces the coherence of groups; when there is doubt over what groups *should* command loyalty all those questioned tend to fragment. Idealization of a group and identification with it are not confined to one society or one period: traditionally among the Nguni people men identified themselves with their lineage, local groups, and chiefdom, and the migrants in town still stress the wisdom and morality of identifying with fellow home-boys, who represent the local group. Some churches and some political parties make a claim to total allegiance, and in certain small groups, or among the most devoted members of larger groups, such as a women's *manyano*, interaction is predominantly with fellow members, but for most townsmen no one group is all-embracing; neither church nor party, and still less 'the service' or 'the firm', commands a man's life. The strait jacket is fashioned by the State, rather than any lesser organization.

Although the splitting of associations goes on, an opposite process is discernible. Many of the independent clubs seek affiliation in local unions (such as the Rugby Board) and they in turn link themselves with like groups in other towns, and national unions commonly, now, seek affiliation with international organizations. A savings circle, or Zionist leader's following, is independent and isolated in all its activities except fund-raising, when it depends in some measure on outsiders; a home-boys' clique co-operates with other like cliques for arbitration in disputes and occasionally in matters concerning a wider home area, such as eastern Pondoland, but in all other matters it acts independently. Most churches, and sports clubs, and welfare societies, however, are linked in national organizations, more and more of which have, or are seeking, international affiliation; thus wide-based groups do, in fact, persist and function in the field of recreation and religion as well as in economic activity.

Some observers looking on the new urban African communities see only chaos, but in fact there are regularities in the breaches of law, logic, and convention. The same types of conflicts recur in Langa, in Broken Hill, in Salisbury, Kampala, Stanleyville; the breaches are within a framework of regularity. What is happening as peasants move into town is part of a process that has recurred again and again in history. It causes some men to despair because they look on the good that is gone, and the present evil; they see the isolated tribal society, or the peasant village, as Arcadia, and compare it with the *tsotsis* smoking dagga and knifing their fellows. But that antithesis ignores half the facts, both in town and country.

In Langa there are *tsotsis*—many of them—but their behaviour does not pass uncriticized. A large category of 'decent people' lives there also, and it judges *tsotsi* behaviour to be bad. In short, moral standards exist. Hence the constant demand for compulsory education for Africans, for technical training, for jobs for adolescents, and the repeated attempts by middle-class leaders to 'look after the interests of the youth in the township' and organize clubs for them.

Something new is growing in towns; its mark is the intense vitality, the aliveness, that appears in dance and song, in the jiving of the *ikhaba*, and the Merry-Macs band, in the irrepressible humour of the townees, and in a flexible changing language.

> *How can we reject*
> *The long last look on the ever-dying face*
> *Turned backward from the other side of time?*
> *And how offend the dead and shame the living*
> *By these despairs? And how refrain from love?*
> *This is a difficult country, and our home.*[9]

[9] Edwin Muir, *The Difficult Land.*

APPENDIX

THE LAW REGULATING
MOVEMENT TO TOWN

Restriction on entry into Cape Town began in 1926. Before that, in 1901, a proposal to exclude Africans had been rejected, and though warnings were issued from time to time about the difficulty of obtaining employment, there was no actual prohibition on entry. In 1926 the municipal area of Cape Town was declared a 'proclaimed area' in terms of section 12 of Act 21 of 1923. All Africans coming into Cape Town were required to report to the registering officer within forty-eight hours of arrival, while all male Africans employed in the municipal area had to obtain a registered contract of service or a casual labourer's permit. Registered parliamentary voters, the owners of certain properties, and certain other specified groups were exempted from these provisions. The local authority could not refuse registration if accommodation was available, and it had to provide accommodation for work-seekers. The right of women to travel to and live in an urban area was not restricted, so that a man could have his family living with him.

Act 25 of 1930 amended the Act of 1923 so as to enable the local authority to apply to the Governor-General for a proclamation limiting the entry of Africans into an urban area under prescribed conditions. Another amendment enabled any municipality to prohibit the entry of a female African without permission of the local authority, but it could not deny permission to a woman whose husband or father had lived and worked in the area for not less than two years, where accommodation was available. Proclamation 231 of 1932 applied some of the restrictions to Cape Town, for instance by limiting the entry of Africans under 18 years of age. But the Council did not use the powers granted to limit the entry of women, nor did it ask the government to apply the more stringent restrictions envisaged by the amending statute.

The Native (Urban Areas) Act of 1923 was further amended by Act 46 of 1937. Its general purport was to vest in the central government the powers of restricting the entry of Africans into urban areas in which the local authority had failed to take such action. One amendment required a woman who wanted to enter an urban area to obtain a certificate of permission from the magistrate of her home district as well as a permit from the local authority. Acting under the powers conferred by the Act of 1937, the government issued Proclamation No. 105 of 1939 in terms of which no African, other than an exempted person, could lawfully enter Cape Town unless he came there to take up employment, or on a temporary visit, or to seek work with the permission of the City Council. The Natives (Urban Areas) Acts were consolidated in 1945 by Act 25. Proclamation 74 of 1946 reapplied the restrictive provisions of the Act to Cape Town, and extended the City Council's jurisdiction under the Act to include the entire Cape Peninsula.

In 1946 the provisions of War Measure 81 of 1943 were applied so as to restrict the sale of railway tickets to Africans wishing to travel by rail from the Cape eastern districts, bounded by De Aar in the north and Mossel Bay in the west, to stations in the Cape western region. Tickets could be sold only to Africans who satisfied the local magistrate that employment was waiting for them at their destination. Exceptions were made for bona fide temporary visitors, scholars, and women wishing to join their fathers or husbands, if they had permits issued by the registering officer of the area to which they wished to travel. After 1 January 1947, the provisions of section 11(1) of Act 25 of 1945 were applied to Cape Town. As a result, Africans who, having satisfied a magistrate that employment awaited them in the Peninsula, were allowed to travel to Cape Town, could not take up work there unless the employer guaranteed to repatriate them on discharge from employment.

Proclamation 105 of 1939 applied to both sexes, but African women living in Cape Town were not obliged to undergo registration. In practice, therefore, the restrictions imposed by the proclamation did not affect them. They were, however, prevented by the War Measure from travelling to Cape Town by rail unless they satisfied the prescribed conditions, and those wishing to take up residence with husbands or fathers had to produce certificates from the City Council to show that suitable accommodation was available for them.

A radical change in the position of urban Africans resulted from the substitution of a new section for section 10 of Act 25 of 1945. The change was made by Act 54 of 1952, and it became an offence for any African to remain in an urban area for longer than seventy-two hours, unless he either fell within the scope of a narrow range of exceptions, or received a temporary permit from an official to be in the area.

The exempted categories consist of Africans born and permanently resident in the area, persons who have worked continuously in the area for one employer for at least ten years, persons who remained for at least fifteen years in the area, and their wives, unmarried daughters, and sons under 18 years of age. It should be noted, however, that exempted persons are not immune from expulsion from the urban area under other sections of the Act. With the Representation of Natives Act of 1959 the special rights of registered voters are obliterated.

In 1954 the City Council began to issue permits to women under section 10 of Act 25 of 1945, and to prosecute women for contravening section 10(4) of the Act, which makes it an offence for an African to be in the area without the prescribed permission or exemption. A reason given at the time for the issue of permits was that employers of African women wished to protect themselves against the danger of prosecution for breach of section 10*bis* of the Act, which makes it an offence to employ an African who is not lawfully resident in the area.

However, the extension of pass law controls to women in the Peninsula acquired a new significance from an address given by Dr. Eiselen, the Secretary for Native Affairs, at the annual conference of the South African Bureau of Race Relations (SABRA) in January 1955. He announced that his Department's policy regarding the immigration of Africans in the western Cape was to expel all 'foreign' Africans, maintain strict supervision over the influx, repatriate families that had recently come into the area, rehouse the lawful residents in municipal houses with the hope that the African population will gradually diminish, and restrict further immigration to migrant and temporary workers.[1]

An even more emphatic expression of a determination to expel Africans from the western Cape was contained in a statement by Dr. Verwoerd, when Minister of Native Affairs, in 1956, to a deputation from the Christian Council, which interviewed him on the subject of migrant labour and the position of Africans in the western Cape in particular.[2] In 1961 the Deputy Minister of Bantu Administration and Development reiterated the official policy, that Africans must gradually and systematically be withdrawn from the western Cape.[3] Movement to town is also controlled through prohibitive rents. In the married quarters of Langa sub-economic rents are charged to the poorest, who pay R2.25 a month for two rooms, and only the more affluent pay the top rent of R9 a month for four rooms with electricity. But in the newly built Nyanga (*Guguletu*) a flat rate of R8.05 is charged for a four-roomed house without electricity. This, together with the fare, amounts to 38 per cent of an unskilled worker's earnings.

[1] SABRA *Referate*, Jan. 1955, pp. 118–19.

[2] *South African Outlook*, March 1956, pp. 40–3.

[3] In an address to Tygerberg Afrikaanse Sakekamer, Bellville. *Cape Times*, 14 March 1961.

SELECT BIBLIOGRAPHY

The following books and papers dealing with various aspects of urbanization in Africa have been found useful. An asterisk indicates those which touch directly on Africans in the western Cape.

*Alexander, Ray, and Simons, H. J., *Job Reservation and the Trade Unions*. Woodstock, Cape, Enterprise, 1959.

Banton, Michael, *West African City: a Study of Tribal Life in Freetown*. London, International African Institute, 1957.

Bascom, W. R., 'The *Esusu*: a Credit Institution of the Yoruba', *J. Roy. Anthrop. Inst.*, LXXXII, pt. 1, 1952. pp. 63–9.

Batson, E., The Poverty Line in Cape Town. Revised edition of Report SS. 3. Report SP. 3 February 1942. School of Social Science, University of Cape Town.

Batson, E., The Distribution of Poverty among Coloured Households in Cape Town. Report SS. 4 1942. School of Social Science, University of Cape Town.

Batson, E., A Re-calculation of the Poverty Datum Line. Revised edition of Report No. SP. 3. Report RS. 203 May 1944. School of Social Science, University of Cape Town.

Batson, E., 'Relative poverty in a peri-urban area: a report from the Cape Flats "Vleiland Survey"', *Journal for Social Research*, 9, 1958, pp. 37–49.

Blair, M. R., 'Selected Budgets. Natal Peri-Urban Bantu Family Basic Income', *Race Relations*, 14, 1947, pp. 159–69.

*Botto, R., Some Aspects of the Leisure Occupations of the African Population in Cape Town. Unpublished M. Soc. Sci. thesis, University of Cape Town, 1954.

Comhaire, J. (Comp.), *Urban Conditions in Africa*: Select Reading List on Urban Problems in Africa. London, Institute of Colonial Studies, 1952.

Comhaire, J. L. L., *Aspects of Urban Administration in Tropical and Southern Africa*. University of Cape Town, School of African Studies, 1953.

De Gruchy, Joy, *The Cost of Living for Urban Africans*. S.A. Institute of Race Relations, 1960.

Epstein, A. L., *The Administration of Justice and the Urban African: a Study of Urban Native Courts in Northern Rhodesia*. H.M.S.O., 1953. Colonial Research Studies No. 7.

Epstein, A. L., *Politics in an Urban African Community*. Rhodes-Livingstone Institute, 1958.

Gibson, Olive, *The Cost of Living for Africans*. S.A. Institute of Race Relations, 1953.

Glass, Y., *The Black Industrial Worker*. National Institute for Personal Research, 1961.

*Hammond-Tooke, W. D., Six Native Churches: A Preliminary Survey of Religion in an Urban Location. Unpublished M.A. thesis, University of Cape Town, 1948.

185

Hellmann, Ellen, 'Native Life in a Johannesburg Slum Yard', *Africa*, 8, 1935, pp. 34–62.

Hellmann, Ellen, 'The Native in the Towns' in *The Bantu-speaking Tribes of South Africa* (ed. I. Schapera). London, Routledge, 1937, pp. 405–34.

Hellmann, Ellen, *Problems of Urban Bantu Youth*: Report of an Enquiry into the Causes of Early School-leaving and Occupational Opportunities amongst Bantu Youth in Johannesburg. S.A.I.R.R., 1940.

Hellmann, Ellen, *Rooiyard: A Sociological Survey of an Urban Native Slum Yard.* Livingstone, Rhodes-Livingstone Institute, 1948. Rhodes-Livingstone Papers No. 13. Cape Town, O.U.P.

Hellmann, Ellen, 'Urban Areas' in *Handbook on Race Relations in South Africa* (ed. E. Hellmann). London, O.U.P., 1949, pp. 229–74.

Hellmann, Ellen, *Sellgoods*: A Sociological Survey of an African Commercial Labour Force. S.A.I.R.R., 1953.

Holleman, J. F., *The Tightrope Dancers* (Report on the 7th Annual Conference, Institute of Administrators of Non-European Affairs, Muizenberg . . . 1958). University of Natal Institute for Social Research, Occasional Reports, No. 2, 1958.

*Horrell, M., *Days of Crisis in South Africa* (events up to 15 May 1960). S.A.I.R.R. Fact Paper No. 5, 1960. Addendum Period 15 to 24 May 1960. S.A.I.R.R. RR 104/60.

*Horrell, Muriel. *The 'Pass Laws'*. S.A.I.R.R. Fact Paper 7, 1960.

*Horrell, Muriel, *The Liquor Laws as they affect Africans and Coloured and Asian People*. S.A.I.R.R. Fact Paper 8, 1960.

Horrell, Muriel, *South African Trade Unionism*, S.A.I.R.R., 1961.

*Horrell, Muriel, and Draper, Mary, *The Group Areas Act—its Effect on Human Beings*. S.A.I.R.R., 1956.

Houghton, D. Hobart (editor), *Economic Development in a Plural Society*. O.U.P., 1960.

Hunter, M., *Reaction to Conquest*. London, O.U.P., 1936.

Johannesburg, *Report on Divorces in Johannesburg*. Social Welfare Dept., 1951.

Kuper, Hilda, and Kaplan, S., 'Voluntary Associations in an Urban Township'. *African Studies*, 3, 1944, pp. 178–86.

*Levin, Ruth, *Marriage in Langa Native Location*. School of African Studies, University of Cape Town, 1947.

Little, Kenneth, 'The Role of Voluntary Associations in West African Urbanization', *Amer. Anthrop.*, 59, 1957, pp. 579–96.

Little, Kenneth, 'The Organization of Voluntary Associations in West Africa' *Civilizations* (INCIDI), 9, 1959, pp. 283–300.

Little, Kenneth, 'Urbanism in West Africa', *Sociological Review*, 7, 1959, pp. 5–13.

Little, Kenneth, 'Some Urban Patterns of Marriage and Domesticity in West Africa', *Sociological Review*, 7, 1959, pp. 65–82.

*Lipschitz, M., and Greshoff, N. M., 'Living Conditions in a Squatters' Camp', *Race Relations Journal*, XXI, no. 4, 1954, pp. 1–38.

Longmore, Laura, *The Dispossessed*: A study of the Sex-Life of Bantu Women in and around Johannesburg. London, Cape, 1959.

*Mafeje, A., 'A Chief Visits Town', *Journal of Local Administration Overseas* (forthcoming).

Mayer, Philip, *Townsmen or Tribesmen*. Cape Town, O.U.P., 1961.

Mitchell, J. C., *The Kalela Dance*, Rhodes-Livingstone Papers 27, 1956.

Mitchell, J. C., *Africans in Industrial Towns in Northern Rhodesia*. H.R.H. The Duke of Edinburgh's Study Conference. O.U.P., 1956.

Mitchell, J. C., *Tribalism and the Plural Society*. Inaugural Lecture. University College of Rhodesia and Nyasaland, London, O.U.P., 1960.

Mitchell, J. C., 'White Collar Workers and Supervisors in a Plural Society', *Civilizations*, X, 1960, pp. 293–306.

Mitchell, J. C., 'The Anthropological Study of Urban Communities', *African Studies*, 1960, pp. 169–72.

Mitchell, J. C., *Sociological Background to African Labour*. Salisbury, 1961.

Mitchell, J. C., and Epstein, A. L., 'Power and Prestige among Africans in Northern Rhodesia. An Experiment.' Rhodesia Scientific Association, *Proceedings and Transactions*, 45, 1957: 13–26.

Mitchell, J. C., and Epstein, A. L., 'Occupational Prestige and Social Status among Urban Africans in Northern Rhodesia'. *Africa*, 29, 1959, pp. 22–40.

Mqotsi, L., and Mkele, N., 'A Separatist Church'. *African Studies*, 5, 1946, pp. 106–25.

Natal Regional Survey, *Small Towns of Natal*, A Socio-Economic Sample Survey. University of Natal. Additional Report No. 3, Cape Town, O.U.P., 1953.

Natal University. Department of Economics. *The African Factory Worker*. A Sample Study of the Life and Labour of the Urban African Worker. Cape Town, O.U.P., 1950.

Natal University. Institute for Social Research. *The Baumannville Community*. A Study of the Family Life of Urban Africans. Cape Town, O.U.P. 1955.

Ngcobo, S., 'The Urban Bantu Family as a Unit', *Race Relations*, 14, 1947, pp. 136–45.

*Olivier, N. S. S., 'Die Naturel in Wes-Kaapland'. *Tydskrif vir Rasse-Aangeleenthede*, vol. 4, No. 2, 1953, pp. 1–12.

Phillips, Ray E., *The Bantu in the City*: A Study of Cultural Adjustment on the Witwatersrand. Lovedale Press (?1939).

Powdermaker, Hortense, 'Communications and Social Change, based on a Field Study in Northern Rhodesia.' New York Academy of Sciences, *Transactions*, 17, 1955, pp. 430–40.

Powdermaker, Hortense, 'Social Change through Imagery and Values of Teen-Age Africans in Northern Rhodesia', *Amer. Anthrop.*, 58, 1956, pp. 783–813.

Reader, D. H., *The Black Man's Portion*. Cape Town, O.U.P., 1961.

Sherwood, Ray, 'The Bantu Clerk: a Study of Role Expectations', *J. Social Psychology*, 47, 1958, pp. 285–316.

Simons, H. J., 'Trade Unions' in *Handbook on Race Relations in South Africa* (ed. E. Hellmann). Cape Town, O.U.P., 1949, pp. 158–70.

*Smith, Prudence (editor), *Africa in Transition*. Some B.B.C. talks on changing conditions in the Union and the Rhodesias. London, Reinhardt, 1958.

South African Institute of Race Relations, 'Problems of African Urban Administration', *Race Relations*, 13, 1946, pp. 21–64.

South African Institute of Race Relations, 'Survey of Urban and Rural Areas—Evidence submitted by the Institute to the Native Laws Commission of Enquiry', *Race Relations*, 14, 1947, pp. 25–78.

Southall, A. W., and Gutkind, P. C. W., *Townsmen in the Making*: Kampala and its suburbs. Kampala, East African Institute of Social Research, 1956. East African Studies No. 9 (roneoed).

Southall, A. W. (editor), *Social Change in Modern Africa*. London, O.U.P., 1960.

Taylor, J. V., and Lehmann, D., *Christians of the Copperbelt*. London, SCM Press, 1961.

Sundkler, Bengt G. M., *Bantu Prophets in South Africa*. 2/e London, O.U.P., 1962.

Sundkler, Bengt G. M., *The Concept of Christianity in the African Independent Churches*. Institute of Social Research, University of Natal, 1958.

UNESCO, 'African Elites', *International Social Science Bulletin*, 8, 1956, pp. 408–98.

UNESCO, *Social Implications of Industrialization and Urbanization in Africa South of the Sahara*. 1956.

Union of South Africa. Department of Native Affairs. *Report of the Inter-Departmental Committee on the Social, Health and Economic Conditions of Urban Natives* (Smit Committee). 1942.

Union of South Africa. Department of Native Affairs. *Report of the Native Laws Commission 1946–48*. Pretoria, Government Printer, 1948. U.G. 28/1948. (Fagan Commission.)

Wilson, Godfrey, *An Essay on the Economics of Detribalization in Northern Rhodesia*. Livingstone, Rhodes-Livingstone Institute, 1941, 1942. Rhodes-Livingstone Papers Nos. 5 and 6.

INDEX

absconder, 60, 72–3
absorption, process of, 29–32, 34, 53, 56–73, 128, 139
Advisory Board, 8, 28, 43
age, 14, 23, 29, 32, 53, 88, 105, 141, 153–4, 157, 160, 172
amagoduka, cf. migrants
amatopi (singular *utopi*) 28–9, 32, 44–5, 101, 153, 166–7
apartheid, *see* segregation, group areas
arbitration, 153–71
associations, 30, 44, 45, 46, 67, 91, 100, 131, 175, 179, 180

bands, 30, 42, 52, 114, 126–8, 132, 143, 178, 180
barracks, 1, 7, 15–16, 29–30, 31, 33, 34, 39, 48, 49–51, 53, 57, 62–3, 153–4
bribes, 9–10, 147
brothers, 83–4
budget, 17, 21, 24

cattle, 90
chiefs, 37–8, 48, 109, 147
choirs, 41, 42, 104, 113–14, 128–30, 132, 143, 144
Christians, 16, 27, 39, 40, 41, 54, 57, 91, 102, 109, 142, 147
church, 6, 27, 36, 39, 41, 42, 43, 44, 45, 46, 54, 58, 60, 64–5, 91–103, 111, 140, 143, 145, 169, 175–6, 179, 180–1
circumcision, 17, 32, 39, 63, 64, 89, 105–9, 146, 155
clan, 76–8, 109, 156, 168
class, 14, 32, 38, 80, 82–6, 101, 137–43, 173
clique, 140
clubs, 30, 54, 55, 113–36, 140, 145, 175, 179, 180
coherence (of groups), 11, 175–80
colour bar, 1, 142, 174
Coloured, 1, 13, 49, 67–71, 115, 121–2, 125, 130, 146
concubinage, 79–81
cricket clubs, 124–5, 177

daughter, 84
'decent people', 15–16, 22–3, 26, 27, 28, 32, 38, 43–4, 79, 101, 137, 146, 150, 181

diviners, 110–12, 154, 161, 170
dress, 16–17, 21–3, 26

education, 14, 21, 30, 39, 54, 72, 81–2, 104, 109, 137–8, 142, 181; cf. schools
élite, 143
employment, 51, 52–3, 82; cf. jobs
'endorsed out', 2, 145
exogamy, 76–8

family, 75, 109, 174, 175
fares, 6, 17
father, 87–9, 157, 160
flats, 4, 15–16, 21, 33, 39, 40, 41, 48, 54, 56, 65, 117, 128, 129
food, 17, 21, 24, 27, 49–50
fund-raising, 131–6, 179, 180

group areas, 7, 56

home-boys, 22, 30, 31, 34, 38, 39, 47–73, 83–4, 114–16, 118, 120, 122, 123, 124, 128, 130, 135, 138, 143, 146, 153, 154, 160, 174, 178, 180
homestead, 75–6
housing, 9; cf. barracks, zones, flats, married quarters

illegitimacy, 27, 43, 78–81, 173
ibari (plural *iibari*), 21, 22, 31, 41, 53, 79, 117, 126, 128, 161, 163–4, 170
ikhaba, 14–15, 23, 25, 27, 41–2, 56, 75, 83, 101, 106, 126–8, 130, 135, 137, 138, 139, 141, 146, 149, 150, 161–2, 170
income, 3, 21, 22, 24, 27

jobs, 20–1, 22, 23, 24, 25, 28, 37, 39–45, 50–1, 56–71, 73, 82, 138, 174

kinship, 74–90, 109, 141, 169, 172, 174–5, 180
kinship terminology, 86–90

language, 17–18, 21–4, 26–7, 34, 38, 41, 68, 86, 149, 181
leaders, 143–52, 176, 179–80
lineage, 76, 109, 112, 180

13

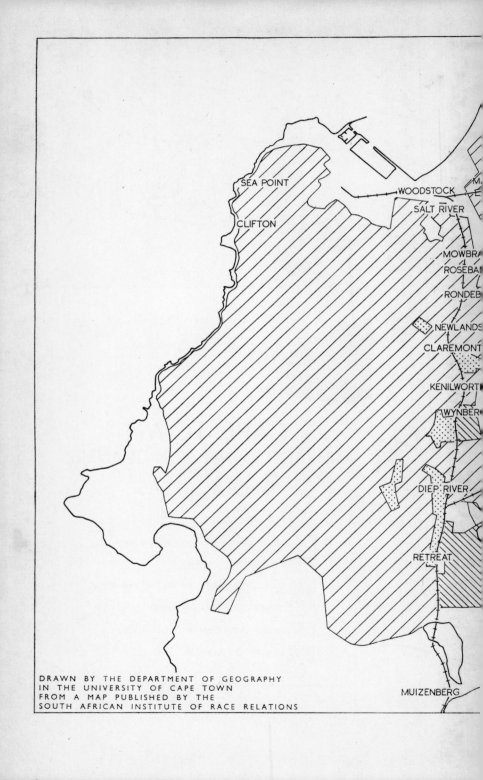

SEA POINT

CLIFTON

WOODSTOCK

SALT RIVER

MOWBRA

ROSEBAN

RONDEB

NEWLANDS

CLAREMONT

KENILWORT

WYNBER

DIEP RIVER

RETREAT

MUIZENBERG

DRAWN BY THE DEPARTMENT OF GEOGRAPHY
IN THE UNIVERSITY OF CAPE TOWN
FROM A MAP PUBLISHED BY THE
SOUTH AFRICAN INSTITUTE OF RACE RELATIONS